THE ACT ITSELF

The Act Itself

Jonathan Bennett

CLARENDON PRESS · OXFORD

1995

Oxford University Press, Walton Street, Oxford OX2 6DP
Oxford New York
Athens Auckland Bangkok Bombay
Calcutta Cape Town Dar es Salaam Delhi
Florence Hong Kong Istanbul Karachi
Kuala Lumpur Madras Madrid Melbourne
Mexico City Nairobi Paris Singapore
Taipei Tokyo Toronto
and associated companies in
Berlin Ibadan

Oxford is a trade mark of Oxford University Press

Published in the United States
by Oxford University Press Inc., New York

British Library Cataloguing in Publication Data
Data available

Library of Congress Cataloging in Publication Data
Bennett, Jonathan Francis.
The act itself / Jonathan Bennett.
Includes bibliographical references and indexes.
1. Consequentialism (Ethics). 2. Act (Philosophy). 3. Human behavior.
I. Title.
BJ1031.B46 1995 170'.44—dc20 94-24341
ISBN 0-19-823548-8

1 3 5 7 9 10 8 6 4 2

Set by Hope Services (Abingdon) Ltd.
Printed in Great Britain
on acid-free paper by
Biddles Ltd.
Guildford & King's Lynn

PREFACE

Moral theorists distinguish the consequences of an act from the act itself, a distinction which is supposed to define the ongoing fight between consequentialism and deontological moralities. Although this book will contain arguments for something like consequentialism, my main concern is not to take sides in that debate but rather to clarify the terms in which it is defined and conducted. I want to offer help in thinking more clearly and sharply about some aspects of human conduct, including the helpful proposal that the concept of 'the act itself' be dropped entirely.

My work in this area, which started nearly thirty years ago, began to accelerate in about 1980 and eventually reached a snail's pace. The themes in this book overlap the materials of several graduate courses, two Summer Seminars for College Teachers under the auspices of the National Endowment for the Humanities, and two sets of formal lectures—the Tanner Lectures on Human Value (Brasenose College, Oxford, 1980) and the John Locke Lectures (University of Oxford, 1992). I warmly thank all three of the above-named institutions for their support and help, and All Souls College for its hospitality in the Trinity Terms of 1991 and 1992. For a year's research leave in 1991 I owe thanks to Syracuse University and, again, to the NEH.

Down the years I have taken on a great burden of intellectual debt to people who have questioned, challenged, argued back, and in other ways helped me to think. Those of whom I have record are Robert Adams, Simon Blackburn, John Broome, Ruth Chang, G. A. Cohen, Andrew Cortens, Ann Davis, Alan Donagan, Philippa Foot, James Griffin, R. M. Hare, Gilbert Harman, Dale Holmes, Jennifer Hornsby, James Hudson, Joel Kidder, Steven Lee, David Lewis, Judith Lichtenberg, Joseph Lombardi, Thomas Loughran, Thomas McKay, Penelope Mackie, Alastair Norcross, Eric Olson, Michael Pritchard, Peter Remnant, Andrew Simester, Thomas M. Scanlon, Jonathan Schonsheck, William Shaw, Michael Stocker, Steven Sverdlik, Richard Swinburne, Michael Tanner, Laurence Thomas, Judith Jarvis Thomson, Henry West, Rick Wiley, Susan Wolf, and Naomi Zack. I am deeply grateful to all of these friends, and apologetic to others—there must be some—who should be on the list.

Over the past thirteen years, Derek Parfit has helped me in my work in moral philosophy, giving it more of his time and energy than I can comfortably think about. My debt to him is inestimable. I am also especially grateful to four friends who commented extensively on the book in its penultimate version, helping me to make many improvements: William Alston, Peter Unger, Dan Radcliffe, and—above all—Frances Howard-Snyder.

I dedicate this book to the memory of Arthur Norman Prior. He was a sturdy friend and an inspiring teacher. Now, nearly twenty-five years after his death, he inspires me still.

J.F.B.

Syracuse
March 1994

CONTENTS

8. OTHER ATTEMPTS

9. DEMANDS

10. ATROCITIES

ERRATUM

In the figure on p. 96, the words 'Survive' and 'Destroy' should be interchanged.

I

ANALYSIS

1. Morality's Grid

Each of us has a working morality by which he or she tries, more or less assiduously, to live. My biggest personal problem with my morality is to obey it more faithfully, becoming a better person by its lights; but I have nothing to say here about that. In this book I shall tackle something easier, though still difficult: I want to understand better some aspects of the morality by which I try to live, hoping thereby to improve it; and I do this in public in the hope that it may help others to understand their morality better too. My topic is the part of morality that judges behaviour—mine or others', actual or possible. Past behaviour is usually of less moral import than possible future behaviour, especially one's own; it is through judgements on the latter that morality helps us to steer our life's course. Still, I take all moral judgements on behaviour as my province.

Whether some way of behaving was, is, will be, or would be right always depends on its non-moral properties and relations:

> It gave him his first experience of friendship.
> It left her feeling betrayed.
> You had promised not to.
> It wasn't true.
> It wasn't yours.
> It got him addicted to the stuff.
> It added twenty years to his life expectancy.
> It hurt.

Moral judgements always have such a basis because the moral supervenes on the non-moral: items that are good or bad, right or wrong, are made so by other facts about them. If that were not so, the following could happen: *What he did was wrong, this being sheerly additional to the non-moral facts about it, just as a thing's colour is additional to its size. He might have behaved in a manner that was like his actual behaviour in every non-moral respect, differing only in not being wrong.* Nobody thinks that this can happen. I labour the point only to make sure that it is clearly before us.

Some of our statements about behaviour are said to involve 'thick moral concepts', which have non-moral and moral components. Terms such as 'treachery', 'murder', 'honourable', and 'courageous' character-ize the non-moral nature of the behaviour, and each conveys something moral as well. Or so it seems, but let us be careful. To call an act 'mur-der' is not *ipso facto* to condemn it: there is nothing conceptually wrong with saying 'If von Stauffenberg had placed the bomb properly, he would have murdered Hitler, and a good thing too!' Plenty of coura-geous acts are deplorable. On the other hand, to say merely that mur-ders are usually wrong is too weak to make murder a partly moral *concept.* The claim has to be an intermediate one: an act's being a mur-der always counts towards its being wrong, is always part of the moral case against it—and similarly with the other 'thick' concepts. Thus understood, the thesis that there are thick moral concepts is true, but it does not spoil the picture I have sketched, because each such concept can be split into two thinner ones, one moral and the other not. From now on I shall pretend that all our thought and talk about behaviour is divided into two classes—one that describes the behaviour without implying any moral stand regarding it, and a second that expresses moral judgements without indicating what the non-moral facts are upon which they supervene.

Substantive morality is the bridge leading to moral judgements from their non-moral basis. It can be expressed in conditionals of the form: 'If any person φs, that counts . . . towards the judgement that he behaves wrongly', where 'φ' stands for a verb phrase whose meaning is entirely non-moral.[1] In the gap goes an adverb of amount—'a little', 'a lot', 'conclusively', or the like. This book is mainly concerned with the antecedents of these conditionals, that is, with the thoughts about con-duct that are the basis for morally judging it.

The concepts involved in those thoughts are worth studying because of their power in our lives. Every human act has countless properties and relations, making it the subject of an infinity of facts; and our

---

[1] I treat 'φ' and its occasional partner 'π' as though they were simple verbs, helping myself to the forms 'will φ', 'φed', and so on. Really, they stand for what linguists call verb *phrases.* An instance of 'He acted wrongly in φing' might be 'He acted wrongly in suing his sister for a share of the inheritance, lying that he needed the extra money, not acknowledging that she had taken care of their parents in their declining years, and using newspaper interviews to blacken his sister's name', and it could go on for pages.

morality selects relatively few of these, which it puts into the antecedents of its conditionals. Most of the questions we confront involve those few. Of course we *can* take account of behavioural facts that are not neatly captured by our main, all-purpose stock of concepts, but usually we do not. Our standard conceptual kit tends not only to shape our answers but also to restrict our questions; its power over us is manifested in what we *do not* as well as in what we *do* think and say. Something with this much muscle is dangerous unless it is understood, which I hope to do through philosophical analysis.

Of the many levels at which we might analytically study the conceptual grid underlying our morality of conduct I choose an extremely abstract one. I shall be concerned with various long lines cutting through the field of behaviour, especially the ones that mark these differences:

making/allowing: between what you make happen and what you allow to happen,

direct/mediated: between what happens through you alone and what happens partly through your effect on someone else,

actual/probable: between what actually comes of your conduct and what the conduct makes probable,

intended/foreseen: between what you intend to make happen and what you merely foreseen will result from your conduct.

Each is a difference between two kinds of relational property of behaviour. I shall make this clearer in Chapter 2, where I shall also discuss behaviour's non-relational, strictly intrinsic properties.

2. *What is Analysis?*

Philosophical analysis has been thought to be the resolving of a complex into its constituent simples, but few would accept that today. The notion of an absolutely *simple* idea or concept looked promising in the seventeenth century but visibly died in the twentieth, at the hands of its friends indeed. Still, without using 'simple' we may use 'simpler'. Typically, an analysis equates a thought with a conjunction of thoughts which are, in a sense, its conceptual parts; and parts must be simpler than the structured whole which they compose; so the analysis resolves a complex into items that are simpler. That cannot be the whole story, however: not every meaning equivalence with a conjunction on the right is an analysis of what is on the left. I owe to Ian Hacking the insight that 'x is a game' is equivalent to 'x is not a physical object and x can be played'; nobody would call that conjunction an analysans of 'x is a game'. For a meaning equivalence to be an analysis it must aid understanding, increasing one's grasp of the item on the left.

Here is an example—a partial analysis of the concept of hurting. The transitive verb 'hurt' is part of the conceptual grid that influences our moral thinking; most of us accept strictures against hurting people. I want a firm grasp, a clear view, of the thought that *she hurt him*. This is hard to get, but it is worth the trouble because the analysis of 'hurt' can be reapplied to vastly many transitive verbs. In analysing 'hurt' we lay bare a conceptual structure in which x *suffers* has a place; in it replace 'suffers' by 'deteriorates' and you have an analysis of 'spoil', replace it by 'recovers' and you have an analysis of 'cure', and so on through thousands of others:

> She kills him, he dies,
> She fells the tree, it falls,
> She compacts the earth, it becomes more compact,
> She raises the roof-beam, it rises,

and so on. Many of these verbs have idiosyncratic further features, but those are negligible. What matters is the shared structure, which I shall investigate in terms of the verb 'to hurt'. All I offer here is a preliminary sketch, which will be refined in later chapters.

The statement that Grandcourt hurt Gwendolen entails that Gwendolen suffered, and Grandcourt could have behaved so that she did not. I shall express that by saying:

(1) Gwendolen suffered in consequence of Grandcourt's behaviour,

which I equate with:

(1) Grandcourt's behaviour was relevant to Gwendolen's suffering.

In my idiolect, a state of affairs is a 'consequence' of someone's behaviour if the person's behaviour made the difference to whether or not it occurred. Also, I stipulate that *relevance* is the converse of *consequence*.

Now, if Gwendolen suffered, and Grandcourt's behaviour was relevant because he could have prevented the suffering but did not, (1) would be true but he wouldn't have hurt her; that is because he would not have made her suffer, but only allowed this to happen. So we need to add:

> (2) The relevance of Grandcourt's behaviour to her suffering was of the making rather than the allowing kind.

However, (1) and (2) could be true through Grandcourt's telling a servant to hurt Gwendolen, which would not make it the case that Grandcourt hurt her. So we must add:

> (3) The causal route from his behaviour to her suffering did not run wholly through someone's will.

I say 'someone's will' and not 'the will of someone *else*' because, as David Lewis has pointed out to me, if at T_1 Grandcourt does something which causes *him* to hurt Gwendolen at T_2, it is not true that he hurts her at T_1. Nevertheless, in my examples it will always be the will of someone else. The emphasis on 'will' is needed. If Grandcourt puts poison into food that the servant innocently takes to Gwendolen, the causal chain between his behaviour and her suffering runs through the conduct, but not through the will, of the servant; so it remains true that Grandcourt hurt her. I hereby adopt 'mediated' and 'direct' as technical terms whose meaning can be gathered from the equivalence of (3) above to this: The causal route from his behaviour to her suffering was direct, not mediated.

This is still not enough, however. I might hurt you by kicking a rock which starts a landslide which crashes into a lake and sends out a wave of water that knocks you over as you stand in the stream, breaking your leg. But now amplify the story thus:

> The kicked rock starts a landslide only because it happens to coincide with a crash of thunder; the wave goes your way only because it happens to reach the junction at one of the rare moments when the control gates are set to the left; and the water catches you only because by chance that is the moment when you are hastily wading across the stream.

The fact that the causal route from my movement to your death involves several intervening coincidences makes it wrong to say that in this case I hurt you, though it remains true that my behaviour has caused you to suffer, in a making and direct way. A final condition is needed, therefore:

(4) The causal chain from his behaviour to her suffering did not depend on a number of intervening coincidences.

This is what David Lewis, to whose help I am indebted in this section, calls the 'stability' condition.[2]

The sentence conjoining (1), (2), (3), and (4) is roughly equivalent to 'Grandcourt hurt Gwendolen': either can be true only if the other is. Our talk and thought about human behaviour teems with active transitive verbs whose meanings have this pattern, so that the meaning of each is pretty well exhausted by four ideas: (1) the conduct has a certain state of affairs as a consequence, in a way that (2) is a positive or active making rather than a negative or passive allowing, (3) does not involve a mediated causal chain, and (4) conforms to the stability condition. In so far as our morality is expressed in such verbs, it gives a privilege to those four ideas: facing a choice where each option would lead to people's suffering but only one involves hurting someone, we shall be inclined away from the latter by the force of the verb 'to hurt'. An analysis of hurting can help us to look critically at this fact about ourselves; it can show us what factors bring the active verb into play, so that we can at least consider whether they should influence us as much as they do. The stability condition (4) plays little part when we are practically deliberating, because a chain involving several coincidences can almost never be foreseen; so from now on I shall drop (4) from my discussions.

I shall later challenge the privilege of the other three factors, arguing (1) that what matters morally is not the actual but the probable consequence of your behaviour, (2) that the difference between making and allowing does not deserve a place in our most basic moral thinking, and (3) that the same is true of the difference between direct and mediated connections between one's conduct and significant upshots of it. All of this will involve moves of a broadly analytic sort.

Explanations must stop somewhere, but I have no criterion that marks off the proper terminus. When a given line of analysis is claimed to have gone far enough, opponents may show that it has not, by showing that the analysans is unclear or confusing or ambiguous, or that it is so complex that we should not regard it as expressing a clear, controlled thought until we have further analysed it. My account of 'hurt', for example, is only partial because it helps itself to the making/allow-

---

[2] For more about it, see my *Events and their Names*, sect. 84, and David Lewis, 'Insensitive Causation'.

ing distinction, which certainly needs to be explained in its turn—not because it is fuzzy, but because even when we are *sure* about *where* to draw the line we are not *clear* about *why*; we do not articulately know what we are doing when we distinguish making from allowing.

I partly analysed hurting through an equivalence which I said is 'roughly' right; and I remarked that the meanings of other transitive verbs are 'pretty well' exhausted by the elements in that analysis. The softening qualifications are deliberate: *I am not interested in the exact meaning of any word.* As will emerge at various points in this book, some facts about the meaning of a word will be negligible from the standpoint of the inquiry I am conducting; when that happens, it is pointless to desert the inquiry in order to stay with the word. I shall continue to speak of analyses in terms of equivalences, but what is being analysed is not the full meaning of the item on the left but rather those aspects of its meaning that are pertinent to the matter in hand. When a purported analysis of some concept does not precisely capture the whole truth about when the concept-word would be the *mot juste*, the question is whether the omitted aspects matter for fundamental moral theory; and sometimes they do not. For example, one aspect of the meaning of 'hurt' is that the propriety of saying 'He hurt her' may in part depend upon a prior moral judgement on his conduct; and that is irrelevant when we are investigating the concepts that are used to characterize behaviour as a *basis* for moral judgements on it. Other examples will turn up in due course.

3. Objections to Philosophical Analysis

My demand for analysis would be rejected by some philosophers, including one who has written that 'in moral philosophy we may often be forced to swallow some quite unchewed metaphysical morsels', where 'unchewed' means 'not fully understood'. I protest. Who or what forces us to swallow something we do not understand? We do not live in one of the countries where, in Locke's words, 'men are forced [to] swallow down opinions, as silly people do empirics' pills, without knowing what they are made of, or how they will work'.

The late Warren Quinn was sceptical about my analytic approach. He wrote:

Bennett is reluctant to assign moral work to any distinction that leaves some cases unclear, especially where there is no theoretically compelling reductionist

theory for the clear cases. But . . . the imposition of such a standard would shut
down moral theory at once, dependent as it is on the as yet unreduced and
potentially vague distinctions between what is and is not a person, a promise,
an informed consent, etc.[3]

If by a 'distinction that leaves some cases unclear' Quinn meant one
with respect to which there are borderline cases, then his opening clause
is false. Because all our linguistic and conceptual apparatus is, in
Friedrich Waismannn's phrase, 'open textured', I hold that every distinction is in principle liable to 'leave some cases unclear' in that sense.
What matters to me is to understand what distinction I am using, in
any context where I rest theoretical weight on it. Of course I can allow
a concept to do 'moral work' without having a clear, deep understanding of what concept it is; many of my moral opinions involve concepts
on which I have only a loose intuitive hold. But when it comes to using
a concept in moral theory, the case is different. I will not assent to
something, claiming it as a fundamental moral principle, unless I have
an adequate grasp of what principle it is, and thus of the concepts it
involves. (This is not to demand a 'theoretically compelling reductionist theory'; that was Quinn's phrase, not mine.) This does not imply
that we should 'shut down moral theory', as Quinn extravagantly
implied. The three examples that he gave—person, promise, informed
consent—are not relied on in every part of moral theory; and even in a
part where one of them is relied upon in a theoretic way, my approach
does not say 'Shut up!' or 'Shut down!' but rather: 'Please make clearer
what you are saying and why you are saying it.'

In the remainder of this section I shall discuss some more principled
bases for objection to the analytic approach in moral philosophy.

It has been argued that 'analysis' and its sibling term 'meaning' are
like 'witch' and 'phlogiston': they may have looked reasonable in their
way, and in their day, but we now know better. This scepticism about
analysis and meaning has stemmed from Quine, whose version of it is
still the best. According to Quine, on an understanding of his position
that is now widely accepted,[4] the sentences we deem to be true lie on
a continuum, with the clearly analytic at one end and the clearly not
analytic at the other, the difference being one of degree. Some sentences
are so placed in our scheme of things that we could easily cope with

[3] Warren S. Quinn, 'Actions, Intentions, and Consequences: the Doctrine of Doing
and Allowing', 361.
[4] W. V. Quine, 'Two Dogmas of Empiricism' and 'The Problem of Meaning in
Linguistics'.

their turning out false; the falsity of others would require some rebuild-
ing of our edifice of belief; and if this went deep and wide enough, we
would break into the language of 'meaning', saying that the sentence in
question was being denied in a different meaning from that in which it
had been affirmed. Those most deeply entrenched sentences are the
ones we call 'analytic': they do not have a property that the 'synthetic'
ones lack; they merely have a high degree of something—embedded-
ness—that everything we accept has in some degree. Quine's position,
properly understood, does not reject the old idea that analytic truths are
those that are true by virtue of their meanings. Rather, it combines that
idea with the view that between what a sentence means and what would
commonly be inferred from what it means there is only a difference of
degree, not a sharp difference of kind.

Quine's view seems to be right, but it does not condemn my project.
All I need are equivalences that illuminate, that help us to understand
our own thoughts at a deep level. To do this they must be—in a phrase
I picked up from Rogers Albritton—*analytic enough*, which is all I aim
for.

Still, the undertaking may be challenged for two other reasons. One
is a general resistance to analytic endeavours as such, and thus to my
search for clarity, understanding, and intellectual control. Richard
Rorty rejects this aim, as is shown when he contrasts two views about
what philosophers of language should be doing. According to one side,
the task is 'to take warm, familiar aspects of the human condition and
look at them coldly and with the eye of a stranger', and ask in that spirit
'what it is for a behavioural system to be a language, or for a sound or
movement to be a sentence'. On the other side is the kind of philosopher who is willing to 'rely on the premise that he speaks a language,
without subjecting it to any kind of explanation or scrutiny', is willing
to 'take that concept on trust, as something whose instances are dropped
into our laps without the need for philosophical work'. The quoted
phrases all come from a philosopher of the eye-of-a-stranger kind,
namely myself. Rorty accepts them as fair to both camps and, in particular, he thinks that the expressions in the second group fit the work
of Davidson, at whom they were aimed. Rorty applauds my saying that
Davidson explains 'language' in terms of 'true' and explains 'true' in
terms of 'language I know', and thinks that he is right to do this:

The question of whether there is anything for philosophers to appeal to save
the way *we* live now, what *we* do now, how *we* talk now, beyond *our* little
moment of world-history, is the decisive issue between representationalist and

social-practise philosophers of language. More generally, it is the decisive issue between an approach to philosophy which takes for granted what Rosenberg calls 'the Myth of the Mind Apart' and one which assumes that something is, indeed, dropped into the philosopher's lap—namely her own linguistic know-how, or, more generally, her own patterns of practical reasoning, the ways in which her community copes with the world. The alternative to this assumption would seem to be that what was dropped into her lap was a gift from heaven called 'clarity of thought' or 'powerful analytic techniques' or 'critical distance'—a heaven-sent ability to wrench one's mind free from one's community's practises.[5]

This stretches to philosophy generally, including ethics. (Rorty once thanked me without sarcasm for helping him to focus his thinking in moral philosophy. My service had been to assert clearly, in a lecture I gave at Princeton, everything he most profoundly disbelieves about morality.) His critique of 'representationalism' about language can easily be aimed against the approach to moral philosophy that I have announced.

The quoted passage is not hard to answer: Of course our linguistic know-how is dropped into our laps; my point was that our warmly intimate relation with our social practices does not ensure that we understand them, and that for *that* we need to stand back and look more objectively. 'Though the familiar use of things about us take off our wonder,' Locke said, 'yet it cures not our ignorance.' The ability to get at a distance, think analytically, and in that way get some understanding of ourselves is a gift that we have, and I am not embarrassed to describe it in Rorty's terms, scornfully though he means them. With one exception: Of course one cannot fully 'wrench one's mind free from one's community's practises'; but one can try, and partly succeed, and the result is a kind of understanding that cannot be reached otherwise.

Rorty would have to agree that we can try, and that something may be achieved in this way; but he would deplore the achievement. He is repelled by the endeavour to stand back from ourselves, get our ways of thinking at a focal distance, and by seeing how they are articulated come to understand them better. Why? What separates him from analytic philosophers is personal, I think. We differ in what we like, want, and hope for, and in what makes us happy. We can go on talking about this, but we shan't settle it by argument or, probably, in any other way.

The second objection to my project is more specific: without opposing analysis, it casts doubt on whether it should make a moral differ-

[5] Richard Rorty, 'Representation, Social Practises, and Truth', p. 158.

ence. If philosophical analysis leaves us feeling estranged from any of our erstwhile moral opinions, according to this line of thought, so much the worse for the analysis. This view is at work in some contemporary moral philosophy, though I have not ever seen it defended. One possible defence should be looked at.

The analytic activity that most concerns me is this: we take some kind of item about which we have a general moral view, and analyse the kind. The aim is to isolate the features of an item that put it in that kind, and to discover which of them contribute, and how, to the moral attitude. This approach does not assume simple moral addition, according to which the badness of a state of affairs is the sum of the badnesses of its several features. Even apart from problems about measurement, simple addition is wrong because how much a given feature contributes to an item's moral status may depend on what other features the item has. This is what Moore called 'the principle of organic unities', according to which something's features may contribute to its overall moral quality not as the weights of the grains do to the weight of the sandbag, but rather as the activities of the cells contribute to the life of the flower.[6] It would be rash to assume that this never happens; so simple addition is not among my premisses.

Still, analysis is atomistic—it tries to clarify the whole by attending to how its conceptual parts are interrelated—and this is not a sure-fire way of getting a better understanding of moral significance. A moral realist, at any rate, may say that our ability to see or sense the moral importance of certain concepts depends on our taking them as unanalysed wholes, and that the analytic lens is really a glass through which we shall see darkly. Having set out his famous determinist account of freedom, Dickinson Miller wrote:

What makes the other party uncontrollably reject all this . . . is the words. They smell of sordid detail. . . . They are not bathed in moral value, not elevated and glowing. In this the opponents' instinct is wholly right; only when they look for the value they fail to focus their eyes aright. It is in the whole act and the whole trait and the whole being that excellence and preciousness inhere; analysis must needs show us elements which, taken severally, are without moral expressiveness.[7]

It might be said, more strongly, that the appearance of value is lost not merely by the elements 'taken severally' but also by the whole when it

---

[6] G. E. Moore, *Principia Ethica*, 27 ff.
[7] Dickinson S. Miller, 'Free Will as Involving Determination and Inconceivable without It', 117.

is looked at as a structure of elements; and this might be extended beyond judgements about the value of freedom. The extended thesis could threaten my analytic programme. When for example I analytically explore the difference between making and allowing, and declare it to be without moral significance, the analysis may have hidden the significance rather than revealed its absence. Anything that my work displays as a negative result might really be a blank visual field caused by an analytic blindfold.

That menacing thesis could be right. If there is such an activity as finding out how we ought to behave, there must be better and worse environments in which to do it, and a philosophical analysis may create bad rather than good discovery conditions. If on the other hand moral non-realism is true, so that arriving at moral judgements is a matter of choice rather than of discovery, it may be that an analysis creates bad conditions for choice. Either way, an unrefuted threat hangs over my whole endeavour. It comes not from Rortyan rejection of analysis as such, but rather from the more specific idea that analysis is not a good method in at least some parts of moral theory. In later chapters I shall argue that certain tendencies in contemporary moral theory are best understood as reflecting just such an attitude to the analytic approach.

4. A Statement of Non-realism

An analytic understanding of our concepts of behaviour is worth having, I have assumed, partly as an aid to substantive moral change. How could that be? My answer depends on my being a non-realist about morality, and I have to explain this. In this section I shall sketch my non-realist position as openly and explicitly as I can. In some contexts one wants to show how like realism non-realism is, but not here. The differences are what matter, and I shall throw camouflage to the winds. Then Sections 5 and 6 will explain how, on a non-realist basis, philosophical analyses can provide reasons for changes of moral view.

I hold that judgements are not answerable to any moral reality, any range of independent moral facts. That lets me off the problem of moral epistemology, which I think is radically unsolved by the realists. They say that they know moral truths by 'intuition', but I cannot find that they mean anything by this except that they do have moral opinions. (If there is anyone who really does do what the so-called 'naturalists' say that they do, namely use moral language only to express propositions of theology or psychology or sociology or the like, then they can lay claim to whatever epistemology is appropriate for theology or psychology or whatever. I do not believe that anyone actually uses moral terminology purely in this way; but if I am wrong, and 'naturalism' is true of some people, then they lie outside the scope of this book.)

I express non-realism by saying that moral judgements do not have truth-values. One can of course use 'true' in thinner ways than this, right down to the point where calling something 'true' is just expressing one's acceptance of it; but it suits me to take the word to involve correspondence with facts.

I accept both main strands in contemporary moral non-realism. One is the view that is best expressed in Gibbard's *Wise Choices, Apt Feelings*, namely that a moral judgement serves to *express* some fact about the speaker's practical attitudes; it does not *state* this fact, and has no truth-value. The other strand, classically presented by Hare in many works, holds that a moral judgement serves as a kind of command, spoken aloud or in one's heart, to others or to oneself, to behave in a certain way.[8]

(What does an attitude or injunction have to be like to count as moral? Part of the story is that it must be universalizable in the sense of Kant and Hare; more about that early in Section 6. Another part has to do with how the attitude or injunction fits in with the rest of the person's life—including the psychic price that person pays for acting against it. That is vague, and is probably incomplete. I do not have a complete and precise account of the boundaries of the moral, but nor does anyone else. This is, of course, a problem equally for moral realists. The only difference is that honest non-realism compels one to face the problem, whereas realism makes it easier to ignore it.)

Both strands of moral non-realism are right: moral judgements are used to reveal oneself, and to affect people; expressivism describes the former use, injunctivism the latter. There are reasons why an utterance that plays either role is apt also to play the other. If I express a favourable attitude to your ϕing, your learning of this will be apt to incline you slightly to ϕ, so that my utterance works somewhat like a request or command or advice. Conversely, if I enjoin you to ϕ, this gives you evidence that I favour your ϕing, so that my utterance reveals an attitude of mine.

[8] R. M. Hare, *The Language of Morals, Freedom and Reason*, and *Moral Thinking: Its Levels, Method and Point*.

The expressivist strand in non-realism does not liken moral judgements to shouts of glee or groans of disgust. On the contrary, it proclaims that they are conceptually structured items using the resources of conventional language. Then why not regard them as true or false *statements* about the speaker's attitudes? Well, that is not in fact how we interpret them—we do not 'hear' them in that way—and this is not a superficial or a fragile fact about them or us. Expressivists should not be troubled by the challenge to draw the fine line between expressing and asserting,[9] nor should they be embarrassed by the charge that 'It is difficult to see that a lot hinges on whether we take ethical statements to describe or express the attitudes of the person making the statement.'[10] The core of their position is clear and straightforward, and a great deal hinges on it. Truth is what we go in for; it is what we care about. If moral judgements were reports on the speaker's attitudes, our interest in them would focus on whether the speaker had those attitudes. As things stand, our focus is quite different: when you let me know that you disapprove of φing, my response will ordinarily not be 'Does he really oppose φing?' but rather the practical question of whether to oppose φing. That is the solid basis for the straightforward idea that moral judgements express but do not describe the speaker's attitudes.

It is widely held that some moral judgements are absolutely necessary. Judith Thomson has cited torturing babies for fun as something that is wrong whatever the surrounding facts are, or *necessarily* wrong, and has used this in a complex argument for moral realism.[11] The argument assumes that what is necessary is necessarily true, which makes possible a simpler route to realism: some moral judgements are necessary, so necessarily true, so true, so truth-valued. For the non-realist this argument—like Thomson's longer one—is blocked at the outset. His case for non-realism gives him reason to deny that any moral judgements are necessarily true. He must admit that we sometimes judge things *as* necessary, and that this seems to be of morality's essence. When we judge that it is contingently wrong to φ, we are relying on some more general moral judgement conjoined with matters of contingent non-moral facts; the former in turn may derive from something yet more general, conjoined with further non-moral facts; but ultimately this must stop, which it can do only at a judgement owing nothing to

[9] See William P. Alston, 'Expressing'.
[10] Richard A. Fumerton, *Reason and Morality*, 24.
[11] Judith Jarvis Thomson, *The Realm of Rights*, ch. 1.

any non-moral contingency. So it is no mere accident that we make judgements like this: 'It couldn't possibly be the case that an act's causing someone to be in terrible agony counts towards its being morally right.' The non-realist must acknowledge that we do properly accept some moral judgements as necessary.

He can take this in his stride. When I judge that it would be wrong to ϕ, I am (in part) expressing a certain attitude of mine to ϕing. When ϕing is testing nuclear weapons in the atmosphere, my attitude depends on contingent facts: I am hostile to ϕing at the world as I believe it to be, and at others suitably like it, but not at every possible world. When ϕing is torturing someone for fun, the attitude I express is unconditioned, absolute, adopted towards anyone's ϕing, no matter what the circumstances; so I accept that moral judgement as necessary. A similar story can be told about accepting injunctions as necessary. So moral non-realism has a necessary/contingent distinction that does not involve the concept of truth, though it is the same concept of necessity that is involved in necessary truth.[12]

This is not to disguise non-realism as realism. I hold—to put it as bluntly as I can—that one's basic morality is partly *chosen*, either in the normal active manner in which one makes a choice, or passively by not choosing to divest oneself of an attitude which one could lose if one chose to. This use of 'chosen' broadens its normal meaning, but that is only for convenience; I shall not exploit the broadening for argumentative purposes.

The source of moral choices, active and passive, is one's personal nature, so they are conditioned by upbringing, biases, prejudices, hopes, and fears; they are choices made by a product of the contingencies of the actual world, and not by a transcendental self that operates from a vantage-point unstained by any touch of the past or the environment. Even in my broadened sense of 'chosen', however, morality is only *partly* chosen, because active and passive choices are circumscribed: I am not psychologically free to choose to be a principled sadist. Many people, indeed, may be almost unable to exercise any significant choice in fundamental moral matters. It would not affect anything much in this book if nobody were free to exercise any choices of this kind. For even then one should still ask: *Why* can we not choose to change our moral stands? I would answer that our inability to choose arose from the contingent facts about our psychological make-up. Such facts are the real

[12] This and other themes of the present chapter are developed in my 'The Necessity of Moral Judgements'.

source of the constraints on our moral choices in the actual world, where we do have some moral elbow-room, though perhaps not much. Those constraints, like the choices made within them, are grounded in our individual natures. We may be troubled by the thought of how contingent our doings and valuings are, but that should be lived with, not veiled in the myth of a free-standing realm of moral fact.

Moral non-realism implies things about how the term 'morality' should be used, and I should align my usage with it. Realists and non-realists alike can use 'morality' as a sortal, speaking of the 'moralities' that different people have. For each of them, the phrase 'Schweitzer's morality' refers—roughly speaking—to the set of moral judgements that Schweitzer accepts. Where the two kinds of moral theorist part company is in their use of 'morality' as a proper name. A realist intends it to refer to something that embodies *the whole moral truth*, the totality of facts about what would be better or worse, right or wrong, vicious or virtuous, and so on. Using the term in this way, a realist might ask 'Does morality condemn her φing?' as a way of asking whether it would be wrong for her to φ. For the non-realist, on the other hand, moral content resides not in something called 'morality' but only in various personally based moralities. When he uses 'morality' as a proper name, as I sometimes do in this book, he refers to a certain form or structure but not to any moral content, and what he says can be warranted only by the concept of morality. It is in that spirit that I say that there is more to morality than judgements on conduct, that parts of morality are absolutely necessary, and so on.

5. Moral Non-realism and Entailment

Non-realism bears, as I said, on how and why philosophical analysis can lead to moral change. Like many philosophers, I think that it can, and I want to be explicit about *how*—about the methods that are used, their rationale, and their powers. The methods I use are common property, being employed as much by realists as by non-realists. My rationales for them, however, depend on my non-realist metaphysic of morals. In particular, the analytic project cannot lead to changes of moral view without using two kinds of move the non-realist rationales for which are unlike any that a realist could offer. In one case, the realist has the easier time of it; in the other, the non-realist.

The first involves the tracing out of the logical consequences of moral judgements, perhaps aided by philosophical analysis, and acting on the results of that. When we trace out an entailment of one of our moral judgements, any of three things may be the case. One is this:

We knew all along that J_1 entails J_2.

If all our results are like that, the whole inquiry is fruitless. Or, secondly:

It had not occurred to us that J_1 entails J_2, but J_2 is something we would have accepted if we had thought about it.

Results of that kind may help us to be clear about what our morality involves, but that is all it can do. Thirdly:

J_2 is something we have rejected, or would have rejected if we had thought about it.

Only this provides a basis for moral change: either we come to reject J_1 or we come to accept J_2. In such a case, we have accepted something that entails something we would have rejected. The entailment was inoperative: it lay there in the logic of our morality, but did not prevail in our minds.

Some philosophers hold that entailments—whether operative or not—require realism: only items with truth-values can entail one another, they say. In fact, entailment is no more confined to truth-valued items than necessity is. Hare showed long ago that injunctions can entail one another. The command 'Bring peace to all people' entails 'Bring peace to all poor people' for exactly the same reason that the statement 'You will bring peace to all people' entails 'You will bring peace to all poor people'.[13] That example is trivial, but the logic is equally good for complex, unobvious entailments which could be inoperative in our minds. The core of this work, which is widely known and accepted, needs no discussion here.

It is perhaps less obvious that there can also be entailments, including inoperative ones, between moral judgements considered as expressing norms, desires, or attitudes. From the sheer fact that I have a certain attitude to all people, doesn't it follow that I have it to each individual person? If so, then there can be no question of my having that attitude to all yet turning out not to have it to the poor. This line of thought, however, rests on a mistake about what general attitudes are. My

[13] For the initial work on this topic, see Hare, *The Language of Morals*, ch. 2. I reviewed much of the subsequent literature in the *Journal of Symbolic Logic*.

hostility to all forms of tobacco advertising, say, is not a fact about how I did or will respond to past or future instances of such advertising. Rather, it is a present attitude to a *kind*—namely, *tobacco advertising*— and it involves me in conceptually representing the kind. So I could have the attitude to the kind, yet discover that I did not have it to some species within the kind; which is to say that general attitudes can have inoperative entailments.

When we find that a moral judgement which we accept, perhaps con- joined with non-moral truths, entails another which we would have rejected, should we do something about that? Obviously, if we don't relinquish the former judgement or accept the latter, our morality will be inconsistent; but what is so bad about that?

For the realist the answer is easy: If a morality is inconsistent then it is not true. The non-realist, who denies that any morality can be true, must answer differently. If he wants consistency in his moral system, he must choose to pursue it as a substantive goal.[14] Even if I know that there are certain instances of φing to which I am not opposed, I can still be in general hostile to all φing; if I do, I must live with a certain tangle within me; but whether to do this, or rather to remove it by alter- ing my moral scheme of things, is something I must decide for myself. Wanting harmony, order, consistency in the moral system by which I live, I choose to oppose the tangle; another person might choose dif- ferently. So I, like the realist, have a basis on which the tracing out of entailments among moral judgements can lead to changes of moral view.

We are to relinquish the entailing judgement or adopt the entailed one. Which? There is no general answer to this, though some moral philosophers seem inclined to give one, at least when the entailing judgement is much more abstract and general than the other. In those cases, indeed, each answer has its supporters, who say things like this. (1) The more specific intuitions are closer to morality's place in every- day life, and are therefore more familiar, and so more worthy of trust, than the highly general ones that come to those who are theorizing in an ivory tower. Thus Nagel, for instance: 'Given a knockdown argu- ment for an intuitively unacceptable conclusion, one should assume there is probably something wrong with the argument that one cannot detect. . . . It is always reasonable in philosophy to have great respect for the intuitive sense of an unsolved problem, because in philosophy our methods are always themselves in question.'[15] (2) Ways of thinking

[14] I learned this from Lynne McFall, 'Happiness, Rationality, and Individual Ideals'.
[15] Thomas Nagel, *Mortal Questions*, pp. x, xi.

that grow out of our dealings with concrete problems in the hurly-burly are likely to be slapdash, approximate, corner-cutting, which makes them less trustworthy than more general principles reached through cool, deliberate, careful moral thinking.

I have used the language of realism—speaking of reasons for 'trust' in a moral opinion, which naturally means trusting it to be true, reliable, in conformity with the moral facts. The debate comes from two hazy epistemological ideals: moral beliefs as nourished by life as lived, moral beliefs as informed by careful inquiry. It is for the realist friends of these views to clarify and justify them.

For the non-realist, the question of which moral opinion to relinquish is practical, not theoretical, and ultimately it is for him to choose. He needs no general view about this, and can judge individual cases as they arise. This is not a matter of superficial snap decisions. It may be hard for the non-realist to decide in a way that fits in with the rest of his morality, and with his sense of himself—his projects, ideals, desires for himself and others, his powers, and his limits.

So much for one kind of move that my project involves: seeing what is entailed by a given moral judgement and acting on the results of that. Realist and non-realist alike can do this, and the issue between them should not affect their practice but only how they describe, explain, and justify it.

6. Unifying Theory

The other procedure that I want to discuss is equally abstract. It is the pursuit of highly general principles from which one's more specific moral opinions follow, perhaps with help from matters of fact. Many of us approach moral theorizing in this way, as scientific theorists look for very general theories that imply and thus explain the empirical data. Why do we do this?

It might be thought that the 'universalizability thesis' is relevant here. I had better explain what that is. Moral judgements supervene on non-moral facts; so if some particular act is wrong, it is made so by some of its non-moral properties and relations, ones that would suffice to make wrong any act that had them. So if you adversely judge an act, this is (for you) a moral judgement only if it is (for you) universalizable—that is, only if, for some value of F, you think that the act is F and judge that every possible F act would be wrong. F may be a long, complicated story, and it may take you ages to get clear about it; but if there is no such F—that is, if your judgement on the behaviour is not derivable from any universal judgement that you accept—then the judgement does not come from your morality.[16]

The universalizability thesis, true though it is, throws no light on the pursuit of high-level theory. The moral intuitions that are our data concern *kinds* of case. Even when the kind is highly specific, having few instances, it still satisfies universalizability's demand that basic moral reasons concern kinds rather than particulars. So we could leave it at that, having a morality consisting of the conjunction of all our low-level, universal but not very general intuitions. What is wrong with that? Do not say 'By examining how our intuitions hang together, we can root out any inconsistencies there may be among them.' The likelihood of outright inconsistency among them is almost nil; there is a significant risk of it only when we conjoin these low-level judgements with more general principles from which they are supposed to follow. So why not stay at the lower level, retaining those moral intuitions and sparing ourselves the arduous search for unifying high-level theory?

A realist might reply that no rationale is needed: it is obvious that a theory should be as unified as possible, and what unifies it is a general proposition under which all the rest falls. That is our attitude in the sciences, where few seriously challenge it. However, as Quine has said on a related point, when scientists pursue generality in their theories they are 'under the welcome restraint of stubborn fact: failures of prediction', whereas in moral theory our procedure 'has only our unsettled moral values themselves to answer to, and it is these that the [theory-building] was meant to settle'.[17] In short, the checkable success of empirical sciences supports the assumption that the basic causal truth about the world is very general, and if it were not so the world would tell us. There is no analogue for this in realist moral theorizing. Realists who pursue moral theory in any of the usual ways must assume that moral reality is so structured as to make some very general theories true, but they do not defend this against the rival hypothesis that moral reality is a mess.[18]

---

[16] The universalizability thesis, traceable to Kant, has been best presented in our century by R. M. Hare, 'Universalisability'. The thesis is inseparable from the supervenience of the moral on the non-moral, and from the necessity of basic moral judgements.

[17] W. V. Quine, 'On the Nature of Moral Values', 45.

[18] This point is forcefully put in Bernard Williams, 'The Structure of Hare's Theory', 196.

From a non-realist standpoint, I can explain my pursuit of high generality. As a personal matter I want to be guided by rather general moral principles. This desire is neither extractable from the concept of morality nor based on insight into the structure of the real. It seems to come from my wish to be whole and interconnected in my person, so that I can understand some of my attitudes as parts or upshots of other more general ones.

Like the tracing out of entailments, the search for general theory can set up strains. It may happen that, finding no general theory implying all our previous moral opinions, we can find one that entails most of them, conflicting with only a few. Should we jettison the few in order to have the theory? Any moral theorist, I suppose, would agree that it could be right to do this; but in practice philosophers vary widely in how much low-level revision they will endure for the reward of high-level unity. Finding no theoretical rationale for this variety, I guess that it comes from differences in personal temperament. I say this about realists too, though only the non-realist is free to avow it openly, as I do. I strongly favour having a morality that is organizable at a high level of theory; I also have many specific moral attitudes; if I cannot reconcile all this, then ultimately I must choose what to relinquish and what to retain.

I have mentioned one reason for being willing to pay for a theoretically unified morality. There is another, which will loom large in this book. It concerns a by-product of the search for highly general moral principles, namely the discovery of reasons for morally discriminating as one does. I may judge that certain ways in which psychologists treat chimpanzees are morally all right, although I am sure it would be wrong to treat humans like that. If I am to retain this stand, I should confront head-on what I take to be the factual unlikenesses of chimpanzees to humans, asking myself whether I consent to letting them make that moral difference. The perceived dissimilarities between the species have caused me to judge them differently, but it is for me to decide whether to let them retain that power in my moral thinking. They pushed me around when I was not consciously focusing on them; until I test their power when they are under the spotlight, I am not properly in control of my own moral nature. This is a low-level example of yet another way in which analysis can help me to test and refine my moral system.[19]

---

[19] In this paragraph I am indebted to Joel Kidder's 'Maxims, Freedom, and Laws'.

7. Levels of Morality

This chapter began with a person's 'working morality' and has lately worked around to my real topic, which is a person's moral theory. These might be differently organized: your moral theory might contain or consist of principles that are more abstract and general than anything you actually work with, down in the trenches, when deciding how to behave. My present concern, however, is with differences not in structure but in content, and indeed with one particular source for the latter—namely, divergences from moral theory which are endorsed by moral theory.

Consider these three views. (1) The ultimate touchstone in judging conduct is how it relates to the virtues: Is it what would be done by a person who is benevolent, who is just, who is temperate . . . ? (2) Anyone who asks herself 'If I φ, how will that relate to the virtues?' will probably go on to think about her own virtue in this situation. (3) Thinking about one's own virtue is apt to make one less virtuous. Some moralists accept (1), and the psychological theses (2) and (3) are plausible. A person who accepts all three, holding that (1) is the correct fundamental morality, has reason to hold that we ought usually not to steer by (1). He should then present some working morality that we can live by, defending its role as a guide to behaviour on the grounds that living by it gives us our best chance of living virtuously. This illustrates the general point that the aims of a given morality may not be best achieved by our thinking much about what we ought to do according to that morality.

Other moralities may be dangerous guides to conduct for other reasons—utilitarianism for example. Here is Sidgwick on that topic:

It is not necessary that the end which gives the criterion of rightness should always be the end at which we consciously aim: and if experience shows that the general happiness will be more satisfactorily attained if men frequently act from other motives than pure universal philanthropy, it is obvious that these other motives are reasonably to be preferred on Utilitarian principles.'[20]

Two dangers especially threaten so-called 'consequentialist' moralities, such as utilitarianism, according to which the required act is the one whose consequences are best overall. Each concerns an impediment to

[20] Henry Sidgwick, *The Methods of Ethics*, 413. This general idea is pertinaciously explored by Derek Parfit, *Reasons and Persons*, ch. 1.

applying the morality properly. (1) Epistemic: It is often—usually? always?—too difficult to get the facts and calculate from them what behaviour will be for the best. (2) Motivational: When we want it to be all right to φ, our desire may lead us to compute, sincerely, that it will be for the best if we φ.

The epistemic danger might be dealt with by adopting rules of thumb—simple principles approximating to the ones that we actually accept. For example, I hold that lying is right in some situations, but it is seldom easy to know that I am in one of those. If I consult my basic moral views about lying, I risk fumbling, delaying, getting it wrong, and so on. It is better to adopt the principle: 'Do not ever lie'. The rare occasions when I tell the truth though really I should lie are a small price to pay for avoiding all the troubles I would be in, and the harms I would cause, if I tried always to steer by my real views about lying. If it is ever quite clear, straight off, that it would be right to lie, I am free to suspend my working rule, and lie. That it how it is with rules of thumb: one can drop them at will.

That is why they cannot solve the temptation problem. Consider sexual fidelity in marriage, for a man whose basic moral convictions do not condemn adultery in cases where (to cut a long story short) it would do no harm. A time comes when he is drawn to a woman who is attracted to him; he is sure that the affair would not dull him as a husband, that his wife would not learn of it, that the other woman would enjoy the liaison while it lasted and then cheerfully move on. In thus concluding that there is no moral objection, he is not consciously insincere; but if we wanted a reliable estimate of the odds in this case, he is not the person we would look to for it. Wishes beget beliefs, especially about probabilities of upshots.

No rule of thumb can obviate this danger. If without such a rule our man would be tempted to miscalculate the facts in his own favour, then with a rule of thumb he will be tempted to suspend the rule and then miscalculate the facts. For his protection he needs something with a firmer grip on his mind than any rule of thumb has. It must present itself to him as having moral force of its own, as something that binds him, not merely as a practical aid that he can use or lay down as he might a hammer.

These ideas have been most fully worked out by R. M. Hare, in his picture of moral thinking as stratified. According to this, the basic morality is a kind of utilitarianism, which we can invoke when we are thinking coolly, carefully, in a theoretic way, about moral issues—

'playing God or the ideal observer', i.e. 'doing philosophy'.[21] A quite different set of moral principles is used for on-the-spot thinking about moral questions as they arise in our lives: what we do here is immediate, engaged, and usually hurried, and for it we need a working morality that is easier to manage and harder to mismanage than utilitarianism. This working morality consists in a rich set of principles whose main purpose is to identify and forbid behaviour of certain fairly simple kinds: maiming, killing, lying, theft, promise-breaking, infidelity, and so on. Hare holds that we should accept these as genuine moral principles: if we break any of them, we should feel that we have behaved wrongly. Yet they are not the basic moral truth, which is utilitarianism. According to that, plus some facts of human nature, our best chance of acting rightly will come from our inculcating in ourselves a sincerely held working morality which forbids actions such as those I have listed. 'We' do this to 'ourselves' across generations: working morality was instilled in us by our parents, and we pass it on.

Hare's view about the two levels of morality seems to me almost certainly right. (I am not endorsing his doctrine that one level contains utilitarianism.) It would be astonishing if our deepest and most careful views about how it is right or wrong to behave were simple enough to be usable in the rush of daily life. Also, if the morality of conduct has something to do with the value of consequences, as most of us think it has, we shall always be tempted to miscalculate these in our own favour; which is another reason for having a working morality in which consequences play a smaller role.

One's fundamental, most carefully considered morality—what one endorses when coolly doing moral theory—could still play a part in the moral life.[22] Looking at past performances in the light of our basic moral theory, we might find that our working morality can be improved upon—that we can see how to bring it closer to what we accept as a matter of basic theory, without making it less serviceable to us. This should lead us to try to alter our moral sense, or that of our children. Also, two accepted working principles may conflict in a particular case. Then, if there is time and opportunity for it, basic morality can be invoked to relieve the log-jam. Thirdly, as philosophers we want to justify our moral convictions as far as we can. Some principles that grip

---

[21] Those phrases are from R. M. Hare, 'Principles'. For a fuller treatment, see his *Moral Thinking*.

[22] For the view that it could not, see Bernard Williams, 'A Critique of Utilitarianism', 128 and 134.

us seem hard to defend in their full strength, but their place in our lives might be explained and justified through a stratified theory. So the upper level in such a morality can have three roles—as reformer, as tie-breaker, and as justifier.

Some philosophers have found something offensively élitist in the idea of a morality which implies that it itself ought not to be widely consulted in daily life. They might have a point if the thesis were that only some privileged few can safely consult the correct basic morality, the rest of us being too stupid and corruptible to be trusted with it. That is not Hare's position, or mine. He says that 'archangels' think carefully about basic morality and 'proles' apply working morality, but he insists that each of us can be more or less archangelic, less or more proletarian, from time to time. This can still be seen as a kind of élitism, in which each of us sometimes condescends to *everyone*, including his or her own past and future stages; and this might be found demeaning, fragmenting, perhaps a threat to the individual person's integrity. It can, however, be seen rather as a tribute to each person's rich variety, the fact that each of us can serve as his or her own guardian, monitor, or pathfinder.

The 'two levels' idea has implications for method in moral philosophy. The conclusions that Hare draws depend on his view that utilitarianism can be proved a priori to be the correct basic morality.[23] His proof has not won wide acceptance and has not convinced me, but I bring it in as a reference point, an aid to steering through methodological space. Because of his proof, Hare thinks that we can study correct basic morality—at what he calls the 'critical' level—without appealing to moral intuitions. These, he holds, are sparks thrown off when working morality is active, which is why he calls it 'intuitive morality'. Those intuitions are our quickly reached applications of that morality to the matter in hand, and they have little authority. When someone makes a moral claim on 'intuitive' grounds, Hare demands evidence that this intuition is not a mere prejudice, an upshot of the person's upbringing, or the like. This is a challenge to show that the intuition rests on something firmer than the contingencies of the person's individual nature. Realists who do not accept Hare's proof must find their own answer to this demand. My non-realist answer is that all my moral opinions *do* rest on my conditioned nature. Some are more than prejudices, and do

---

[23] For a brief statement of the proof, see Hare, *Moral Thinking*, ch. 6. For a hard-edged, technical reconstruction of it, see Allan Gibbard, 'Hare's Analysis of "Ought" and its Implications'; also R. M. Hare, 'Comments on Gibbard'.

not reflect unconscious pathological states; I have arrived at some through careful thought and feeling, and others—though not reached reflectively—are open to change on the basis of further thought and feeling. Still, all of these share the metaphysical status of vicious or shallow prejudices.

That goes for intuitions in working morality and in abstract theory. Some moral opinions that grip me strongly are ones that I cannot, in a thoughtful and controlled way, justify in their full extent: I can think of cases where they would give the wrong answer. I do not try to shake these opinions off, and would indeed be alarmed if their hold loosened; but when I am trying to get clear about what I most basically think about right and wrong, I have to block my ears to some of this intuitive clamour, treating it as possibly belonging to the level of working morality and not high-level moral theory. If its proper place is at the former level, then it is a poor guide to the special cases I have mentioned—not because it comes from intuitions, but because of what intuitions it comes from. Applying the latter to these recherché situations is like using a screwdriver as a scalpel.

This could affect how we view certain results of our analyses. Suppose that our down-to-earth moral judgements show that we attach moral significance to a certain distinction, but when we analytically hold it up to the light we cannot in good conscience say 'Yes, that *does* make a moral difference.' In Section 5 I said that if that happens, something must give, but if there is any truth in Hare's two-levels theory then our morality might come through unscathed. For it might be that although the distinction in question has no basic moral significance that would show up in a careful analytic scrutiny, it does figure in our working morality as a stand-in for some more complex distinction which really is significant and would seem so to us if we could properly hold it in our minds.

2

FACTS ABOUT BEHAVIOUR

8. How the 'By'-Locution Works

Our rich repertoire of things to say about how people behave is not a mere assemblage of atoms. Atomic reports can be combined into molecules, held together by relations that we are interested in. One of these is temporal succession: He spent the money *and then* he worked to earn it; She married him *before* having her baby. Another is the relation involved in the 'by'-locution: He signalled by waving his arm; She rescued the village by diverting the flood; He betrayed Essex by prosecuting him on a capital charge. These 'by'-statements are answers to 'how?'-questions; the questions are often of great importance to us, as are the answers. The 'by'-locution is a powerful, flexible, tremendously useful conceptual device that we have for stitching together things we say about how people behave. My main project will go better if we have a clear understanding of how the locution works. That will be my task in the present section.

Each instance of the 'by'-locution comprises three elements: (1) a complete sentential clause ('She signalled'), (2) 'by', (3) a subjectless gerundial phrase ('waving'). I associate (3) with a second complete sentential clause ('She waved'); I shall say why later.

The first clause always means something of the form 'Something that *x* did had RP', where RP is a relational property. For example, 'He broke a promise' means that some fact about his behaviour conflicted with a promise he had made. What the remainder of the 'by'-statement does is to produce an instance, a value of the 'Something . . .' (or 'Some fact . . .') which makes the initial clause true. Thus, 'He broke a promise . . .' means that *some* fact about his behaviour conflicted with a promise he had made, and '. . . by coming home late' says what it was. Thus,

He broke a promise — by — coming home late

analyses into

Some fact about his behaviour conflicted with a promise he had made — namely the fact that — he came home late.

Similarly, 'He overcooked the stew . . .' says that some fact about his behaviour causally led (in a certain way) to the stew's being overcooked, and '. . . by leaving it on the fire for too long' says what. In each case, the whole content could be expressed without using 'some' and 'namely': 'His coming home late conflicted with a promise he had made', 'His leaving the stew on the fire too long led to its being over-cooked'. My more prolix 'some'/'namely' version has two merits: it brings out in a perspicuous way what is common to all instances of the 'by'-locution, and it explicitly states the two trivially entailed proposi-tions—that he broke a promise and that he came home late, that he overcooked the stew and that he left it on the fire for too long.

When we say that someone ɸed by πing, the proposition that he πed may also mean something of the form 'Something that he did had RP', so that it can be fed into a new 'by'-statement. This lets us make chains: 'He spoiled the party by insulting the host, which he did by insinuat-ing that the host gave the party only to further his career, which he did by saying "I see that nobody higher than vice-president is here; don't you wish you had saved your money?" ' The last term in that chain would be hard to specify further with help from 'by', though one might say that he uttered that sentence by moving his vocal organs in certain ways. I shall return to this in Section 11 below.

Such chains can be enormously long: we can report behaviour in ways that involve relation upon relation. Reports of causal chains are striking in this respect. When someone's conduct has a certain causal upshot, this will have others in its turn, and so on indefinitely; and these more remote consequences can often be reported in statements that do not use 'cause' or 'consequence' or the like. So in answer to 'What did he do?' we can often choose how far to go along the causal chain. Joel Feinberg has called this phenomenon 'the accordion effect'.[1] What did he do? *He saved the village. He prevented a flood. He diverted the stream. He blocked an outlet. He felled a tree. He moved thus and so with a saw.* These can all be true because of a single set of movements that he made: He saved the village by preventing a flood, which he did by diverting the stream, which he did by . . . and so on. Also, links can be omitted: He saved the village by felling a tree, he prevented a flood by moving thus and so with a saw.

---

[1] Joel Feinberg, 'Action and Responsibility', 134 f.

My 'namely'-analysis seems to be a pretty good account of how the 'by'-locution works. It is clearer than any of its predecessors, and unlike them it covers all the territory.[2] If this simple proposal is right, why has it been so long in coming? The surface answer is that previous workers on the problem (including myself) did not dig into the initial clause of the 'by'-locution so as to uncover the existential quantifier; until that comes into the open, 'namely' has nothing to grab on to. The idea of digging came easily, once I had realized that 'by'-statements do not relate human *acts* to one another.

This was part of the still larger discovery—as I think it to be—that the act concept should not predominate in any inquiry into our thought and talk about how people behave. Much analytic philosophy about behaviour has, I believe, been cramped and thus distorted by reliance on the act concept, and many aspects of this book reflect my having broken free from it. The act concept proved to be an obstacle to understanding in the areas I shall explore; in no philosophical inquiry have I found it helpful. Before showing how it impedes understanding of the 'by'-locution, I should first explain what concept it is.

9. 'Act'

Acts can also be called actions, and we could speak of 'the action concept', but then we must be wary. My topic is the concept of *actions* or of *an action*, not that of *action*, with which I have no quarrel. The two differ grammatically as count noun and mass noun, as do 'puddle' and 'water': the former can be pluralized and takes articles while the latter does not; the latter can be preceded by 'a quantity of . . .' and 'a sample of . . .', while the former cannot. Puddles are things we count, while water is a kind of stuff that comes in stretches or quantities or amounts. Similarly with machines and machinery, shoes and footwear, snowflakes and snow, loaves and bread. Many nouns can be used in either way: there are three *roads* leading out of town; we walked along miles of bad *road*. 'Action' is such a noun.

---

[2] See for example J. L. Austin, *How to Do Things with Words*, lecture 10; Alvin A. Goldman, *A Theory of Human Action*, ch. 2; Judith Jarvis Thomson, *Acts and Other Events*, 204 (formula T-S_7) and 218 (formula T-S_{12}); and Carl Ginet, *On Action*, 16 f. Thomson's ingenious account is confined to cases where RP involves causation, and cannot be extended to cover the likes of 'He divorced her by signing a document' or 'He tried to escape by disguising himself'. The analysis offered by Patrick Francken and Lawrence Brian Lombard, 'How not to Flip the Switch with the Floodlight', 39, is similarly limited.

When used as a mass noun, 'action' has the same grammar as 'water' and 'snow', occurring in the singular without any article. It does not of course refer to material stuff, but it does refer to *some of what goes on*, or, we might say, to *stuff that is done*. For example:

> She sprang into action.
> There was a lot of action here this morning.
> That was a gratifying course of action.

To get a sense of action as stuff that is done, partly comparable with material stuff, compare that first sentence with 'She bathed in milk', the second with 'There was a lot of fog here this morning', and the third with 'This is a profitable line of footwear'.

We also use 'action', in a grammatically mass fashion, to stand for a universal—namely, whatever it is that an item must have in order to count as action. Used like that, 'action' means the same as 'agency': we speak of an episode as 'an instance of action', or say that some philosopher is exploring the field of 'action'—not meaning 'stuff that is done', but rather the conditions something must satisfy if it is to count as *done*. Agency matters greatly in philosophy. The morality of conduct concerns what we do, as distinct from what happens to us—the movements we make, not the spasmodic twitches that we cannot avoid—and there are philosophical problems about just what this involves. I take this concept on trust, however, making it the frame of my whole inquiry; and in my rare mentions of it I shall call it 'agency', not 'action'. That frees 'action' for use purely to designate stuff that is done, in contrast to 'act', which is my vehicle for the count concept, the notion of individual, countable things that are done.

An act is an event of a certain kind. The shout that he gave was an event; if his giving it was an exercise of human agency, then it was also an act. Thus:

> An act is an event that is an instance of agency.

We do not yet deeply, analytically understand the concept of *agency*, and that limits our grasp of *act*, which contains it.[3] What unfits the latter for theoretical use, however, is its well-understood ingredient,

---

[3] I disagree with this: 'If . . . actions are events, a proper understanding of action—including intentional action—requires a proper understanding of events' (Alfred R. Mele, 'Recent Work on Intentional Action', 199). We need to understand *event* to understand *actions* (which I call *acts*), but not to understand *action*—whether this is stuff that is done or the universal agency.

namely the event concept. This concept behaves well when kept in its place, but that is not in disciplined theories.

Students of it often refer to acts through gerunds, that is, verb derivatives ending in 'ing'. They are apt to refer to *the catch he made* as *his catching of the ball*. That, although correct, is risky because it gets confused with *his catching the ball*, which does not name an event at all. This mix-up has led some into philosophical error. To get an intuitive sense of how the two differ, consider how 'his catching of the ball' behaves like 'the cover of the ball' or some other phrase standing for a thinglike entity:

It includes an indirect object ('*of* the ball').
'His' can be replaced by articles ('the catching of the ball', 'a catching of the ball').
An adjective can precede the gerund ('his lucky catching of the ball').

For reasons like these, 'his catching of the ball' is called a *perfect* nominal, meaning that it has become perfectly nounlike, its parent verb having lost all its nature as a verb. In contrast, 'his catching the ball' has a conflicting set of grammatical properties, which it shares with the propositional 'He catches the ball'.

It includes a direct object.
An adverb can precede the gerund ('his brilliantly catching the ball').
It can be negated ('his not catching the ball').
It can be modified with tenses ('his having caught the ball').
It can be modified modally ('his having to catch the ball').

No articles, no '*of* the ball', no preceding adjectives. 'His catching the ball' is called an *imperfect* nominal, because although it behaves in some ways like a noun phrase—e.g. it can be the subject of a sentence—its parent verb is, in Zeno Vendler's phrase, still 'alive and kicking' inside it.[4]

If this quick survey leaves you unconvinced, it need not matter much. I shall keep out of trouble by referring to events not with gerunds but rather through so-called 'derived nominals'—event sortals such as 'appointment', 'birth', 'collapse', 'departure', 'earthquake', and so on. Here are some that are specifically kinds of acts:

apology, argument, baptism, burial, climb, dance, dismissal, fight, frown, gesture, greeting, hug, intervention, kick, lockout, punch,

---

[4] Almost everything in the present section is derived from Zeno Vendler, 'Facts and Events'. These ideas of Vendler's have been widely accepted and further developed, most recently by Alessandro Zucchi, *The Language of Propositions and Events*.

quip, refusal, resignation, shout, smile, speech, stroll, tackle, take-
over, theft, tracheotomy, transplant, visit.

Those words are perfectly nouns: they take adjectives, can be pluralized, and take articles; 'ingratiating smile', 'refusals', 'a transplant', 'the
speech'. The kick that he gave her is grammatically on a par with the
ring that he gave her; so is the apology that she extracted from him.
Events are things that happen.[5] Physical objects are things that do not
happen. That is not a mere fact about how we use 'happen': there is a
metaphysical basis for it, though I shall not go into it here.

The event concept is good for giving small, vague bits of news, but
not for use in hard-edged theories. Two things go wrong, for example,
when a philosophical inquiry into behaviour is expressed in terms of the
act concept. (1) The analysis loses scope, because much of the truth
about how people behave is not about their acts. For example, we might
be concerned with the fact that *She did not warn him*, or that *She closed
at least one of the gates but not more than three*. In neither case can we
cleanly say what act of hers interests us. Behavioural facts that are naturally expressed with help from negation or disjunction usually lie
beyond the reach of the act concept, which thus tethers us, preventing
us from ranging across our whole proper territory. (2) The event/act
concept creates needless problems. Intending to slap him mildly, she in
fact slapped him hard: was *the slap* that she gave him intentional? You
can make a case for Yes and one for No; or you can say that 'The slap
was intentional' is true in one sense and false in another, or that the
slap was intentional under one description but not under another. The
question must be faced if the act concept is your topic; but if your concern is with intentions, you need not slog through all this. There is no
mystery about the case. What happened was that she intended to slap
him mildly, and did slap him hard. If we say, more stiltedly, that she
intended it to be the case that *she slapped him mildly*, and in fact she
slapped him hard, we make explicit that she intended one fact to obtain
but made a different one obtain instead. That is the whole story. We
had a 'problem' only because we forced our account of her intention
into the constricting mould of the act concept, which pushed it out of
shape and then dropped it into quicksand. I shall return to this in more
detail in Section 63 below.

Anything useful we can say with the event concept we can say without it; it is everywhere dispensable. Truths about events supervene log-

---

[5] This phrase is the perfect title of J. E. Tiles's book *Things that Happen*.

ically, and in a simple way, on truths about things and their properties: there was a quarrel because some people quarrelled; there was a shower because rain fell; and so on.[6] The only event-using statements that are not simply expressible in other terms are the ones that stir up dissension among theorists: 'When he wins the event with his final jump, the jump is the victory'; 'Two events cannot have exactly the same causes and effects'; 'The fall of this sparrow could have occurred later', '. . . could have had a different trajectory', '. . . could have been the fall of a different bird'. These have to be wrestled with when the event concept is one's *topic*; but they do not lie across the path to my present goal of finding the best way to think about behaviour.

If my present work has an obvious predecessor, it is Lars Bergström's *The Alternatives and Consequences of Actions*. That work's chances of being helpful are lessened by the heavy use it makes of an act concept. Also, the concept is peculiar: if I reply loudly, Bergström would have it that my reply is one act and my loud reply is another; and he speaks of one act as a 'version' of another, as though acts were stories.

10. The Grammar of the 'By'-Locution

Previous writers on the 'by'-locution have nearly all approached it through the act concept, asking what the sentence 'She signalled by waving her arm' says about how her *signal* related to her *arm-wave*. I, for one, wasted much time peering at 'by' through the lens of the famous thesis that if she signals by waving then her signal is her wave. We were all wrong to force the act concept into a story so inhospitable to it. I say that for two reasons.

(1) One is that plenty of 'by'-statements clearly have nothing to do with acts as ordinarily understood. He fulfilled her fears by never once thinking of her during the whole voyage. He did his duty by continually remaining sensitive to any slights to her good name. These are normal 'by'-statements, but the phrases '[his] never once thinking of her during the whole voyage' and '[his] continually remaining sensitive to any slights to her good name' don't strike one as reports on *acts* that he performed. There are countless such examples: He broke the record by not speaking to anyone for five weeks; He upset her by how loudly he

---

[6] Donald Davidson argues, on the contrary, that we should unpack 'Adam and Eve quarrelled' into 'There was a quarrel, and Adam and Eve took part in it', not vice versa. For references and counter-arguments see my *Events and their Names*, ch. 11.

cracked his knuckles; She kept him off balance by treating him nicely every second time they met. There is no clean way to handle these as relatings of act to act.

(2) 'She signalled by raising her hand' does involve acts, because it entails that a signal and a gesture were performed. Even it, however, has no trace of the act concept on its surface; if that concept is to enter the story, it must be dragged in. The sentence has the surface form which I have noted as common to all 'by'-statements: a fully sentential clause ('She signalled . . .'), the word 'by', and a subjectless gerundial nominal ('. . . raising her hand'). Such triples give us 'He broke the record by pushing a railroad car at 10 m.p.h. on level ground', 'He let the apples spoil by leaving them in the barrel', 'She brought down the government by not intervening in the debate', and 'She signalled by raising her hand'. The first item, obviously, states a whole proposition about how the person behaved. It might report an act, but often it does not: the 'by'-locution as such does not force the act concept into that initial sentential clause.

The third item, the noun phrase containing a gerund, is trickier. It seems clear that in 'She signalled by raising her hand' the gerundial phrase is short for '*her* raising her hand', with 'her' being deleted because it co-refers with the subject of the whole sentence. To stop the co-reference, put the first clause into the passive—'A signal was given . . .', and then we have to put 'her' back in: 'A signal was given by her raising her hand'. Analogously, we delete 'himself' from 'He wants himself to go to the concert' but we do not delete 'her' from 'He wants her to go to the concert'. The best way to see 'She signalled by raising her hand', therefore, is as ending with the complete gerundial nominal 'her raising her hand'. That is an imperfect nominal, which refers to the fact that she raised her hand; or so I have argued, pointing out a series of grammatical features which it shares with whole sentences and not with such act-names as 'the movement she made with her hand'.

So the 'by'-locution as such does not involve the act concept. The form of it is: *a proposition about behaviour*—'*by*'—*a proposition about behaviour*. That is precisely the form of the analysans in my 'namely'-analysis.

I have expressed the latter using the phrase 'something that he did', which could quantify over acts; so it might be thought that I have acts lurking in the background after all. If that were right, my analysis would not cover all the ground: as we have already seen, 'He fulfilled her fears' had better not mean anything of the form 'Some act of his had RP'. To avoid being hemmed in, I construe 'something that he did' to mean 'some fact about his behaviour'. I have said so explicitly a few times, and I now declare that to be the position I am taking. Each 'by'-statement, I assert, means something of the form: *Some fact about x's behaviour has RP, namely the fact that* . . . This requires that the relational properties in question be ones that facts can have. So indeed they are, as I shall show in Section 13.

When I speak of 'facts about behaviour', I seem to imply that I have in my ontology some stuff called 'behaviour'—or 'action', a term we have already encountered standing for stuff that is done. Perhaps I could accept that implication, on this basis:

> There is no trouble in the concept of *what is done*. The clumsy awkwardness of the act concept comes from its way of cutting up what is done into things that are done, that is, comes from its nature as a count concept. Behaviour or action is of the same ontological kind as acts, differing from it only as mass from count—as grass differs from blades, footwear from shoes, money from coins. So although I refuse to work with the act concept, I have no qualms in quantifying over items or portions or stretches of behaviour.

Even if that is right, though, I do not want to owe you a metaphysics of behaviour. Of course there is behaviour, some of which can be sliced into acts; but I need not give either of these a ground-floor place in my enterprise. What I call 'facts about behaviour' are really about people, specifically about how they behave, just as facts about heights are about how high things are. If I ask you to 'tell me about her behaviour', you are less likely to begin 'Her behaviour was . . .' than to begin 'She . . .'. In Section 15 below we shall find an extra merit in this way of looking at things.

11. Intrinsic Behavioural Facts

'She thatched the cottage.' 'How?' There must be an answer to this: Nobody could thatch a cottage without there being some other fact about her behaviour which resulted in the cottage's having newly placed thatch on its roof. 'He raised his hand.' 'How?' There must be an answer to this too. It might be 'He raised his hand by holding it in his other hand and hoisting it like a flag', or 'He raised his hand by tying it to a crane-hook and starting the crane'. It is of course more likely that no such intermediate behaviour was involved, and that he raised his hand by just raising it, and not through any other mode of behaviour that he could have embarked on as a means to getting his hand up. In such a case I shall say that he *immediately* raises his hand.[7] Even when he raises his right hand by hoisting it with his left, he immediately moves the latter. Most human behaviour involves immediately moving one's limbs or vocal cords.

Or so I believe, but some philosophers disagree. According to them, all action starts with a voluntary *act of the will* or *trying* or *setting oneself to* φ or the like, which does not consist in one's moving.[8] This implies that we never immediately move our limbs or vocal cords. I shall assume without discussion that this minority view is wrong; if it is right, I could revise this book to fit it.

It is sometimes uncontroversially the case that behaviour starts with the person's voluntarily doing something other than moving, e.g. redirecting his thoughts. (The verbal question whether turning one's thoughts is properly called 'behaviour' is negligible.) Suppose for example that I want you to stop talking, and I think that my best chance is to get you to think that you have embarrassed me. I deliberately turn my thoughts onto some shaming episode in my past, making myself blush. If my plan works, then *I have quietened you*, which entails that some fact about my behaviour has resulted in your being silent; and it is not a fact about how I moved. From now on I shall simplify things by setting aside all cases like this, and pretending that all behaviour involves moving. The only harm that this pretence might do to the work will be noted in Section 33.

When Agent immediately raises his hand, the question 'How?' has an answer: 'He raised his hand by immediately raising it'. This is unlike most instances of the form 'He φed by πing' in that here 'He πed' entails that he φed. There is no mystery about that, however. Whenever someone φs mediately, there is some value of π such that (1) 'He πed' does not entail 'He φed' and (2) he φed by πing. That is what it is to do something mediately. When Agent raises his hand immediately, there is *ex hypothesi* no value of π satisfying those two conditions— merely one that satisfies (2).

---

[7] When Agent φs by πing, I shall say that he πs *more immediately* than he φs. We can thus easily define the uncomparative use of 'immediately' out of its comparative use. This use of '(im)mediate' has of course nothing to do with the direct/mediated distinction that I discuss in other chapters.

[8] H. A. Prichard, 'Acting, Willing, Desiring'; Jennifer Hornsby, *Actions*, ch. 3.

Does any plain English sentence mean, for some value of φ, that the subject φed immediately? Here are some candidates:

He nodded.
She clapped her hands.
She snapped her fingers.

Someone might get his head to move back and forth by attaching it to an eccentric gear etc., but that would not be *nodding*, it seems; the meaning of 'nod' rules it out; and similarly with the other two. It does not follow that 'She nodded' means that she moved her head immediately. (I thought it did, until Thomas McKay came to my aid.) Suppose that someone has an infirmity which has destroyed her proprioceptive body image: she has lost her sense of how it feels, from the inside, to move thus or so. On a certain occasion she gets her head to move up and down, meaning this as Yes to a question. Unable to do this immediately, she achieves it by watching herself in the mirror, rapidly trying out various micro-movements, and eventually hitting on the right ones to get her head to move as she wants it to.[9] Looking at her, we would say 'She nodded', and when she explained how she did it we would not retract. The verb 'to nod', in short, does not permit such a wide range of values of π as does 'to raise one's hand'; nor do 'to clap', 'to kick', and some others. Yet the ordinary meanings of these verbs, though narrow, still leave *some* room for 'How?' to receive answers other than 'By doing it immediately'.

If I am wrong about that, so be it. The point does not matter greatly, because it only concerns what meanings are provided for in plain English. There are what we might call *intrinsic facts* about behaviour, namely the ones I report in the form 'She immediately φed'. We need to be clear about how these relate to non-intrinsic facts, such as that she boiled the eggs or kept faith with her friend; but whether English can express them without help from 'immediately' is of no great moment.

Philosophers have sometimes spoken of 'basic acts', in a sense which connects with intrinsic facts about behaviour. When Agent immediately raises his hand, they would say that he thereby performs a basic act. Here as so often the act concept makes needless trouble. If someone signals by waving her hand, and if the wave is a basic act, then is the signal the wave? If it is, then the signal is basic, which makes every act basic, rendering 'basic' idle. If it is not, then the person in waving

---

[9] For details, see Oliver Sacks, 'The Disembodied Lady'.

performs two acts—a signal and a wave—and the floodgates are open to her performing hundreds. Wrestling with this conundrum is a high price to pay for the *dis*advantage of working with the act concept. Facts about behaviour create no such difficulty. That she signalled is different from the fact that she waved, but who would doubt that there are thousands of facts about how a person behaves at a given time?

12. Relational Features of Behaviour

We need a shared understanding of what sorts of relational properties behaviour can have, and of how they are involved in the meanings of some of the things we say. There are three relations that matter for moral judgements, I believe; let us look at them in themselves first, before examining how they figure in our meanings. Consider this simple tale:

David stretches out his arm in front of him. (1) As he extends it, his arm knocks a vase off the table. (2) Betsy expected him to stretch out his arm. (3) He extends his arm because he thinks this is likely to ease the pain in his elbow.

The behaviour we are to consider is David's extending his arm. We have been told here about three of its relational properties. (1) It relates causally to a certain consequence: we get from the arm's moving to the vase's fall through the world's unfolding in accordance with causal laws. (2) It relates non-causally to a state of affairs which it makes obtain, namely the fulfilment of Betsy's expectation. David's extending his arm may have the causal consequence that Betsy thinks he has done what she expected; but the mere fact that her expectation *has* been fulfilled is a non-causal consequence of David's behaviour. The fact that he moves thus, conjoined with the already obtaining fact that she expected him to, adds up to the further fact that her prediction is fulfilled. I count C as a non-causal consequence of Agent's φing just in case: C is entailed by (Q & Agent φs) and not by either conjunct alone, where Q is a contingent fact which does not entail any causal laws. (3) It relates to a belief (and by implication a desire) by which it is explained. He extends his arm because he thinks this to be conducive to his goal of easing the pain. Note that (1) and (2) concern what is partly explained by the behaviour, while (3) concerns what explains it. Now let us see how these three occur in analyses of plain talk about behaviour.

(1) Vastly many of our reports on behaviour mean things of the form: *Something that he did caused . . . it to be the case that P.* He felled the tree, she rescued the village, he overcooked the stew, she renovated the barn, he mowed the lawn. Each means that a certain state of affairs causally resulted . . . from some fact about how the person behaved. The ellipses stand for extra constraints, of which some are common to all the cases (see Section 2 above), while others are not: 'She painted the wall' entails that her movements led, *without any complex intervening causal chain*, to there being paint on the wall; the emphasized condition does not enter into the meaning of 'She ruined the wall'.

(2) Other reports mean things of the form: *Something that he did led non-causally . . . to its being the case that P.* In the initial scenario, the statement that David fulfilled Betsy's expectations is like that. We have three facts:

A: David extended his arm.
Q: Betsy expected David to extend his arm.
C: Betsy's expectation was fulfilled.

C is entailed by A conjoined with Q, and not by either alone; so C is a non-causal consequence of David's extending his arm. If Betsy had expected that David would break the vase, both sorts of consequence would be involved. The fulfilment of that expectation would ensue causally from his extending his arm and non-causally from his breaking the vase. Another example: 'He broke the promise he had made to her'. This requires that some fact about his behaviour, conjoined with some fact about a promise he had made, resulted non-causally in the promise's being broken. Did some other fact about his behaviour result causally in the same promise's being broken? That depends on what the promise was. If it was *to make no noise*, then Yes; but if the promise was *to keep still*, then No.

(3) Many reports on behaviour, while not explicitly mentioning beliefs, desires, goals, or the like, mean something of the form *Something that he did was explained . . . by his thinking that P and wanting G.* I could have presented the initial scenario by saying 'David tries to ease the pain in his elbow', which means that something he does is explained by his thinking it is apt to ease the pain. Another example: 'He hunted for lions' means 'Something that he did is explained . . . by his thinking it would be conducive to his goal of catching or killing lions'; 'He tried to escape' means 'Something that he did is explained . . . by his thinking it would be conducive to his goal of escaping', and

so on. It is easy to see how these fit into the 'by'-locution on my analysis of it: He tried to escape by disguising himself as the chaplain; Something that he did is explained . . . by his thinking it would be conducive to his goal of escaping, namely disguising himself as the chaplain. As always, the ellipses stand for further constraints; they are needed because (for example) he doesn't count as having tried to escape if he got no further than asking whether the prison had a chaplain.

In the initial scenario, you were invited to think that David immediately extends his arm, rather than that he manipulates it with his other hand. Reports in this third category, however, are neutral about the difference between mediate and immediate behavioural facts. Consider the statement that he tried to escape from prison by disguising himself as the chaplain. The fact that he so disguised himself is not immediate; it is the fact that he moved in ways that caused it to be the case that he looked like the chaplain. However, if *that* fact about his behaviour is explained by his thinking it would be conducive to his goal of escaping, then so also are the (more) immediate facts about the movements he made that led to his being disguised. In general, when a belief and desire explanation applies to a certain behavioural fact, it will apply also to the more immediate facts that underlie it. It will not necessarily apply to the less immediate ones. David did not knock the vase off the table because he thought that this would ease his pain.

13. Fact Causation

What I have called relational properties of behaviour are properties of facts about behaviour. In this section I shall show how this can be. Here are the three classes of relational properties, rearranged for expository reasons: (1) . . . is explained by the person's believing that P and wanting G; (2) . . . has the non-causal consequence that P; (3) . . . has the causal consequence that P.

(1) Facts about behaviour are the best, least controversial bearers of properties in class (1). Those properties can also be had by acts: his desire to upset her can be adduced to explain *the answer* that he gave her, that being an act. But we can also, and more informatively, adduce it to explain his answering her rudely, or his answering her in Russian, or his answering that he preferred Donald Duck to Greta Garbo, which are facts about his behaviour.

(2) Facts are the natural bearers of properties in class (2). The best account I can find for non-causal consequences is in terms of entailments between propositions, and facts are true propositions. What led to its being the case that (C) he had broken his promise was (A) his arriving home late and (Q) his having promised not to arrive home late; and (A) is just the imperfect-nominal way of referring to the fact that he arrived home late.

(3) It has been widely thought that the canonical form of singular causal statements is 'Event$_1$ caused event$_2$'; but fact-causation statements are also possible and indeed better. For one thing, they are more informative. The rainstorm was nocturnal, cold, long, heavy, noisy, irregular, windy, driven in from the north, the first one in years, and so on; the sentence 'The rainstorm caused the landslide' does not tell us which of those features was causally relevant to there being a landslide. The language of fact causation lets us say more: There was a landslide because three inches of rain fell in two hours on dry ground. Of course we can report this by saying more about the event: The landslide was caused by a rainstorm, which had that effect because it involved three inches of rain in two hours on dry ground. This, however, brings us back to fact causation.

The latter is stronger, subtler and more versatile than event causation. Here is an example. The dynamite will explode if current flows through the wire, and there are ten switches, hooked up in parallel. All ten close at the same instant, and the bomb goes off. Which event—which making of contact—caused the explosion? None, because no contact made any difference. Well, then, perhaps the explosion was caused by a 'decacontact', a composite event whose parts were the ten contacts. Even if there is such an event, however, that answer smudges the difference between this case and the one where all ten contacts are needed for the bomb to explode. Although good philosophers have been exercised by analogues of this 'problem', it is illusory. It comes from trying to force into the receptacle of event-causation material that has the wrong shape for it. Move to fact causation and all is clear: the bomb went off because *at least one of the switches closed.*

That example succeeds because facts, being propositional, can be disjoined, conjoined, negated, and adverbially modified with respect to time and place and in other ways. This lets what we say in the language of facts, including fact causation, be more refined than the coarse 'events' idiom can manage. There is no unique event corresponding to the fact that at least one of the switches closed. Again: if she caught the ball, there was a catch; but if she did not catch the ball—which may be a momentous fact about her behaviour—there is no corresponding event or act.[10] That last example presupposes that negative facts can have causal consequences, and so they can. Consider this example: *A gate is swinging shut, and comes to be shut at T_2; at T_1, about a second earlier, I could have grabbed the gate, held it, and thus stopped it from shutting at T_2; I did not do that.* We would not say I 'caused' the gate to shut, but my not grabbing it at T_1 relates in a causal way to its being shut at T_2—it leads to the gate's closing a second later through the world's unfolding according to causal laws.

We do not say things like 'The fact that the bread was left out in the rain caused the fact that it became soggy'; but we do say 'The bread became soggy because it was left out in the rain', 'The bread's becoming soggy was a consequence of its being left out in the rain', and 'Its being left out in the rain caused the bread to become soggy'; those are fact-causation statements.

I should pause briefly on that last example, where I treat 'the bread to become soggy' as a way of referring to the fact that the bread became soggy. The noun-infinitive form is one of our commonest and most comfortable ways of referring to facts, as I think you will agree after pondering a few examples, along with the one about bread. If I want it to be the case that the weather is fine tomorrow, I can express that by saying 'I want the weather to be fine tomorrow'. If I expect it to be the case that you win the race, I can say so in the words 'I expect you to win the race'. If further evidence is needed, consider this. Classical Latin does not have a construction that works like the English form '. . . that [S]' where S is a whole sentence. It does have the noun-infinitive form: though it does not have the form 'He believed that she was honest' it does have 'He believed her to be honest'. Now, it is universally accepted among Latinists—it is utterly received doctrine—that the noun-infinitive form is the classical Latin way of doing *exactly the same work* as we do with 'that [S]'. If this were wrong, it would have been noticed by now. I add only that what holds for the Latin noun-infinitive is likely to hold also for the English one, which is derived from it.

---

[10] For an overview of the merits of fact causation, see Hugh Mellor, 'The Singularly Affecting Facts of Causation'.

14. 'Itself'

Moral philosophers sometimes contrast the consequences of an act with the act itself. Some say, and others deny, that the nature of the act itself bears more strongly on the morality of conduct than do its consequences; and a whole literature for and against 'consequentialism' has grown up around the issue. Never mind the occurrence in this of 'act'; I have finished with that, and turn now to the apparent line between *behaviour* and *what results from it*.[11] That, one would think, is one part of the line between intrinsic and relational facts about behaviour, because facts about consequences are one subspecies of relational facts. When someone announces an interest in this, one might wonder about the rest of the intrinsic/relational line. Are we to hold a species of relational fact in one hand, all the intrinsic facts in the other, ignoring the remaining relational facts? It seems odd.

It seems even odder when one recalls how impoverished are the strictly intrinsic facts about how people behave. Nearly everything we say about behaviour attributes relational properties to it, and that includes everything with moral significance. An intrinsic account of how Agent behaved would give only the geometrical or balletic qualities of his movements. Such facts might matter if we held it to be fundamentally wrong to make (say) circular movements with one's left hand; but nobody accepts such a morality.

Perhaps that is being too strict about what is 'intrinsic'. Then let us relax the latter somewhat, and see if that brings us to a notion that really is at work in the standard contrast between behaviour and its consequences. Perhaps 'the behaviour itself' is meant to include all its instantaneous properties, including relational ones. That would include (1) the facts about why the person φed, and (2) non-causal consequences that the behaviour has because of facts then obtaining. Causal consequences would be shut out, in theory, because they all take time; but our moralists are surely not going to fuss about nanoseconds! Any line of thought that brings within 'the behaviour itself' its strictly instantaneous relational properties will be apt also to include (3) the ones that the behaviour acquires through very short causal chains. 'Never mind the consequences—just tell me what he did.' 'Well, he knocked a piece

---

[11] In brief: I have dealt with 'the act' and now turn to 'itself'.

off the sculpture with one blow of his hammer.' To the casual ear, that might sound fairly intrinsic.

Unfortunately, this does not come close to describing what the moral theorists have in mind. Their debates about behaviour and consequences involve examples like the following: *In a certain vexed political situation, Agent can probably save many lives by procuring the judicial execution of someone he knows to be innocent. He needs only to sign a certain report; then the causal chain will unroll, through many predictable legal stages, to the victim's execution a year later.* This is a famous example, to which I have added one detail: it would take a year for the victim's death to ensue from Agent's movement. That will not stop anyone from seeing this as a debatable case in which the wrongness of behaviour is challenged by the value of its consequences. The temporal way of marking off 'the behaviour itself', though possible, is not what is going on. I have done my best with the notion of intrinsicality, starting strictly and then relaxing it in the most plausible way; but the result is useless. We must start again.

My view about what happens when moral philosophers contrast the consequences of behaviour with the behaviour itself is best stated in three steps.

Step One. For particular values of ϕ they are contrasting ϕing with the consequences of ϕing. There is nothing difficult or problematic about that; in drawing that line, *for a given ϕ*, we need have no thoughts about intrinsicality. The meaning of 'hurt', for instance, tells us how much of what goes on falls within the province of Agent's hurting Patient, and how much should be relegated to the causal and other consequences of his doing so. Similarly for any other value of ϕ, unless it is vague or ambiguous.

That, however, is not enough to support any *general* debate in which behaviour is distinguished from its consequences. For such a debate to have meaning, the combatants must agree about where in particular cases the line falls between behaviour and consequence; but according to Step One, anything that comes under 'consequences' relative to one value of ϕ comes under 'behaviour' relative to another.

Step Two. In doing what is described in Step One, these moral philosophers always work with silently agreed constraints on what kinds of value ϕ can take. That might support a general debate, for some of the upshots of Agent's way of moving on a given occasion may not be describable in the form 'Agent ϕed' for any ϕ that meets the constraints. To complete the account we need only to say what the constraints are.

Step Three. The constraints are guided, I believe, by what is common to the meanings of simple transitive verbs like 'hurt', 'help', 'betray', 'reward', 'harm', and so on. I do not mean that our moral philosophers confine themselves to values of φ expressible in such terms, for plainly they do not. There is more to 'Agent knowingly procured the judicial execution of a man he knew to be innocent' than any one English word expresses. What the simple verbs have in common is that the intrinsic facts about Agent's behaviour lead to a certain consequence (1) in a making rather than an allowing manner, (2) and in a direct rather than a mediated way. (See Section 2 above.)

Those two ideas, I submit, are the whole intelligible content of the debate about the relative moral significance of behaviour and of its consequences. They are, therefore, the whole intelligible content of the debate between so-called deontologists and so-called consequentialists.

Chapters 4 to 10 of this book will be mainly concerned with the making/allowing distinction, and secondarily with the direct/mediated distinction. In Chapter 11 I shall turn to another relational property of behaviour, namely its being explainable through a certain kind of intention. Some philosophers accord moral significance to that, and this view cannot owe anything to the influence of word-meanings. The meanings of the transitive verbs in our standard repertoire are silent about what Agent knew or wanted, and therefore about what he intended; so the source of an emphasis on intention must be sought elsewhere. I shall discuss this in Chapter 11.

3

MORAL JUDGEMENT

15. First- and Second-Order Morality

Some moral judgements belong to first-order morality, others to second-order. First-order morality issues judgements of the type 'It would be right for me to ф', 'He acted wrongly in фing', and so on; second-order morality judges whether the person deserves credit or discredit—perhaps including praise or blame—for фing. All of my examples have come from the first order, which is the chief concern of this book; but before moving on, I need to devote a section to exploring the boundary between the two orders of morality.

The two orders are often distinguished by saying that the first judges *behaviour* ('That was the wrong thing to do') while the second judges *people* ('He is to blame for doing that'). If we rest weight on this, we need an account of what behaviour is (see the end of Section 10 above); but it is better not to, because the behaviour/person or act/agent way of distinguishing the orders of morality is superficial. What it calls a judgement on behaviour is really one kind of judgement on a person: when we say that *what he did* was wrong we mean that *he* acted wrongly.

The two kinds of judgements on people are associated with two ways in which people can relate to one another. First-order judgements go with such roles as those of guide, counsellor, steersman, map-reader—especially the self-guiding that comes from deliberating about how to act. Second-order judgements speak in the voice of a victim or beneficiary of conduct, or a spokesman for victims or beneficiaries; they essentially express feelings, especially those of resentment or gratitude.[1]

This use of the terminology of 'first-order' and 'second-order' comes from Donagan. It is appropriate because judgements of the type 'He acted wrongly' do come first—they are more basic than ones that assign (dis)credit. Consider these:

---

[1] I rely here on P. F. Strawson's classic 'Freedom and Resentment'. For a plainer presentation of Strawson's ideas, see my 'Accountability'.

(1) He ought to φ.
(2) He ought to have φed.
(3) He is to blame for not having φed.

Of these, (1) is a prospective first-order judgement, and (2) a retrospective one, while (3) belongs to the second order. We could not (3) blame people unless we had views about (2) how they ought to have acted, which requires our sometimes judging (1) what a person ought to do. The converse does not hold. A morality might be used only in its prospective or action-guiding role; or it might, like Spinoza's morality, be used like that and also for retrospective judgements on conduct, but still with no thoughts of credit or discredit. Nobody could start at the bottom, with second-order judgements, without going all the way up. So first-order morality really does come first.

Vastly many moral matters do not fit comfortably into either order as I have described them. To give three examples out of thousands: Your moral scheme of things comes into play when you reflect on the role of your career decisions in your life as a whole, when you consider whether some change in temperament means that you have matured with age or merely softened, when you meditate on what price in hunger is worth paying for freedom. I do not underrate the importance of these topics, which lie outside the domain of the present work, or of course the significance of second-order morality.

I have been taking it for granted that someone might act wrongly yet not be to blame. There are many ways to block the inference of 'He is to blame' from 'He did the wrong thing', including the famous three:

> He is durably mentally incompetent to a degree that makes it inappropriate to judge him morally.
> He acted during a morally incapacitating mental episode of some kind.
> He acted under extreme duress.

The inference may also be blocked by facts about what the person knew or believed; and those, unlike the other three, can also block an inference in the opposite direction. Suppose that in ways that were predictable though he did not foresee them, Agent's wicked attempt at cruel revenge did nothing but good. In such a case, although Agent is intensely to blame, he did what any informed and decent person would have hoped he would do, would have urged him to do, and so on; which justifies saying that he acted rightly. That is a freak occurrence, however. Most behaviour that discredits the agent is morally wrong.

There are competing views about what state of knowledge or belief is needed for a person to be blameworthy. If someone acts wrongly because his ϕing has relational property RP—for example, because he moves in ways that lead to someone's suffering avoidable pain—it may be held that he is to blame just in case

(1) He expected his behaviour to have RP, or
(2) If he had behaved as he ought, he would have expected his behaviour to have RP, or
(3) He could (easily) have found grounds for expecting his behaviour to have RP.

Of these, (1) is plausible, but a case can be made for moving to (2) instead. Suppose that someone picks up a shotgun, guesses from its weight that it is unloaded, points it at his brother, and pulls the trigger with lethal effect. By the 'actual belief' standard of (1), this oaf is not to blame for killing his brother: can that be right? The friends of (1) can say Yes: if this reckless person is to blame, it is not for pointing and shooting but rather for jumping to the conclusion that the gun was unloaded. Whether he is to blame even for that depends on what he believed at the time: if he really thought that feeling the weight was a safe way to tell whether a gun is loaded, then he is not to blame for that epistemic conduct either, though he may be for something still earlier. Proponents of (2) will respond that that is not how we actually do apportion blame. We would blame the person, they will say, for *firing the gun on the evidence that it was not loaded*, rather than blaming him for *trusting that evidence* while exculpating him for *firing the gun*. I do not pretend to settle this dispute.

On the other hand, I do not hesitate to reject (3). Here is a new story: Agent had only to turn the canoe over before dragging it out of the water, and he would have seen that it was booby-trapped; the evidence of impending disaster was easily within his grasp. But there was no reason to suspect that there would be a booby-trap, so he is not to blame by any sane standard. To think otherwise you would have to hold that everyone ought always to learn everything that he can about where his behaviour will lead. That is absurd, and when Prichard implied it he can't have been thinking.[2]

Condition (1) has been thought by some to be necessary not only for

---

[2] H. A. Prichard, 'Duty and Ignorance of Fact', 37.

an agent to merit blame but for an action to be wrong.[3] That view closes one part of the gap between *wrong* and *blameworthy*, that is, between first- and second-order morality. It deserves a fuller day in court than I can give it here, so I set it aside without discussion. The facts that make behaviour wrong, I shall assume, do not include any that concern the agent's state of mind.

That was an approximation, and is not quite right as it stands. There are some first-order moralities whose most basic concern is with love or respect or benevolence or some other motivating frame of mind. In the context of these moralities, judgements about right and wrong can of course be supported by facts about agents' states of mind. Acting with a wrong motive relates to a love-enjoining morality in just the way that causing avoidable pain relates to utilitarianism. These are *basic* concerns for these moralities; and if they involve states of mind, so be it. What I have wanted to deny is this: if a first-order morality's basic concern is to oppose behaviour that has relational property RP, that does not give it a derivative concern with beliefs about or attitudes towards RP. For example, a morality's having a basic concern with the causing of pain does not give it a derivative concern with beliefs about the causing of pain. Such beliefs are relevant to judgements in the associated second-order morality, but not to first-order judgements of wrongness.

This position seems to be held by most moral theorists. I have not argued for it, but merely declared myself an ally. In developing it, I shall set aside first-order moralities whose basic concerns involve motivating states of mind. The points I shall make apply to them too, but if they are taken into account everything becomes harder to express accurately. For ease of exposition, then, let us confine ourselves to first-order moralities whose basic concern is to oppose behaviour that has relational property RP, where this is not a relation to a motivating state of mind; it might, for instance, be the relation of causing such-and-such consequences.

16. Knowability and First-Order Morality

With those preliminaries out of the way, I now approach the main topic of the present chapter. Taking my stand on the ground that a first-order morality which has no *basic* concern with agents' states of mind has *no*

---

[3] The best defence of this position that I know of is James Hudson, 'Subjectivization in Ethics', to which my discussion of condition (1) is indebted.

concern with them, I shall nevertheless maintain that the judgements about right and wrong issued by such a morality do depend in part upon facts about what the agent could have known. A fact about what someone could have known is not a fact about his state of mind.

Consider a first-order morality M which opposes the causing of disasters (I am using shorthand), and which pays no attention to knowability. Agent ϕs, and this starts up a causal chain that leads to a disaster; but the chain includes indeterministic elements whose outcomes were highly improbable. Not only did Agent not expect the disaster: nobody at that time could have foreseen it; conditions making it inevitable or even likely did not exist in the world at that time. Still, according to M, Agent acted wrongly in ϕing.

Do not reject this because it is not fair to Agent; such judgements about fairness belong to second-order morality, which is not in question here. M does not accuse or condemn or blame Agent for causing the disaster—it merely judges that he acted wrongly in doing so. Even those who are not confused about fairness, however, will also reject M, and rightly. We all agree that, in the case I have described, Agent in ϕing behaved *disastrously* but did not behave *wrongly*. Why? Is it merely that we sense 'wrong' not to be the *mot juste*? If so, the issue is trivial— a matter of verbal propriety. For the question 'Does P entail a judgement of wrongness?' to have substance, 'wrong' must be anchored in something solid. I shall offer a suggestion about its anchoring in our thought.

In the case I described, the whole prima-facie case for calling Agent's ϕing at T morally wrong lies in its proving to be disastrous in the upshot. However, at time T that case could not have been made: nobody, however skilled and well informed, could have been in a position to advise Agent not to ϕ, to comment on the undesirability of his ϕing, or anything like that. Furthermore, Agent cannot pointfully look back on his ϕing in the light of its terrible outcome in the hope of learning how to do better in future. In the case as described, there may be nothing that he overlooked or slighted when he decided to ϕ.

In the foregoing paragraph, I offer a generic thought: someone does not act wrongly at T unless this is made to be the case by facts that obtain at T—that is, (1) facts that pertain to T and (2) facts that pertain to other times but are deterministically implied by the world's state at T. I also offer two specific supports for this: a wrong action must be one which a well-enough-informed bystander could in principle have advised against, condemned, or deplored at the time of acting; and an agent who has acted wrongly should have at least a theoretical chance of learning from the wrongness of his action, seeing how he could have done better and may do better in future. The bystander's-comment and chance-of-learning desiderata both require that the marks of the behaviour's wrongness be laid down in the world at T; and that constitutes at least part of the reason why behaviour is not wrong unless the facts that make it so are registered in the world at the time of acting.

I have illustrated this in terms of the improbable but actual upshots of Agent's φing, but for some kinds of first-order morality the issue arises also with respect to the other temporal direction. (My thesis about knowability and first-order morality is a formal one; it holds for all first-order moralities, whatever their moral content.) Consider for example a morality with a basic concern for the keeping of promises; Agent has promised not to φ; and the world now contains no trace of that promise—nobody's memories or brain states, nor any other facts about the world, provide a basis from which a perfectly informed supergenius could infer that Agent once promised not to φ. My treatment of the 'future' version of the problem implies that in this 'past' case it would not be wrong for Agent to φ. I am content with this conclusion, though the 'past' version of the problem is hard to think about realistically because the issue will never actually arise. Once the traces of Agent's promising not to φ are lost, they are gone for ever; no one will ever be in a position to say: 'Although Agent couldn't realize it at the time, when he φed he broke a promise. Did he then act wrongly?' Still, there might be an earlier time at which people could have predicted the loss of traces, and have had the thought: 'Although Agent won't be in a position to realize it at the time, if he φs at T he will be breaking a promise. Will he then be acting wrongly?' I say No, but the case is so *outré* that it is hard to think about efficiently. Let us set it aside and concentrate on the 'future' kind of case.

Morality M, which leaves knowability out of its conditions for wrongness, gives the wrong answer—I have argued—in cases where behaviour leads improbably to a significant upshot. This can happen only in an indeterministic world. In a world where deterministic laws reign, any upshot of a bit of behaviour is in theory predictable from the world's state at the time of acting; it will always be true that a well-enough-informed bystander could have advised against the action, and that the agent upon looking back could in principle learn things which would guide him towards doing better in future. In vastly many cases, however, the well-*enough*-informed bystander is a purely theoretical entity, the relevant facts about the world's state at T being such that nobody remotely like a human being could possibly discover them and work out what they imply for the future; and the possibility *in principle* of Agent's learning from his wrong action is often not a real possibility, for the same reason. Most of us, I think, have a concept of moral wrongness which requires that the relevant facts not merely be registered upon the world at the time of acting but be such as might be known and understood by human beings. We can strengthen this in various ways, requiring that the relevant facts be such as could have been known by the agent himself, or could without much trouble have been known by the agent himself, and so on. Each of these strengthenings corresponds to a somewhat more robust notion of bystander's comment and of possibility of learning. I have nothing to say about how to choose amongst these proposals, and shall lump them together under the label 'knowability constraints'.

A knowability constraint on wrongness widens the gap between wrong behaviour and behaviour that turns out to be disastrous; at a world that is deterministic in both causal directions it *creates* that gap.

When I say that P's being the case at T_2 was 'knowable' at T_1 I mean that at the earlier time there were states of the world from which it could have been correctly and reliably inferred that P would be the case at T_2. I do not take it that someone knows that P only if he is entitled to perfect confidence that P, or anything like that. The idea that knowledge entails freedom from possibility of error arises from a failure to understand why there is something wrong with saying things of the form 'I know that P, but I might be wrong about this'. As for the much-discussed possibility that someone might be led by normally reliable means to a true conclusion, by a route that involved a couple of errors that cancel out—I have nothing to say about that.

17. Concepts of Probability

Because wrongness is tied to what can be known, it is tied to probability. The only way anything can be known at T_1 about what will contingently be the case at T_2 is through probabilities, including inevitabilities. Let us see what kind of probability we should be talking about. In discussing this I shall confine myself to probabilities of propositions about the future, and especially ones about the causal consequences of behaviour. That does not exhaust the moral territory; the

fact which Oedipus needed to know at the crossroad was not about consequences.

At a determined world, the concept of probability can have two uses.
(1) There are subjective probabilities: *your* probability for its raining
tomorrow is 0.75, meaning (roughly) that you are three-quarters of the
way to being quite sure that it will rain tomorrow. This can be sharp-
ened by an analysis in terms of the odds you would give if you were
rational and willing to bet. (2) There are objective relative probabilities:
the probability that it will rain tomorrow, given that the weather today
is thus and so, is 0.75; the probability that he will pick a black card,
given that he will draw two cards from a normal pack, is 0.75. A world
that is not strictly deterministic has room for (3) objective non-relative
probabilities, as reported in the statement 'The probability now that it
will rain tomorrow is 0.75', where this is not said relative to a specified
belief state or body of evidence. Let P be the proposition: *Radioactive
particle* x *will decay at some time in the next thirteen years.* Given the
indeterminism of such processes, P could now have the probability
0.5—not *for* someone or *relative to* such-and-such evidence, but objectively and absolutely. We can define this in terms of one of the other
concepts by calling it (1) the probability of P for someone who knows
all about the world's present state and can compute perfectly, or (2) P's
probability given all the facts about how the world is now. But we do
not need either of those versions: we can quite well speak simply of the
probability that P has. At a determined world, of course, the only objective non-relative probabilities are 1 and 0.

The second and third kinds of probability are subjects of debate, for
example about whether and how they involve frequencies. Fortunately,
the uses I shall make of the probability concept will not drag me into
that.

Now, the facts about consequences that first-order morality attends
to are all and only the . . . knowable ones (the ellipses are a reminder
that we are generalizing across all the knowability constraints: what is
in theory knowable, humanly knowable, knowable by the agent in question, and so on). They are, then, facts involving one special kind of
relative probability, namely: P's probability relative to everything that
is . . . knowable at a given time. From now on, I shall call this 'probability', simply. Thus, to say 'When I signed the agreement, there was a
better than even chance that the firm would go bankrupt' is to say that
the probability of bankruptcy, given the totality of facts that were then
. . . discoverable, was above 0.5. This concept of probability has . . .

knowability built into it; the only parameter that needs to be specified is the time. (I use 'likely' etc. and 'chance' etc. to mean the same as I do by 'probable' etc.)

In practice, of course, one must also remove the ellipses and opt for some one kind of knowability. That involves a choice of concept of wrongness that I have no present need to make. Indeed, I shall from now on speak of knowability *simpliciter*, thereby generalizing across all the different knowability constraints. When I speak of probability, therefore, I am also generalizing across a corresponding range of relative probabilities.

To say that Agent's conduct was dangerous is to say that he did something that had a certain non-causal consequence. A fact about his behaviour, conjoined with ones already obtaining, created a pattern which made it likely that something bad would happen. The pattern has that significance only by virtue of causal laws: if the physics of the actual world were different, that same arrangement of particles might be quite safe. But the fact of danger is not a causal consequence: the behaviour completed it instantaneously, not through how the world developed from then on.

Agent's ϕing could lead to a probability's existing later on, like this:

At T_1 when Agent left the gate of the railroad crossing open, there was no significant danger because the company had decided not to use that line any more. Against the probabilities, however, an escaped convict stole a locomotive and drove it towards that crossing at T_2, four hours later. At T_2 there was danger, to which Agent had contributed at T_1.

In this case, the probability of harm was a causal consequence of Agent's behaviour. The route from (1) the gate's being left open at T_1 to (3) the existence of danger at T_2 runs entirely through (2) the gate's being open at T_2, and the route from (1) to (2) is causal. I shall argue shortly that, just for that reason, it is irrelevant to the morality of Agent's behaviour.

18. The Probability Principle

The actual causal consequences of your behaviour are different from its probable ones. Your ϕing may make probable something which it does not cause, and may cause something which it did not make probable. Here is an example:

The factory is on fire. It is unlikely to spread to the warehouse, but there is a 0.001 chance of its doing so if a certain fireproof door remains open. Agent slams the door shut. By a one in ten chance, the bang of the door's closing coincides with the sound of a falling beam, and that double noise activates a burglar alarm; by a one in ten chance, the electrical demand of the burglar alarm comes at an instant when that circuit is already at the limit of its load, and a fuse blows; the blowing of that fuse creates a tiny pocket of heat which, by a one in ten chance, occurs in the presence of some highly flammable gases which catch fire and ignite the warehouse.

Each of the one-in-ten chances is the probability, *at the time* (T_1) *when Agent acts*, that the beam will fall precisely at T_2, that the circuit will be fully loaded at T_3, and that the flammable gases will surround the fuse at T_4. I stipulate that the warehouse could not have caught fire in any other way, given that the door was slammed shut. In this case, therefore, Agent's conduct created a 0.001 likelihood of a warehouse fire by this route, and eliminated a 0.001 chance of fire via the only other possible route; in short, his behaviour made no difference to the likelihood of fire; it also caused the warehouse fire. I adapt this story from one of David Lewis's, in which the behaviour that causes the disaster reduces its probability.

In the story as I have told it, Agent's conduct in slamming the door is not made wrong by any facts about its consequences, because the only ones that might condemn it were not knowable when he slammed the door. Consider this: *If Agent slams the door shut at T_1, the warehouse will catch fire at T_5.* Some philosophers think this is true just because its antecedent and consequent are true. Even if they are right, the picture does not change. Understood in that way, the conditional is a truth that is not humanly knowable at T_0 because its truth comes solely from *The warehouse catches fire at T_5*, which is not knowable then. I conclude that Agent's causing a fire in the warehouse does not discredit him or even make his behaviour wrong by the most severe defensible standard for this.

This applies also when the behaviour does make the bad outcome more likely. Suppose that a host gives his guest too much to drink, thus increasing the chance that she will have a traffic accident as she drives home. Then consider four ways that events could unroll as the guest proceeds homeward:

Likely Causal Chain: She has an accident that is caused in the probable way by her inebriety.

Unlikely Causal Chain: She happens, improbably, to inhale fumes from a leaking sewer, and these combine with her blood alcohol to cause a muscular spasm, loss of control, collision with another car.

Other Cause: She has an accident which is caused by an earthquake.

No Effect: She gets home safely.

The moral quality of the host's behaviour, I have implied, is the same each time. It is wrong even in No Effect, because it makes the guest significantly more likely to have an accident on the way home; and it is wrong *only* in that way in the other cases, right up to Likely Causal Chain, for everything else is a matter of sheer, extrinsic luck—of how events unrolled, not registered in any fact obtaining at the time when the host offered the drinks.[4] If in Likely Causal Chain another guest had said 'Don't give her any more. If you do, she'll have an accident on the way home', he might later say 'See? I was right!' However, even if that was true when he said it, its truth was not knowable when the drink was offered, so it does not contribute to the conduct's being wrong.

The warehouse fire and the tipsy guest lead us to what I call the probability principle: *The only facts about consequences that have any bearing on the moral status of behaviour are ones about what consequences it makes probable*—how good or bad they would be, and how probable the behaviour makes them up to and including its making them inevitable (giving them probability = 1). This concerns the consequences that are made likely by the intrinsic facts about the person's behaviour, which ordinarily means the facts about how he or she moves. If Agent's way of moving causes a dangerous situation S without having made it likely that S would obtain, this fact is irrelevant to any moral judgement on Agent's behaviour.

So facts about actual causal consequences have no direct role in morality, being displaced by facts about certain non-causal consequences, namely probabilities. The dislodged concept, however, retains an essential though secondary place in the story: probabilities are important just because they are probabilities of causal consequences. (That remark is not trivial, for my φing can make upshot U likely with-

---

[4] I am ignoring a further source of wrongness in all the cases, namely that each drink does neural damage.

out creating any chance that U will result from my ϕing. Here is a fictional example:

> In men, taking up smoking in the sixties is a predictor for Alzheimer's disease in the seventies, because that behaviour tends to be caused by a birth trauma which also tends to cause Alzheimer's later on. If I start smoking in my sixties, that increases the likelihood of my later getting Alzheimer's, though there is no chance that my smoking will cause me to get it.

That increase in likelihood is irrelevant to the morality of my ϕing, because it does not concern the likelihood of something's being caused by my ϕing.[5])

The probability principle is based on a view about how moral status relates to luck. Thomas Nagel has helpfully distinguished four ways in which luck may affect someone's performance.[6] It is partly a matter of luck that he is this kind of person, that he is in these circumstances, that such-and-such causes act upon him at the moment, and that his conduct has the effects that it has. According to a certain attractive Kantian view, a person's moral standing cannot depend in any way on luck; but we have been unable to build this into a credible morality. Apparently we cannot honour the three-quarters of the Kantian view that concern *where the person's behaviour comes from*: the kind of person he is, his life circumstances, and the particular causes that act on him.[7] However, we can still hold that nobody is culpable for *what comes from his behaviour* as a matter of luck. This last element in the attractive idea poses no threat to a coherent morality; we have no reason to challenge its hold on our minds, and therefore none to accord moral significance to actual consequences.

Knowability is a ladder which, now that we have climbed it up to the concept of probability, we should kick away. I started with the likes of this:

(1) Agent's closing the door at T caused the factory to burn,

and argued that for Agent's behaviour to be wrong we need something stronger:

---

[5] For more on this, see the papers in part III of Richmond Campbell and Lanning Sowden (eds.), *Paradoxes of Rationality and Cooperation: Prisoner's Dilemma and Newcomb's Problem*.

[6] Thomas Nagel, 'Moral Luck', 28.

[7] There is a fine, brief exposition of this matter in Bernard Williams, 'Morality and the Emotions', 228.

(2) It was knowable at T that Agent's closing the door then would cause the factory to burn.

I have now moved from this to something that is not stronger than (1) but merely different from it, namely:

(3) It was probable at T that Agent's closing the door at T would cause the factory to burn.

Unlike (1) and (2), this does not entail that Agent's closing the door caused the factory to burn. Furthermore, (3) is what we need for our moral purposes: whether the factory actually burns is altogether irrelevant to whether Agent acted wrongly in closing the door. That is why the knowability ladder must be kicked away. As for the ways in which 'knowable' might be qualified—humanly, easily, by Agent, and so on—these generate different kinds of relative probability which might have a place in one's morality. So they are still potentially with us, even after knowability has gone.

19. Morality and Bad Luck

Although we have excellent grounds for basing our moral judgements on probable consequences and not on actual ones, it seems that we *do* admit the latter, defying the edict banishing luck from the moral domain. That edict should hold in both orders of morality: actual consequences do not affect right and wrong, and are even further removed from credit and discredit. Or so it seems, yet our assignments of blame—or of something like it—are sometimes affected by our beliefs about actual consequences. This issue seems closer to second-order morality, but it could spill over into first-order, and I shall pause to discuss it.

The phenomenon of 'something like blame' for actual consequences falls into two parts that are to be explained differently. One part is not much like blame; it involves coolly holding a person responsible for actual consequences while knowing that he is not to blame for them. Following Susan Wolf, let us look at this first from the point of view of the agent.[8] Suppose that you cause harm to someone without being in the least at fault: a small child dashes into the path of your car, which hits and hurts her. The probability principle allows you to treat this

---

[8] Susan Wolf, 'Moral Luck', forthcoming.

accident as though you were not involved—stopping to help the child, no doubt, but only as you would do as a concerned bystander. In fact, though, you are likely to have a sense of being especially obliged to care for the child—to see that she gets to hospital and that her parents are informed, and to contribute to the cost of care if the parents cannot easily afford it. The difference between the two courses of behaviour could come from differences in degree of altruism: the extra care for the victim might be exhibited by some Good Samaritan who was not causally involved in the disaster. My topic, however, is the difference between two ways of acting on the knowledge that one is causally involved: a minimalist one based on the judgement 'The accident was in no way my fault, so I am not especially obliged to help', and another based on the judgement 'I did it, so I should help'.

Susan Wolf illuminates this difference by comparing it with two attitudes that one might take to payment for a shared meal in which one has consumed less than the others. A person so placed is entitled to ask for separate bills, so that he pays only for his share; but one might brush entitlement aside and offer to split the bill evenly, so as to keep things simple. Someone who does that for that reason exhibits *generosity* in the broad sense of that term in which Claudius describes Hamlet as 'most generous, and free of all contriving'. This virtue shows itself in a careless breadth of conduct and feeling, an unwillingness to do the sums needed to mark the boundaries of one's rights and entitlements. In the person who causes unforeseeable harm it will show in his taking upon himself some responsibility for the harm that has been done, rather than computing his way to a conclusion that exculpates him. In conclusion, Wolf suggests that if we as onlookers have a sense that the person's moral status is affected by his having caused the harm, however blamelessly, that reflects our sense of how he will see his situation if he is generous. The term 'generosity' is mine, not Wolf's; but the core of this account is hers, and it seems to me right.

It leaves untouched, though, the more heated phenomenon in which morally faulty behaviour is met with a heightened degree of rage, resentment, or the like if it leads to actual harm. It is obvious why we blame a person who drives his car while drunk, persuades children to play Russian roulette with live ammunition, or takes a manhole cover home as a souvenir, even if no harm is done. But why do we blame a risk-maker more severely if he drunkenly hits someone on the road, if one of the children is shot, if a blind person falls down the manhole? Speaking for myself: I do not. For me, the actual harm serves only to make vivid how wicked the behaviour was because of the danger it created. Although I do not think that every drunken driver should be penalized as harshly as one who kills, that is for reasons of policy, not because of any moral distinction. If there are people who really do blame the drunken driver more severely if he has a victim, I think they err: they could not reconcile this with their own most basic moral convictions or attitudes.

Still, there is an intelligible source for their directing towards the harm-causer something that feels like blame. It can be seen more clearly in a case where the fault level is lower. The motorist who hit and injured my child was driving quite circumspectly and only slightly above the speed limit; I often drive like that myself; but if he had been a little more careful the accident would have been averted. It will be natural for me to be angry and resentful towards this motorist, and this feels like a moral reaction.

I suggest that it is not really moral. Although in the general mess of imprecision of feeling it is hard to know what is going on, I offer the following diagnosis. When some actual consequence of behaviour is bad, we have something to grieve over, which can then turn our minds against a related item through a simple association of ideas. The item need not be causally involved—I might hate a place just because I was once miserable while there, not being made so by the place—but causation makes the mechanism kick in more strongly. I shall not follow Locke in giving the association of ideas 'so harsh a name as madness',[9] but I agree with him that it is not reasonable. I am saying that this reaction is natural, not that it makes sense.

It has nothing to do with blame. Association may sometimes seem to augment blame, but really it is redirecting grief. Not long ago, near where I live, a man accidentally killed his son in a hunting accident, and a few minutes later he shot himself to death, leaving a widow and a second child. This was intelligible behaviour; even the widow said 'I understand'. Without condoning what the father did, we can understand his doing that, without supposing that he had been in the least careless with his gun.

Now here is another story. In a gross episode of macho display, a man recklessly mishandled his gun and seriously risked killing his son; then, realizing how badly he had behaved and wanting to be free of that burden, he killed himself. You don't believe this, and indeed it is not

---

[9] John Locke, *An Essay Concerning Human Understanding*, II. xxxiii. 4.

true. It would not be intelligible for a person to kill himself for that reason. Our reaction to the actual father's suicide cannot have to do with
any moral judgement. We do not picture him as escaping a burden of
guilt, but rather as suffering from misery over an outcome and an
unbearable association of the thought of it with the thought of himself
as cause. Locke recounts someone who 'could never bear the sight' of
a man to whom he was profoundly grateful for restoring his sanity
through 'a very harsh and offensive operation'. The sight of his benefactor, Locke says, 'brought back with it the idea of that agony which
he suffered from his hands, which was too mighty and intolerable for
him to endure'.[10] One wonders what the operation was, and what kind
of madness it cured; but the general point survives doubts about the
details.

[10] Ibid. II. xxxiii. 14.

4

MAKING/ALLOWING

20. *The Difference Between Making and Allowing*

As I noted in Section 2 above, ways in which a state of affairs can be a consequence of behaviour divide into two species:

She fells the tree.	She lets the tree fall.
She causes it to fall, or makes it fall.	She permits it to fall, or allows it to fall.
It falls because of something she does.	It falls because of something she doesn't do.
It falls because she intervenes in the course of nature.	It falls in the course of nature.

Those are not the only ways of marking the distinction, but they will do to go on with. The consequential states of affairs are endless: she cures the patient (lets him recover), she spoils the cheese (lets it deteriorate), she compacts the earth (lets it settle), she kills the wasp (lets it die), and so on.

Why say that these turns of phrase mark one distinction? Well, if I had put any one of them in the opposite column, you would have seen that as a slip; so there is something systematic going on here. Perhaps each column is unified only by a 'family resemblance', so that the difference between the two, although systematic, cannot be expressed in a clean, unitary analysis. I would not settle for that, though, without first trying to do better. In his famous panegyric in favour of family resemblances, Wittgenstein seems to have assumed that if we 'look at the differences' amongst some items we will stop thinking they have something significant in common; but why should we?[1] This inference of Wittgenstein's is one of several mistakes in that passage. What actually moved him, I believe, was not a reason or argument but rather an aspect of his temperament: he was more interested in differences than in com-

---

[1] Ludwig Wittgenstein, *Philosophical Investigations*, pt. 1, sects. 66 ff.

monalities, more drawn to the particular than to the universal, and out-right hostile to the 'craving for unity'. Against this, I think it matters greatly to know whether the above turns of phrase do involve a unitary distinction and, if they do, what it is.

I shall refer to the item in question, in a loose and non-committal way, as the distinction between making and allowing. That is not to give a privilege to 'make' and 'allow': we shall not get to the bottom of this distinction by tracing out the precise meanings of any pair of verbs. Or so I believe, but of course I must listen if anyone offers to show that some one word or phrase is the key that will unlock this door. I decline, though, to examine the details of the meaning of any word just 'because it is there'. Some philosophers have energetically sought the whole truth about when it is correct to apply certain words, assuming that some good will come of this. Here is one, tracing the semantic outlines of selected words and expecting to read off moral truths from the results:

Is turning off the respirator an instance of causing death or permitting death to occur? If the patient is beyond recovery and on the verge of death, one balks at saying that the activity causes death. It is far more natural to speak of the case as one of permitting death to occur. . . . We are inclined to refer to the respirator as a means for prolonging life; we would not speak of insulin shots for a diabetic in the same way . . .[2]

This seems to give authority to word-meanings in the shaping of moral judgements, as though we might be helped to know what to do by dis-covering the *mot juste*.

Why should facts about what 'we are inclined' to say be enlisted in the struggle with a moral problem? The only answer I have seen is from the same source: 'As native speakers of English, we are equipped with linguistic sensitivity for the distinction between causing harm and per-mitting harm to occur. That sensitivity reflects a common-sense per-ception of reality; and we should employ it in classifying the hard cases arising in discussions of the prolongation of life.' Presumably this means 'and *therefore* we should employ it . . .'. Why does it follow? The mean-ings of our words no doubt reflect aspects of how we see the world, but are they aspects that matter in moral hard cases?

One might look for help to J. L. Austin's reported reason for study-ing the delicately nuanced complexities of correct English. These semantic patterns are an artefact that our forefathers created down the

[2] George P. Fletcher, 'Prolonging Life: Some Legal Considerations', 94.

centuries, Austin is said to have thought, so they probably meet real needs and reflect real differences, and it would be wasteful not to avail ourselves of this resource.[3] Applied to moral theory, this seems weak. Our meanings might reflect needs and interests of our ancestors without being closely tailored to their moral views: morality is not the most likely reason for choosing a way of classifying human conduct. Also, any moral views that are reflected will belong to our ancestors' working morality, developed to cope with the bustle and trouble of everyday life, not their best and deepest thoughts in a calm hour. Finally, even those best thoughts can be criticized; we should try to assess our moral inheritance, seeing whether we can improve upon it. I conclude that attention to inherited semantic patterns, though it could help in our moral thinking, is not likely to do so.

Apart from the Austinian one, I can think of three other possible bases for letting linguistic intuitions influence moral theory.

(1) Some people think that all morality is based on God's commands, and some of *them* think that God has addressed his creatures in human languages. Not all: Suárez thought that God sometimes lets us know what he wants more directly.[4] Still, the idea of divine commands as spoken, and as morally authoritative, is respectable, and would be a reason for steering by semantic details either of the language of the commands or of one into which it had been reliably translated.

(2) Others think that morality ultimately rests on a contract—not an explicit one drawn up in English, but an implied one, consisting in facts about how people would behave if they believed this or that. Word-meanings can shape and prune people's thoughts, and so they could easily affect which of the contractualist's conditionals are true, and therefore—according to this sort of contractualism—could have an effect on basic moral truth.

(3) Richard Brandt holds that the basic form of moral question for anybody is not *Is it wrong for me to ϕ?* but rather *Should I accept and advocate for general acceptance a moral code that forbids ϕing?*[5] That

[3] G. J. Warnock, 'John Langshaw Austin: A Biographical Sketch', 18 f.

[4] 'Such instruction as to [the lawgiver's] intention consists of some utterance, the term "utterance" being understood to include any indication or manifestation whatsoever, given to another person, of an internal act.' 'We should bear in mind that the natural law . . . is not always formulated in the mind according to those general or indefinite terms in which we quote it when speaking or writing.' (Francisco Suárez, *Laws and God the Lawgiver*, 57, 262; I. iv. 13, II. xiii. 6.) I am indebted to Joseph Lombardi for this reference.

[5] Richard B. Brandt, *A Theory of the Good and the Right*, chs. 9 and 10.

could let meanings have an effect on basic morality, because semantic facts could influence what codes have any chance of acceptance.[6]

Lacking one of those premises, I can find no reason for basing morality, and to that extent life, on linguistic sensitivity to the meanings of any verbs. Philosophers have discussed in print the complexities of the proper use of 'kill', 'fell', 'hurt' etc., and of 'let die', 'permit to fall', 'allow to suffer', etc., as though we had to get these straight in order to know what to do with this patient in this hospital bed.[7] I cannot see how they could justify this way of proceeding. 'What matters is whether a certain act, about whose nature we are quite well enough informed, is right or wrong, not what we are to call it. Philosophers are, among other things, concerned with the use of words: they should use [their] skill . . . to *prevent* our wasting time on disputes about words, not to bog us down more deeply in them.'[8]

21. Trouble with 'Allow' and 'Let'

Without unduly deferring to word-meanings in general, we might expect that our grip on making/allowing would be firmer if we attended to 'allow' (or 'let') on the one hand and to 'make' (or its active-verb relatives) on the other. This strategy is suggested by philosophical work on the making/allowing distinction that has been done under the label 'killing versus letting die'. It turns out to be a bad strategy, however, as I shall explain in this chapter.

(1) Statements of the form 'Agent allowed [Noun] to [Verb Phrase]'—'She allowed him to leave', 'They allowed her to stay in ignorance', 'He allowed the beer to go flat'—entail that Agent did or should have known that [Noun] was likely to [Verb] if not prevented from doing so. It is part of the meaning of 'allow' (as of 'let') that you *allow* to happen only what you knew or should have known was apt to happen if you did not stop it. That creates a disparity between curing and allowing to recover, raising and allowing to rise, felling and allowing to fall. In thousands of such pairs the item on the left entails nothing about

---

[6] Not that Brandt admits them by that or any other route. See ibid. 2–10.

[7] Eric D'Arcy, *Human Acts*, *passim*; John Casey, 'Actions and Consequences'; and others, some to be mentioned later.

[8] R. M. Hare, '*In Vitro* Fertilization and the Warnock Report', 102 f. For a good criticism of the linking of semantics with morality see Rolf Sartorius, *Individual Conduct and Social Norms*, 40 ff.

what the person knew or should have known: it is no part of the meaning of 'She cured him', 'She smashed the barn', 'She cleaned the floor',
that she knew that her conduct was likely to lead to his recovery, to the
barn's being in pieces, to the floor's being clean. Knowledge and intention are conspicuously absent from my partial analysis of 'hurt' in
Section 2 above. We shall lose our balance if we try to understand
making/allowing in terms that are epistemically loaded on one side of
the line.

What a person knew about the likely consequences of his behaviour
heavily affects our moral judgements on him and perhaps on it. Any
facts about this must be taken into account. But we risk confusion if we
express them separately on the making side of the line while burying
them in the meaning of 'allow' on the other side. From now on I shall
understand the distinction in such a way that nothing epistemic is
essential to either side of it; and that is one respect in which I cut it
loose from the details of the meaning of 'allow'. Philosophers who state
their problem in terms of 'killing' versus 'letting die' also silently
restore the epistemic symmetry, by confining their attention to killing
(curing, cleaning, etc.) where Agent *does* have the relevant knowledge.

Isn't there another unwanted difference? 'Allow' seems to imply that
Agent is reluctant or the speaker disapproving or surprised—or, anyway, to presuppose that the question of Agent's preventing [Noun]
from [Verb]ing has somehow come up. One might naturally say 'He
allowed them to put a garland around his neck', thinking that he would
be embarrassed by this; or 'He allowed her to kiss him on the mouth',
thinking that he ought to have offered his cheek; but it would be strange
to say, in an ordinary case, 'I allowed the delivery man to hand me the
parcel'. This looks like a further unwanted imbalance between the two
sides of our line, because there is nothing like it on the 'making' side.
That would interfere further with our project, which is to study a certain factual distinction between two ways in which conduct can relate
to an upshot, in order to learn whether it is a legitimate *basis* for moral
judgements.

Perhaps we can allay this fear, though, for the 'question arising' idea
may not be an ingredient in the meaning of 'allow'. The statement 'I
allowed the delivery man to hand me the parcel' might be an odd thing
to say yet still be true, as is 'The delivery man did not stand on his
hands and sing "Rule, Britannia" while giving me the parcel'. Each
statement is foolish because there is no point in saying something that
everyone would take for granted; and this has nothing to do with the

meaning of 'allow' in particular. (See Section 42 below for more about this.) In contrast, the epistemic element cannot be explained away in this fashion. It pretty clearly belongs to the meaning of 'allow'.

(2) A further troublesome element in the meaning of 'allow' and 'let' can be illustrated by three short stories in each of which a vehicle is on ground that slopes down to a cliff top. One story continues like this:

> *Push*: The vehicle stands, unbraked, on the slope; Agent pushes it; and it rolls over the cliff edge to its destruction.

The second goes like this:

> *Stayback*: The vehicle is already rolling; Agent could but does not interpose a rock which could stop it; and the vehicle rolls to its destruction.

The third is this:

> *Kick*: The vehicle is rolling to a point where there is a rock that can bring it to a halt. Agent kicks away the rock, and the vehicle rolls to its destruction.

In each case we have a person, a time, and a vehicle's smashing at the foot of a cliff. All would agree that in Push the relevance of conduct to upshot belongs on the left (positive, active-verb, 'making') side of the line, and that in Stayback it belongs on the right (negative, passive, 'allowing') side. In Kick the facts are more complex. Although the relation of conduct to crash belongs with Push on the left of the line, it is natural to say that in Kick Agent lets or allows the vehicle to roll on down: 'He kicked away the rock, letting the vehicle go its way'. This shows that even apart from the epistemic element, 'allow' and 'let' do not draw our line in the right place.

What is going on when we characterize Kick in terms of 'allowing'? Setting the epistemic element aside, it might seem right to say that 'Agent allowed [Noun] to [Verb]' means: (*a*) *Agent could have prevented [Noun] from [Verb]ing, but he did not*. That is true in Stayback, and not in Push (or so it seems reasonable to think), but it does not accurately track the use of 'allow'. In Kick it is right to say that Agent in kicking away the rock *allows* the vehicle to roll on down, but (*a*) is not true: there is no opportunity in Kick for Agent to prevent the vehicle from rolling. What is true is that if he had left the rock in place, *it* would have prevented the vehicle from rolling. Cashing in on that, we might suggest that 'Agent allowed [Noun] to [Verb]' means, in addition to the epistemic element, this: (*b*) *Agent could have so behaved that* [*Noun*] *was prevented from* [*Verb*]*ing, but he did not.* That is true not only in Stayback but also in Kick, where Agent could have behaved so that the rock prevents the vehicle from rolling on down.[9] Tying 'allow' to 'prevent', then, it seems that to allow something to happen is so to behave that it isn't prevented from happening—not necessarily by oneself.

But then in Push, when the vehicle was standing motionless, that was because it was prevented from rolling by small stones, hollows in the ground, wet grass, and so on; so Agent in pushing the vehicle was preventing these things from preventing it from moving; yet in this case we do not say that in pushing the vehicle he allowed it to move. What makes the difference? I am not sure; though it seems to involve the difference between removing obstacles (Kick) and enabling something to overcome obstacles (Push). Enough of this! We should not look for help from the meaning of 'allow', which is a complex, shallow mess.

If we tie our inquiry to the likes of 'killing versus letting die', therefore, we risk being pulled off our path by 'let' and 'allow'. We may also be distracted by two ways in which 'kill' and its like also fail to line up with the making/allowing distinction. I shall give them a section apiece.

22. *The Bubble Phenomenon*

Sometimes we can use an active-verb phrase to report what is in fact an allowing rather than a making. When our moral or quasi-moral notice is strongly attracted to Agent's not preventing something that he could have prevented, we may report this in active, positive, 'making' language. He *killed* the house plants by letting them die, when it was his job to keep them alive; she *saved* the Jewish family by not reporting them to the SS, when it was dangerous to keep quiet; he *destroyed* the government by not intervening in the debate, when everybody expected him to speak. In each case the language of allowing is appropriate—he let the plants die, she allowed the family to stay in safety, he let the government go down—but what is notable is that the language of making is also appropriate.

This is a standard, legitimate way of using 'kill' and other verbs. Some philosophers who maintain that the making/allowing distinction is morally neutral, so that letting people die is basically no better than

---

[9] This detail in the meaning of 'allow' is described in Philippa Foot, 'The Problem of Abortion and the Doctrine of Double Effect', 273.

killing them, dramatize their stand by playing fast and loose with active verbs. John Harris, for instance, calls all allowings-to-die 'negative killings', and speaks of failing to shield someone from injury as 'injuring' her.[10] My topic is not these licentious uses of 'kill' and 'injure' but rather a fact about their conventional use which I have described and shall now explain.

Part of what is going on is a judgement that the behaviour in question was striking, surprising, notable; perhaps that it was notably wrong, or right, though the judgement need not be overtly moral. We have here a bubble forced on to the surface of our language by pressure from an underlying agitation.

Such pressure is not alone enough to create the bubble, however. Suppose it is my job to keep the gate open, I see it swinging shut and know I can easily stop it, I deliberately stand aside and watch it close, and the results are calamitous; you are shocked at my behaviour. However agitated you are, though, you will not say that I closed the gate. Similarly for 'fell the tree', 'crumble the cake', 'flatten the carton', 'disperse the leaves', 'pile up the dust', 'dirty the carpet', 'light the fire', 'put out the fire', and so on.

What makes the difference? You might think that my inaction is causally closer to the gate's shutting than the politician's silence is to the government's fall; but such differences in causal structure are irrelevant. Suppose that the government is under pressure in a parliamentary debate to declare war; one influential statesman, a virtual pacifist, is relied upon by the peace faction to intervene decisively; but he sits in silence. The debate runs its course, and the government has to yield: war is declared. It is not natural to say that this man has *pushed* the government into declaring war, yet the causal structure is just like that of the situation where we will say that a non-intervening politician *destroyed* the government.

In this last story, however, we can properly say 'He *harmed* the peace faction' and 'He *helped* the warmongers'. The 'bubble' phenomenon, it seems, requires a certain kind of situation and a certain kind of active verb. The bubble reaches the surface with help of a highly charged verb, such as:

kill, save, destroy, harm, help,

and unlike:

[10] John Harris, 'The Survival Lottery', 258; 'The Marxist Conception of Violence', 211.

close, fell, crumble, flatten, disperse, pile up, dirty, light, push.

If a speaker is to express his agitation, he cannot do it merely by using the language of making (as against allowing)—why ever should that have the expressive effect he is after? What he needs is to use that language with a verb that commonly has moral or evaluative force. That is why we can report an allowing in the words 'He harmed the peace faction' but not in 'He pushed the government into war'.

If that is wrong, I'll bet that this phenomenon can be explained in some other way that still does not give it any importance. It must be noticed by someone whose topic is the actual uses of 'making' etc. and 'allowing',[11] but in moral theory it matters only in a prophylactic way: if we do not grasp that it merely concerns the surface of word-use, we may strain to respect it in our *thinking* about making/allowing. If we do that, we shall get lost. The same holds for the next topic.

23. *Propositional Matches*

First, I must introduce the concept of a *propositional match* between a behavioural fact and some proposition contained in a human item—a state of someone's mind, a speech act, or a social artefact such as a law, convention, written record, verbal tradition, or the like. Here is an elementary example.

She said that he would win the race, and he did; her prediction's being fulfilled was a noncausal consequence of his winning. One part of the pattern that his winning created is a match between the content of her prediction and his winning the race. Keeping tenses out of this, the proposition *He wins the race* both expresses the content of her prediction and states the fact about what he did. My 'match' concept covers not only propositional identity but also contradiction: if she predicted that he would not win, and he did win, there was what I call a propositional match.

Many of our ordinary statements about behaviour entail that a propositional match occurred. Here are some involving people's states of mind: *He disobeyed an order*; *He fulfilled her fears*; *He belied their hopes*. It is obvious how matches are involved in those. It may be less obvious how they are involved in relations with social artefacts: *He broke the law*; *She broke the record*; *She married the man*; *He disinherited his child*. You

---

[11] e.g. Earl Winkler, 'Is the Killing/Letting-Die Distinction Normatively Neutral?'

can break the law only because the law says that you are to do or not do certain things. To break a record—in one sense of that phrase—you must relate suitably to a history text which *says that* up to now the fastest or highest etc. has been such and such. Similarly with the legal procedures of marrying and disinheriting; what you do must relate suitably to the appropriate law, and buried in there somewhere will be a match. It may take a little digging to find it. For example, to show how 'He broke the record for the 80-metre dash' involves a match, we must represent it as saying: '*He ϕed*, for some value of ϕ such that the records for the 80-metre dash entail that it is not yet true of anybody that *he ϕed*'. The awkwardness of that is justified by the theoretical benefit of bringing the case under the conceptual natural kind—matches between behavioural facts and propositions contained in human items.

Causal chains can help to create matches, as when someone breaks a noise law by starting a siren. It is also true that matches can start causal chains, as when someone causes deaths by shouting that the theatre is on fire. This person ϕed for a value of ϕ such that the meaning conventions of her language say (roughly) that if you ϕ you say that there is a fire in your vicinity; and it was because of that match that people died. A match has causal consequences only through someone's thinking that the match obtains. The deaths in the theatre would not have been caused by her shout's having that meaning if nobody had attributed that meaning to it. Another example: What she did counted legally as marrying the man; but *that* fact won't make him happy or miserable, or further his career or slow down hers, unless someone believes that what she did counted as marrying him. Similarly with breaking the law, telling an untruth, keeping a promise, and all the rest. I have many examples of this, and no counter-examples. I suspect there is a reason why it must be so, but I have not found one.

24. The Match Phenomenon

Now consider these statements, reporting two causal and two noncausal consequences:

> I disappointed her by not coming home until midnight.
> He hurt her feelings by not phoning on her birthday.
> She broke the law by not paying National Insurance.
> She signalled her assent by not saying 'Non placet'.

In each of these an upshot is explained in terms of a negative fact about behaviour—something the person did not do, a failure or omission or refraining or neglect or the like; and yet it is natural to report each not in the language of 'allowing', but rather 'makingly', with an ordinary active verb. I shall explain why.

These are four out of countless instances of what I call 'the match phenomenon'. Each involves a propositional match. For example, when I disappointed her by not coming home before midnight, her disappointment arose immediately from her thinking that *I did not come home before midnight*; and that belief arose from a certain fact about my behaviour, namely that *I did not come home before midnight*. And in each case the propositional match helps to explain why the active-verb 'making' terminology is appropriate and why the language of 'allowing' is not.

That last clause marks off the match from the bubble phenomenon. In the latter, something that can be reported in 'allowing' terms can *also* be reported using an active-verb phrase. The match phenomenon, on the other hand, disqualifies the language of 'allowing' and requires the use of an active verb. It would be weird to say that in not phoning on her birthday he allowed her feelings to be hurt, or that in not paying National Insurance she failed to prevent the law from being broken. Instances of the match phenomenon feel like makings rather than allowings—not only in our semantic intuitions but also in other ways. Some moralists think that the making/allowing distinction makes a basic moral difference: the moral import of my so behaving that someone died depends in part—according to them—on whether my conduct caused her to die or merely allowed her death to occur. But none of them will say that the gravity of your hurting someone's feelings may depend on whether you did it by saying S or by not saying S; or that the wrongness of my breaking a promise may depend on whether I broke it by φing (I promised not to) or by not φing (I promised to φ).

Thus, in every instance of the match phenomenon where the relevant behavioural fact is negative, (1) it is appropriate to use the language of 'making' and not to use that of 'allowing', and (2) the behavioural fact matches a proposition contained in a human item somewhere on the chain from conduct to upshot. I suggest that the match is what quells the intuition of allowingness, that is, that (2) explains (1).

For evidence, consider two ways for it to be true that *she suffered psychologically because Agent did not come home before midnight*. In each case, we assume for simplicity's sake that Agent knows that his not coming home before midnight is likely to have her suffering as a consequence.

(*a*) We naturally hear the emphasized sentence as saying that she was upset *that* he did not come home earlier; then the route from conduct to upshot ran through her thinking that he did not etc., which means that there is a match. Understanding the case in that way, we do not think of Agent as letting her suffer, but rather as hurting her, making or causing her to suffer. (*b*) The true story might instead be that she suffered psychologically because of an obscene phone call at midnight, from which Agent would have shielded her if he had been there. In this case we intuitively relate his absence to her suffering in the 'allowing' way; in not coming home earlier, he let her be afflicted. His behaviour is as much an allowing of her suffering as if she had suffered physically when hit by a brick which Agent could have deflected.

So here we have two stories in which psychological suffering is a consequence of a negative fact about Agent's behaviour. Only one strikes us as an allowing; and only in the other is there a propositional match. These two facts are presumably connected, but I have not been able to find out exactly how.

5

MORAL SIGNIFICANCE

25. *Basic Moral Significance*

The making/allowing distinction is mostly discussed in causal contexts, where it separates hurting someone from letting him be hurt, curing someone from allowing her to recover, knocking down a wall from not preventing it from coming down, and so on. It is, however, richly relevant to at least one kind of non-causal consequence, namely the relation between behaviour and resultant probabilities. Agent may create a danger by removing a secure fence or by not repairing a broken one, and that is a difference that we notice. That contrast holds firm, and the risks are real, even if no actual harm is done; but if I confine myself to cases like that, or even emphasize them much, I shall be constantly bringing the probability principle under the spotlight. Not wanting to do that, I shall focus on cases where the behaviour does actually cause what it makes probable; and for simplicity's sake I shall talk about causal consequences rather than the non-causal creating of probabilities of those consequences. Thus, for example, I may contrast (1) a case where Patient is hurt because Agent fells a tree which falls on her with (2) a case where she is hurt because he does not warn her that a tree is about to fall; and it is to be understood that in (1) Agent's handling of his axe made it likely that the tree would fall on Patient, and that in (2) at the last moment when a shout by Agent could have made a difference it was likely that the tree would hit Patient if she did not move. What really matters morally is the likelihood; but it will ease the discussion if I handle the cases in terms of the consequences.

I have already mentioned this question in moral theory: if someone's behaviour has a bad state of affairs as a causal consequence, is the morality of his conduct directly affected by whether he made the consequence obtain or only allowed it to do so? The answer No means that the difference between making and allowing is *neutral*, by which I always mean 'basically morally neutral'. The question arises with regard to both first- and second-order moral judgements: Which sort of conduct is worse or more likely to be wrong? Which brings greater discredit on the agent? I shall bring in elements from both orders, with more emphasis on the former.

If we approach the question by comparing pairs of cases, one of making and one of allowing, we must ensure that they differ only in that way. It is not illuminating to compare a case where Agent maliciously hurts his wife with one where he unknowingly allows her to suffer, or a case where he mildly embarrasses his sister with one where he neglects to save her from being mutilated. This general point about seeing that 'other things' are 'equal' is obvious, but some of its instances need to be watched. Three morally potent differences are especially apt to get mixed up with making/allowing, because they tend to accompany it. They concern second- more than first-order morality, but still we should look at them.

(1) It is in general easier to avoid doing a specified thing than it is to do one; easier to obey 'Don't do A!' than to obey 'Do B!' At times when I could have closed the gate but did not, I may have been lecturing or making love or closing another gate; or the gate might be so heavy that in closing it I would have hurt myself; or I might have needed to sprint to reach it in time. On the other hand, if I caused a bad state of affairs by closing the gate, I could probably have not closed it without much inconvenience, pain, or difficulty.

Difficulty of avoidance has a place in our moral thinking, and deserves its day in court. It should speak clearly in its own voice, however, not mumblingly through its link with making/allowing. That link is loose, anyway, because some issues about difficulty, pain, cost, etc. have nothing to do with making/allowing; and, conversely, negative ('allowing') relevances are not *always* harder to avoid than positive ('making') ones. We should leave avoidance costs out of our present inquiry, which concerns making/allowing itself, not its usual associates.

(2) The making/allowing distinction also tends to be accompanied by differences of motive. This follows from the difficulty point. If my not φing has a bad upshot, the reason for my conduct may well be the cost to me of φing, rather than a malign intent. When something bad results from my φing, on the other hand, it is less likely that it would have been hard for me not to φ, and that increases the likelihood that I φed for evil reasons. Motivational differences matter in second-order morality, and perhaps even in first (see Chapter 11 below); but they are not essentially tied to making/allowing. Whether her behaviour was

relevant to his drowning because she pushed him out of the boat or because she did not throw him a lifebelt, the question what she believed, wanted, intended is separate. Either way, she might have been innocent and unknowing, with no intention to injure him; equally, either way, she might have been moved by malice or greed.

(3) The two kinds of relevance tend to differ also in respect of what is or could be known. To take an extreme example: A woman would have been saved from death by smoke inhalation in Zagreb last night if someone had telephoned her at midnight and woken her. She died, then, because nobody woke her: I did not and you did not and nor did the Emperor of Japan. This does not put us in moral trouble, because we had no reason to suspect that by calling that number at that moment we could save someone's life. Most of our fairly immediate allowings are like this: we could have prevented a bad thing from happening, but we had no evidence that this was so; whereas in our fairly immediate makings we tend to know more about the consequence in question. This too is extrinsic to the difference between making and allowing, and should not be allowed to clutter our thoughts about it. (For reasons given in Section 21 above, it would not be right to say that you or I 'allowed' the woman to die in Zagreb, because that word requires knowledge or special responsibility. Still, our conduct relates to her death in a manner that belongs on the allowing side of the line I want to explore.)

Finally, we should distinguish moral from legal significance. In anglophone countries the criminal law is severely asymmetrical along the making/allowing line: it forbids vastly more than it enjoins. It does lay upon us duties of care towards our infant offspring, requires us to report crimes we have observed, and so on for certain other special ties and circumstances. But the asymmetry is strong. Suppose that while basking beside a lake I see someone drowning, when I could easily throw him a lifebelt; and I let him drown because I am lazy, or I hate him, or I am curious to see a drowning. In most countries the criminal law will not lay a finger on me for that behaviour. In some lands that is not quite so, but in none is the law symmetrical along the making/allowing axis.[1]

This aspect of the penal code can be justified without according basic

---

[1] For facts about the variety, see John Kleinig, 'Good Samaritanism'; Charles O. Gregory, 'The Good Samaritan and the Bad: The Anglo-American Law'; André Tunc, 'The Volunteer and the Good Samaritan'; Aleksander W. Rudzinski, 'The Duty to Rescue: a Comparative Analysis'.

moral significance to making/allowing.[2] Any attempt to make the law symmetrical would run up against a problem about relative cost. A criminal law that comprehensively enjoined help as well as forbidding harm would have to say what cost a law-abiding citizen must pay for bringing what benefits to others. As we have no uniform way of measuring costs or, therefore, of weighing them against benefits, the law cannot do this in a fine-grained way. Some cases of allowing harm (= not helping) morally deserve to be made criminal—e.g. the drowning example—but the penal code cannot cover these unless it is either (1) arbitrarily selective, picking out a few disgraceful kinds of case almost at random, or (2) unduly onerous, enjoining action in too many kinds of case, or (3) intolerably complex, in an endeavour to steer between (1) and (2). This problem is solved in some countries by making the law suitably (4) vague, speaking of how it is 'reasonable' to expect people to behave. I conjecture that such a law can work only when previous known cases give the populace some intuitive sense of where the limits lie. The alternative solution is for the law to turn its back on wicked allowings as such. It can also cost something to behave in a negatively relevant fashion, e.g. to refrain from doing harm; but the law can deal with these cases as they arise, forbidding the main kinds of detrimental action, and then dealing piecemeal with the rare cases where, for instance, someone steals food rather than starve to death. I conclude that the shape of the law is not good evidence for the moral significance of making/allowing.

26. Intuitions about Cases

Some philosophers have thought it useful to adduce pairs of cases where the distinction seems intuitively to make a moral difference, and others have described ones where it seems not to. Even if the pairs are devised with scrupulous care, however, with none of the mistakes I have warned against, they are still a bad basis for settling this issue. Here is a typical example of what happens on the neutrality side of the debate.[3] One man out of hatred and greed kills his wife by poisoning her; another

---

[2] For some other explanations see Kleinig, 'Good Samaritanism'; James Barr Ames, 'Law and Morals'; Herbert Fingarette, 'Some Moral Aspects of Good Samaritanship'; Antony M. Honoré, 'Law, Morals and Rescue'. For further useful references, see Eric Mack, 'Bad Samaritanism and the Causation of Harm', pp. 230–4.

[3] See e.g. Michael Tooley, 'Abortion and Infanticide', 59; James Rachels, 'Active and Passive Euthanasia'.

finds that his wife has inadvertently taken poison and, out of hatred and greed, does not give her the available antidote. We are invited to agree that the two behaviours are morally on a par, although one is a making and the other an allowing; from which we are to infer the moral neutrality of that difference.

This argument is far from conclusive. For one thing, it compares two bits of vile behaviour; perhaps a real moral difference escapes our moral sensors because it is swamped by all that wickedness. When we try to remedy this by taking a milder pair of examples, the desired intuitions are less readily forthcoming.

Some examples have been thought to count overwhelmingly against the neutrality of making/allowing. Suppose that four people are bound to die unless they get organ transplants today; their only chance—and it makes their survival certain—is to take the heart and both kidneys and liver from a single healthy person who owes them nothing and is not offering this sacrifice. Most people would condemn a surgeon who killed this man and did the transplants, rather than letting the four die. They would prefer his allowing four deaths to his making one occur; and, since four are worse than one, that is evidence that making bad things happen is much worse than allowing them to happen.

That can seem overwhelmingly conclusive, but Judith Thomson has shown otherwise by comparing it with this: A runaway train is careering down the hillside on a line where there are four people who must die if it reaches them; all we can do is to throw a switch to divert the train on to a line where it will kill one person.[4] Once again: allowing four to die, versus making one die. Yet everyone judges the train case with a different intensity, and most judge it in the opposite direction, from the transplant one, although modulo the making/allowing distinction they are the same case. Our resistance to the quadruple transplant must come from something other than a moral discrimination between making and allowing.

Seeing the transplant collide with the train, we can learn that pairs of examples are not good aids to understanding our own moral thinking. However well such a pair succeeds in eliciting certain intuitions, with however little help from extraneous factors such as cost, knowledge, etc., *we still don't know what is going on*. To know what place making/allowing should have in morality, we need a good analytic understanding of what distinction it is—an account of it in terms that

---

[4] Judith Jarvis Thomson, 'Killing, Letting Die, and the Trolley Problem', 80 f.

are clear, objective, and deeply grounded in the natures of things. Clear so that we can think effectively, objective so that we can think communally, and deeply grounded so that the issue about moral significance will not be trivialized.

Objection: 'We already know that we have a morally significant making/allowing distinction, and your analytic approach could not show otherwise. If a certain distinction is clearly neutral, that proves that it is not what underlies people's uses of the turns of phrase through which you have (in Section 20) identified the making/allowing distinction.' If that were right, conceptual analysis could never help us to move forward in moral theory; but it can, by uncovering inconsistencies which have lurked, unrecognized, in our system of moral principles. We could easily be making a moral mistake in our present area. It could be that the longest, strongest common thread running through the Section 20 locutions is neutral, and that people think otherwise because they are not clear in their minds about what they are saying, going by, committing themselves to, when they talk and think in those ways. The truth might be this:

> Whenever someone discriminates morally on the basis (she says) of the difference between doing and letting, causing and allowing, or the like, she has something in mind that she thinks is present in the case and believes makes a moral difference there; but she is wrong if she thinks that *this difference comes from a single factor that is present and operative in all these cases.*

The italicized clause belongs to abstract moral theory rather than down-to-earth moral belief; it is the sort of thing about which intuition might well be untrustworthy; there could easily be evidence that it is wrong. This should be agreed to even by those who place a good deal of reliance on intuitions.

27. Sometimes but not Always?

A different objection against arguments from examples should be looked at now. Suppose some pair of cases convinces us that we judge two behavioural episodes differently, that we are right to do so, and that this difference in judgement comes purely from making/allowing. That would show that *in this one instance* the distinction makes a moral difference, refuting the claim that it never does so. This is a tiny result.

Philosophers who argue from pairs of examples are always after bigger game than that. In fact, they have mostly assumed that making/allowing either always makes a basic moral difference or never does. This assumption, without which arguments from pairs of examples would lose their last vestige of interest, has been challenged.[5] Perhaps, it has been suggested, our distinction makes a moral difference sometimes but not always.

It might be thought that this cannot be so. 'Something makes a moral difference by providing a reason for some change in one's moral judgements,' this line of thought goes, 'and what is ever a reason is always one, since reasons are essentially universal.' That is not right as it stands. Even if there is some truth in 'Reasons are essentially universal', it is undeniable that a given kind of factor can be a reason for φing in one context and not in another. Shall I go for a late-night swim? No, because if I do *I will be tired tomorrow morning*. That is a reason against the swim this time, because I am to lecture tomorrow and I will do it badly if I am tired. In contrast, the fact that a late swim last night would have left me tired this morning was not a reason against it, since I have no commitments requiring alertness today.

Most of our practical reasons are like that, applying in some circumstances and not in others. I infer that where they do apply they are not the whole reason, but conjoin with other facts to make up a whole reason. The thesis 'Once a reason, always a reason' is true not of partial reasons ('It would make me tired in the morning') but of complete ones ('He could not have known', 'It would make him angry and resentful', 'It would hurt'). This may be trivial, but it is a truth.

Our present topic, then, can be called 'the partial reason thesis' about the making/allowing distinction. It says that when someone's behaviour has a notably good or bad consequence, its moral status is never affected just by the fact about whether it made the consequence obtain or merely allowed it to do so, but is sometimes affected by that combined with some further fact. The two must together yield a complete moral reason which is not provided by either alone.[6] I do not know whether this thesis is true.

If it is, then the following can happen: Agent's φing is relevant to

[5] First, so far as I know, by Philippa Foot, 'Killing, Letting Die, and Euthanasia'.

[6] For discussion of two kinds of partial reason—I call them 'stepping-stones' and 'signposts'—which are not in this way independent contributors to the morality of the situation, see Jonathan Bennett, 'Positive and Negative Relevance'. Most of the present section is drawn from that paper.

upshot U, and the fact about whether the relevance was positive or neg-ative serves as a partial reason for a moral judgement on that conduct. Moral theorists who give pride of place to the concept of rights think that this can happen, because they hold that rights are positive/negative asymmetrical: I have a right not to be killed, they say, but not one to be kept alive, a right to marry but not one to have a wife found for me. They do not say that the very concept of a right has a mak-ing/allowing asymmetry in it, for they think we have some rights to be helped, which could be 'allowingly' violated; but there are, they hold, far more rights which could only be 'makingly' violated. Philippa Foot, using the point to defend the partial reason thesis, endorses the 'prin-ciple . . . that the right to non-interference extends further than the right to have one's purposes furthered by others'.[7] If that is correct, facts about kind of relevance can be partial reasons. We can have a com-plex fact R about you and me and relations between us, including the fact that my conduct was relevant to your suffering some harm; to this we add a premiss K saying what kind of relevance it was, namely that I did not allow you to suffer but rather made you suffer; and out rolls the conclusion that I violated one of your rights, which does not follow from either R or K alone.

That, however, does not automatically confer on making/allowing the sort of moral significance I want to discuss—the sort that concerns how good or bad, right or wrong, conduct is. To explain why, I need a little technical terminology. Consider a case V in which Agent violates Patient's right to life, and set out in detail the facts that make this the case, including the fact that the relevance of Agent's conduct to Patient's dying prematurely is of the making rather than the allowing kind. Now consider a case DV in which the facts are exactly as in V except that now Agent *allows* Patient to die prematurely rather than *making* this happen. I shall say that in DV Agent 'dual-violates' Patient's right to life. This is the making/allowing dual of violating a right to life. It is what you get if you dismantle the latter far enough to expose the concept of 'making', replace that by 'allowing', and then reassemble.

Now, the fact about kind of relevance makes the difference between violating and dual-violating a right, and the latter of these is not a kind

<hr />

[7] Foot, 'Killing, Letting Die, and Euthanasia', p. 160. For more on this, see Judith Jarvis Thomson, 'A Defense of Abortion', esp. 8 ff. For some of the controversy over the making/allowing asymmetry of rights, and for further references, see Jeff Jordan, 'Why Negative Rights Only?'

of violation. However, it may be as bad as one. It may indeed be the case quite generally that no positive violation of a right is, *ceteris paribus*, any worse than its making/allowing dual would be. This would not discredit the rights concept. Even if positive rights violations are no worse than their duals, there may be good reasons for distinguishing the two: the making/allowing distinction might matter for moral theory even if it does not carry basic moral weight.

Of the moral theorists who take rights seriously, few would settle for this eirenic suggestion. Most would say that when judgements about rights embody a making/allowing asymmetry, the latter makes a difference to degree of moral severity. Rights violations, they would say, are systematically worse than their making/allowing duals. Why? This view needs to be defended. It does not follow from the fact that most rights violations are on the 'making' side of the line. Apparently no rights theorist has tried to fill this gap in the argument. Some, I think, might respond as follows: 'There is a degree of making/allowing asymmetry in the truth about what rights there are; and you have conceded this. To that I add my intuition, insight, knowledge, that it is especially gravely wrong to violate someone's rights—worse than "dual-violating" them, as you tendentiously put it. Argument has to stop somewhere, and mine stops there.' We ought not to rest content with this. Someone who holds that making/allowing, without always being morally significant, becomes so in the context of rights ought to wonder how the trick is worked, what the chemistry is of this moral molecule, what rouses the distinction from its moral lethargy in this context but not in others. Argument must indeed stop somewhere, but this seems an unduly early place to stop it.

28. The Difficulty Excuse

A draft of unpublished work by a distinguished philosopher clearly committed itself to the partial reason thesis: 'Blame for a positive act does not depend on how difficult not acting would have been. Blame for an omission must take account of the difficulty, inconvenience, etc. of the omitted act.' The word 'blame' belongs to second-order morality, though the writer meant to be talking about first-order as well.

Omissions belong on the allowing side of the line: if you omit to prevent upshot U your conduct is relevant in the negative or passive or allowing manner to U's obtaining. So the writer was implying that if someone's conduct was relevant to the obtaining of U which is bad, the excuse 'It would have been hard for him so to behave that U did not obtain' may reduce blame if the relevance was on the allowing side of the line but not if it was on the other. That fits the pattern I am exploring. The upshot's being hard to avoid combines with the relevance's being negative to generate a reason for a blame-reducing judgement on the person. Each conjunct in the reason is needed: if you delete the fact that the relevance was negative, the other conjunct does not reduce blame, since 'blame for a positive act does not depend on how difficult not acting would have been'.

The writer was not drawing on any views about rights, saying on the contrary: 'If someone is wronged, he has a right which is violated. But the wrongfulness of murder seems to be the basis of the right, rather than vice versa.' We have here a genuinely new proposal, not a disguised version of the rights thesis. The claim is that if my conduct is relevant to something bad, and if it would have been hard or costly for me to behave so that the bad thing did not happen, the latter fact does not affect my (dis)credit if I made the bad thing happen, though it may do so if I allowed it to happen. It is as though making does—whereas allowing does not—smooth the moral surface so that facts about difficulty of avoidance can get no purchase on it. This is striking, but why should we believe it?

We should not. The thesis implies that no facts about difficulty, inconvenience, etc. can reduce blame for positively making bad things happen; but that is too much to swallow, and it conflicts with something said earlier in the same draft: 'There is sometimes good excuse for . . . doing what will lead to deaths; e.g. having a system of rail or air transport.' The excuse for having such lethal systems must be the inconvenience of not having them, so we cannot accept, just as it stands, the thesis that 'Blame for a positive act does not depend on how difficult not acting would have been . . .'. When that material was published in a joint work whose authors are identified only collectively, the inconsistency had been removed: 'Blame for a positive act seldom depends on how difficult not acting would have been. Blame for an omission must take account of the difficulty, inconvenience, etc. of the omitted act.'[8] The only change is the insertion of 'seldom': from a philosophical point of view this is disappointing, since it weakens not by clear

---

[8] Working Party, *Euthanasia and Clinical Practice: Trends, Principles and Alternatives*, ch. 3.

restriction but by softening; it fends off counter-examples without throwing light.

Still, if it is true there should be a discussable thesis lurking behind it. The rare positive cases where the difficulty of avoidance *does* reduce blame are presumably marked off by some feature F that they all have and that others do not. Then we should have a thesis of the form: 'Blame for a non-F positive act never depends on how difficult etc., whereas blame for any omission, even a non-F one, must take account of the difficulty etc.' That would restore the clean contrast, if we had a value for F. I cannot find one. Indeed, the thesis strikes me as implausible even in its soft ('seldom') form. I am puzzled by anyone's venturing to assert it without giving reasons.

Perhaps it results from confusion. Perhaps this vibrant, challenging thesis:

(1) A *truth* of the form 'It would have been difficult not to' is more likely to *excuse* an omission to prevent harm than to excuse a positive causing of harm

has not been properly distinguished from this tame offering:

(2) A *proposition* of the form 'It would have been difficult not to' is more likely to *be true of* an omission to prevent harm than to be true of a positive causing of harm.

The thesis (2) that it is in general harder to obey 'Do A' than to obey 'Don't do B' is common ground, and is quite different from the controversial (1). Whereas (1) contrasts the making and allowing territories in terms of what moral force they allow to facts about difficulty of avoidance, (2) contrasts them in terms of how many such facts they contain. The writing in question certainly implies (1), but (2) may be what the author had in mind.

I introduced the partial reason thesis as something whose truth would further condemn arguments from pairs of examples, but those are condemned anyway. My preferred alternative approach, starting with a good analysis of the difference between making and allowing, might also help us finally to come to terms with the partial reason thesis. The prospects for defending the thesis in that way are not good, it seems to me; but I have not worked hard on the question.

6

POSITIVE/NEGATIVE

29. 'Negative Acts'

Let us seek a clearer view of the moral significance of making/allowing by first getting a better understanding of what distinction it is. Apart from an unhappy remark by Bentham, to be discussed shortly, the earliest attempt to clarify the distinction may have been one that I made in 1966 and improved some years later.[1] Although it has had many critics, and has won few converts that I know of, I shall argue that it captures a part of the truth. The critics all rely on a single type of alleged counter-example, which I shall evaluate in Section 32 below, explaining why I do not recant in the face of it.

The perceived failure of my analysis of making/allowing may have triggered the subsequent spate of rivals to it. The best of these was the late Alan Donagan's; I shall devote Chapter 7 to it, and to relating it to my analysis. Our analysantia, although formally as different as chalk from cheese, turn out to be almost coextensive; and the supposedly fatal counter-example to mine counts equally against Donagan's. In Chapter 8 I shall critically discuss some other offerings, showing how each can be repaired, turning it into something that its author may have been aiming at in the first place. Significantly, each of the improved versions approximates to Donagan's analysis or to mine—more often to his.

When philosophers refer more or less casually to the making/allowing distinction, they often use the terms 'positive' and 'negative', or ones closely allied to these. I align myself with this tradition, making those terms central to my analysis; but I do not follow the common practice of characterizing *acts* as 'positive' and 'negative'. Indeed, of all the benefits that accrue from keeping the act concept out of one's theories (see Section 9 above), the most dramatic are right here. I shall explain.

[1] Jonathan Bennett, 'Whatever the Consequences', and 'Morality and Consequences', lecture 1 (47–72).

When in Section 28 I quoted a philosopher as contrasting 'blame for a positive act' with 'blame for an omission', I choked back two questions which I now ask: What is a positive act? What is an omission? The gate was open, and I could have closed it, but instead of doing that I went on with my digging. This involves an omission (I omitted to close the gate), but if any sense attaches to 'positive act' then I also performed a positive act, namely digging. Two acts at once, then? But if there are two, there are more: I omitted to start reciting 'Maud', and to sit on the gate, and to throw my shovel over the gate, and so on indefinitely. Must we conclude that at every moment one performs countless acts— a few of them positive all the rest negative? No friend of the act concept would say so, but many commit themselves to it.

In fact, there could not possibly be conduct which was, in itself, negative: it is an error to try to divide items of conduct into those that are and those that are not negative acts or refrainings or forbearances or omissions, as though we had '. . . is negative' or '. . . is a refraining' as a monadic predicate of acts. Writers who have tried such a division have come to grief. Bentham, for one, seems to have thought he could peer at a person's behaviour at a given time and declare it to be intrinsically, monadically negative. This led him to view the negativeness of an act as consisting in the extreme of inaction, something that brackets the person with corpses: 'Acts . . . may be distinguished . . . into positive and negative. By positive are meant such as consist in motion or exertion: by negative, such as consist in keeping at rest; that is, forbearing to move or exert one's self in such and such circumstances.'[2] This makes 'positive' and 'negative' nicely monadic, for we do have the monadic predicates of acts '. . . does not involve movement' and '. . . involves movement'. Not surprisingly, though, Bentham did not believe his own account of 'negative act', for he went straight on to say: 'Thus, to strike is a positive act: not to strike on a certain occasion, a negative one.' Obviously, you can not-strike yet still keep moving, so 'keeping at rest' is not after all necessary for 'negative acts'.

If 'negative' or any of its kin is to be seriously employed in our present context, it must be applied to *facts about behaviour* rather than to *acts*. At any given moment, one's behaviour is the subject of countless facts, infinitely many of them negative: that is easy to accept, unlike the

[2] Jeremy Bentham, *An Introduction to the Principles of Morals and Legislation*, 72 (ch. 7, sect. 8). In sect. 9 Bentham distinguishes 'absolutely' from 'relatively negative', which sounds promising; but he explains and illustrates this in such a way that no light is thrown on anything.

boast that at every moment one performs infinitely many acts. As I present my analysis, 'negative fact' will show its paces; at intervals we shall see evidence of the toxicity of 'negative act'.

Some philosophers have endured terrible troubles in the service of the latter. Bruce Vermazen, writing at length about negative acts, feels constrained to say that 'Negative events do not, strictly speaking, exist.'[3] Donald Davidson remarks: 'We often seem to count among the things an agent does things that he does *not* do: his refrainings, omissions, and avoidances.'[4] It is wrong—and may be libellous—to count things I do not do among the things I do. It is all right to include my omissions, but they are not things I don't do. What Davidson should have said is that in describing a person's behaviour we often include negative facts about it.

John Kleinig has quoted this from a writer early in this century: 'An omission is not like an act, a real event, but merely an artificial conception consisting of the negation of a particular act.'[5] This is not bad as far as it goes, but 'artificial conception' is a rather hapless way of referring to something that is quite straightforward, namely a negative fact about conduct.

When Davidson alludes to 'things that he does not do', it may be that although he thinks he is writing about negative acts, really he isn't. The phrase 'things that he does not do' can function as an idiomatic way of referring to negative *facts* about a person's conduct. For example, it is sometimes said that when Agent allows upshot U to come about, it comes about 'because of something he doesn't do'. I used that turn of phrase in my introductory lists of locutions in Section 20, and I doubt that you winced. Yet that is absurdly wrong if it uses 'something' to quantify over acts. Consider the Stayback story that I told in Section 21, where a vehicle goes over a cliff because Agent did not interpose a rock that could have stopped it. If the disaster occurred because of *something he did not do*, meaning *some act he did not perform*, what act is it? In fact there is no act such that (1) he did not perform it and (2) the disaster occurred because of it. His interposition of the rock satisfies (1) but not (2). His *not* interposing the rock satisfies (2) but not (1), and anyway it is not an act. Of course there is nothing wrong with 'It happened because of something he did not do' taken as an idiom whose

[3] Bruce Vermazen, 'Negative Acts', 100.
[4] Donald Davidson, 'Reply to Bruce Vermazen', 217.
[5] A. Stroud, *Mens Rea; or, Imputability under the Law*, 4.

literal meaning is that it happened because of a negative fact about how he behaved.

Similarly with '(act of) omission', though here there is an extra wrinkle. On the face of it, if we allow that there are acts of omission, we must conclude that at each waking moment one performs millions of them. Although I can cite no references, I have seen philosophers use 'act of omission' in a way that blocks this conclusion. They count behaviour as an 'act of omission' only if it involves the agent's *notably* not φing—usually because he ought to have φed. That rescues us from having to credit people with performing countless acts of omissions all at once; but it makes 'act of omission' worthless in our present inquiry into the *bases* for our moral judgements on behaviour.

30. Negative Relevance

In developing my analysis, I shall refer back to two of the three cases I introduced in Section 21 above: *Push*, in which a vehicle stands, unbraked, on a slope, and Agent gives it a push that starts it rolling to its destruction; and *Stayback*, where the vehicle is already rolling, and Agent could but does not interpose a rock which could stop it. An analysis of making/allowing should at least get those right, and make clear how it does so.

My analysis identifies making/allowing with what I call the positive/negative distinction. I use 'negative' primarily in the phrase 'negative proposition' and thus also in 'negative fact' (facts are true propositions). I could amplify Stayback, for instance, so that it says that Agent moves his fingers, makes a daisy chain, and smiles; also, he does not resign his job, he does not stand on his head, he does not interpose the rock; three positive facts about how he behaved, and three negative ones. Given 'positive' and 'negative' as predicates of facts or propositions, we can define the relations '. . . is positively relevant to . . .' and '. . . is negatively relevant to . . .' between behaviour and upshots. These definitions are the first of the three stages in my analysis. In giving it, I use 'T_1' to name the moment when Agent pushes the vehicle in Push, and the last moment when he could usefully have interposed the rock in Stayback.

I now begin the first stage of my analysis. Suppose we wanted a full T_1-dated explanation of the vehicle's fate in Stayback—that is, facts about how the world is at T_1 from which it will follow causally that the vehicle is destroyed at T_2. Let E be the environmental portion of this material: it is the proposition about Agent's surroundings that is needed for the causal explanation that we seek. What must we add to E to complete the explanation? That is, what is the weakest proposition A about Agent's conduct at T_1 such that (E & A) causally imply that the vehicle is destroyed at T_2? The answer is that we need A = the negative fact that Agent does not interpose the rock. There are positive facts about how he behaves at T_1, but none fits the description 'weakest fact that, when added to E, yields a complete causal explanation of the disaster'. The fact that Agent smiled at T_1 does not yield a complete causal explanation; the fact that he turned and walked away does yield one, but it is not the weakest fact that does so. The negative fact that Agent does not interpose the rock is exactly what is needed: it is just strong enough to complete the explanation.

Now look for a T_1-dated explanation for the disaster in Push. Here there are countless negative facts about how Agent behaves at T_1, but none is strong enough to complete the explanation. For that we need the positive fact that he pushes the vehicle hard enough to start it moving.

In short: Agent's behaviour in Push is *positively relevant to* the destruction of the vehicle: the weakest fact about his conduct that suffices to complete a causal explanation of the vehicle's being destroyed is positive. Agent's conduct in Stayback is *negatively relevant to* the disaster: the weakest fact about the conduct that suffices to complete a causal explanation of the vehicle's being destroyed is negative.

(In my chosen examples, the behavioural facts are causally relevant to the upshot, and the explanations are causal. The analysis, however, is not confined to the causal realm. What I have said about Push can be reapplied to a case where Agent *puts someone in danger* by removing a warning sign: to explain the existence of the danger at T_2 we must mention Agent's removing the sign at T_1. Similarly, my treatment of Stayback can be simply adapted to fit a case where Agent *leaves someone in danger* by not putting up a warning sign: to explain the existence of the danger at T_2 we must mention Agent's not putting up the sign at T_1.)

The second stage of the analysis explains what it is for a fact or proposition to be negative. We can call a *sentence* 'negative' if it contains an odd number of negating expressions, but that is not useful. When sentence S is negative in that sense, either that is a symptom of an underlying feature of the proposition it expresses, or it is not. If it is not, then a distinction depending on the negativeness of sentences would be negligible in moral theory: the rights and wrongs of conduct could not ultimately depend on facts about sentence wording. If on the other hand the negativeness of S reflects some deeper feature (which seems unlikely, given such equivalent pairs as 'George is not in the armed forces any longer' and 'George has become a civilian'), then the deeper feature should be appealed to directly. So, granted that negativeness won't fall from propositions down on to acts or events, I need to prevent it from floating up on to sentences. That is, I need a concept of negativeness in propositions. Frege doubted that one can be had:

> For logic at any rate, a distinction between affirmative and negative thoughts is wholly unnecessary. . . . We see what tricky questions the expression 'negative judgement (thought)' may lead to. The result may be endless disputes, carried on with the greatest subtlety and nevertheless essentially sterile. Accordingly I am in favour of dropping the distinction between negative and affirmative judgements or thoughts until such time as we have a criterion enabling us to distinguish with certainty in any given case between a negative and an affirmative judgement. When we have such a criterion we shall also see what benefit may be expected from this distinction.[6]

Roderick Chisholm has sought to meet this challenge with an analysis according to which, if P and P* are complementary states of affairs, then P* is negative if: *Necessarily, whoever conceives P* conceives P and It is not the case that: necessarily, whoever conceives P conceives P*.*[7] In short: a negative proposition is one that cannot be thought without thinking its contradictory. What are we to make of Chisholm's modal 'cannot' or 'necessarily'? If it speaks only of something that we humans cannot do, then that limit on our powers—making us unable to think *It is not the case that bananas are yellow* without having the thought *Bananas are yellow*—must result from underlying facts about us and those two propositions. The relevant fact about the first proposition, I should guess, is that it is negative. Thus interpreted, the account does not get to the bottom of the matter.

Probably, however, Chisholm is using 'necessarily' to express absolute necessity, implying that if P* is negative then no being at any possible world can think P* without thinking its contradictory P. This strong claim would have to rest on the assumption that a negative proposition is composed of its contradictory and a negator (as the sen-

---

[6] Gottlob Frege, 'Negation', 125 f. A Fregean 'thought' (*Gedanke*) is not a mental item; it is a proposition.

[7] Roderick M. Chisholm, *The First Person*, 124 f.

tence 'It is not the case that bananas are yellow' is composed of its last three words and its first six). That would make it impossible to think the negative proposition without thinking its contradictory; you cannot think the whole without thinking each part.

I side with those who hold that propositions are not structured items with component parts, but it would take me too far afield to go into that.[8] If we are wrong about this, that transforms the 'negative proposition' problem, opening the door to Chisholm's account and to some others. If we are right, Chisholm's analysis fails, and—I now add— Frege's scepticism about the problem still looks reasonable. I shall not meet it head on. Rather than trying to define an all-purpose concept of *negative proposition*, I shall aim for something more limited that still meets my needs. Because my treatment will not imply that negative propositions have structure or parts, the distinction I shall define is not as deep as we might like: its roots don't all run down to logic or basic metaphysics. Still, they go below the surface of the language, giving my distinction a fair degree of depth and objectivity. The idea underlying it has occurred to philosophers as disparate as Berkeley, Kant, and Ayer.

I'll present it through Venn diagrams. Let all the ways Agent could move at time T—including staying still—be represented by a square. Each point on the square represents a proposition attributing to him some absolutely specific way of moving. A region of the square represents the disjunction of the propositions represented by the points in the region. Start, for example, with the proposition that *He walks fairly slowly northwards*. Take every point proposition—every absolutely specific way of moving—that would make it true that Agent walks fairly slowly northwards; identify the points that represent those; then the region of the square that represents our original proposition is the region that contains just exactly those points.

A line across this square represents a pair of propositions which are complementary within the square. They are not strictly contradictories because each entails the existence of Agent at that time. I offer to define propositional negativeness only with respect to that framework.

I propose this: A proposition about how Agent moves at T is negative if it is fit to be represented by a region that covers nearly the whole of the space of possibilities for him at that time. That is, a proposition and its complement are positive and negative respectively if they divide

[8] For a superb treatment of the matter, see Robert C. Stalnaker, *Inquiry*, chs. 1–4.

the Agent's behaviour space (as I shall sometimes call it) extremely unevenly; the highly informative one is positive, and its almost empty complement is negative. This is the idea that is at work in Kant's account of why the judgement 'The soul is non-mortal', which has the positive form 'S is P', is negative in content. Its predicate 'non-mortal' is negative, Kant says, because it picks out only 'the unlimited sphere of non-mortal beings':

Nothing more is said by [this] proposition than that the soul is one of the infinitely many things which remain over when I take away all that is mortal. The infinite sphere of all that is possible is thereby limited only to the extent that the mortal is excluded from it, and that the soul is located in the remaining part of its space. But, even allowing for such exclusion, this space still remains infinite, and several more parts of it may be taken away without the concept of the soul being thereby . . . determined in an affirmative manner.[9]

This explains the familiar fact that negative commands are in general easier to obey than positive ones, negative plans easier to execute, and negative hopes easier to realize. To obey a positive command or execute a positive plan (become a teacher, go to Sri Lanka), you have to actualize some one of a relatively small range of possibilities, and it may be that each is costly—or that most are and it would be hard to identify any that are not. On the other hand, to execute a negative plan (don't become a teacher, keep out of Sri Lanka), you need only to pick a behaviour out of a vast range of possibilities—so vast that it is probably easy to find costless ones amongst them.

31. A Metric for the Behaviour Space

The third and final stage of my analysis offers a metric for the relevant space of possibilities—a basis for saying that one proposition is consistent with more possible states of affairs than another. This is easy to provide when one entails the other, but otherwise it is hard. I need a basis for saying, of two complementary propositions, that they divide up their total space of possibilities unevenly, and for saying which corresponds to the larger subspace. We cannot do this by counting the number of points in each, for there will usually be infinitely many

---

[9] Immanuel Kant, *Critique of Pure Reason* A 72 f. = B 97 f. I use Kemp Smith's version, except for rendering Kant's *Raum* by 'space' rather than 'extension'. See also A. J. Ayer, 'Negation'; and this: 'But, in effect, what is all this negative knowledge better than downright savage ignorance?' (George Berkeley, *Alciphron*, 54).

points on each side of the line—e.g. infinitely many ways of walking fairly slowly northwards and infinitely many ways of not doing so. There are two ways of trying to stave off this threat of infinity.

(1) If space and time were granular, there would be only finitely many positions that a person's body could be in, so that we could after all have finitely many points on each side of the line. That would free us to base our metric on counting points. For all I know, space and time are granular, but I would not risk keeping any eggs in that basket.

(2) Because our concern is with the movements that a person could *make*—movements that are within his repertoire as an agent—infinity can be kept at bay in another way, suggested to me by Alastair Norcross. How Agent could have moved at T is determined by the intersection of (*a*) the neuronal events that could have occurred in his brain at T, and (*b*) the facts about wind, gravity, magnetic fields, falling meteorites, and so on, and internal non-neuronal factors such as the temperature of his blood, the different conditions of his various muscles, and so on. The members of (*b*), not being under Agent's voluntary control, are the same throughout the square of possibilities; the variability in how he could have moved comes entirely from (*a*). The number of distinct possibilities in (*a*) is finite, because it is determined by how many neurons Agent has and how many relevantly different states each can be in, both numbers being finite. So there are, after all, only finitely many points in Agent's behaviour space, and our metric can be got by counting them. This provides the basis for a real metric for the space of a person's possible voluntary movements. Like discrete space and time, however, it is too far from our actual thoughts to be usable in an analysis—even a revisionary one—of any distinction that we actually possess.

Those two bases for a 'finite number of points' metric probably yield the same results as one another, and as the metric I now offer, which does not suppose the number of points to be finite. I propose that two propositions about how Agent moves at a particular time are to be accorded the same amount of the behaviour space if they are *equally specific*. This will not work with every determinable, e.g. with colours, because for them we have no agreed objective measure of specificity; but we have such measures for space and time, and thus for movement and for specificity of propositions about movement. This enables us to say that a given complementary pair divides the possibilities so unevenly that one is positive and the other negative. For example, *He walks northwards* and *He does not walk northwards* are positive and negative respectively, because the former is much more informative, much more specific, than the latter. The fact that one is and the other is not expressed with help from 'not' has nothing to do with it.[10]

This is not a definition of negativeness for every kind of proposition for which we can measure degrees of specificity or for which the number of points is finite. If it were, we could apply it to propositions about cardinalities, saying that *There is one F* and *There are about 137 Fs* are positive while *There is at least one F* is negative: if we take a square of possible cardinalities for the Fs, with each point corresponding to one cardinal number, the existential proposition corresponds to the entire square minus one point. If I had to define 'negative' for such propositions, that is how I would do it, biting the bullet and arguing that existential propositions really are negative. But I neither want nor need to. We have no positive/negative distinction for cardinalities, or for colours, or for hosts of other determinables. The only positive/negative distinction that looms large in our thought and talk, it seems, is the one that applies to propositions that are either explicitly about how someone moves or—like 'He pushed the vehicle towards the cliff top'—are made true by facts about how someone moves.[11]

If someone's behaviour is (in my sense) relevant to upshot U, the space of his possible ways of moving can be divided into those that satisfy *If he moved like that, U would obtain*, and those that satisfy *If he moved like that, U would not obtain*. The line between these is what I call 'the U-line'. For example, the disaster line through Agent's space of possible conduct has all the vehicle-smashes movements on one side and all the vehicle-survives ones on the other. (For simplicity's sake, I am pretending determinism, so as to get rid of probabilities between 0 and 1.) Now, what makes Agent's conduct *positively* relevant to the disaster in Push is the fact that the disaster line separating his vehicle-is-destroyed options from his vehicle-survives ones is like that in Figure 1. That is, of all the ways in which he could have moved, only a tiny

---

[10] David Lewis has pointed out that my metric for the behaviour space was anticipated in John Bigelow, 'Possible Worlds Foundations for Probability'. Bigelow has a numerical measure for the degree of similarity between worlds, and then defines a circle of radius r_n in a two-dimensional possibility space as the set of worlds that are similar to some given world in degree n or greater.

[11] The colour difficulty is discussed by Ayer, *Negation*, 61–3; by Richard Gale, *Negation and Not-Being*, 22–5; and by David H. Sanford, 'Negative Terms'. Gale's section 'Criteria for Positive and Negative Propositions' gives many references to the previous literature.

proportion were such as to lead to the vehicle's destruction; virtually all would have had its survival as a consequence. In Stayback, on the other hand, Agent's conduct is relevant to the disaster in a *negative* way, represented by Figure 2.

Although it seems intuitively obvious that Figure 1 is right for Push and Figure 2 for Stayback, I need to defend it in the face of a difficulty which I have so far kept out of sight. Even when two propositions are purely about how one person moves at one time, it may be impossible to say which is the more specific. For example, one may state the precise trajectory of the person's right hand, while the other more vaguely describes how he moves his whole body. For my apparatus to work cleanly, it must be handled in terms of pairs of propositions that are not like that, that is, pairs that really can be compared for specificity. I now defend my claim that Figure 2 is right for Stayback, doing this purely in terms of comparable pairs.

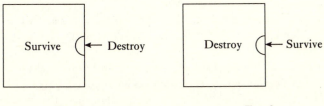

FIG. 1   FIG. 2

Consider the proposition that Agent interposes the rock, and think about the different physical ways he could have done this: a few dozen pairwise contrary propositions would pretty well cover the possibilities, each identifying one fairly specific sort of movement which would get the rock into the vehicle's path. Thus, Survive in Figure 2 can be divided up into a few dozen smaller regions, each representing some kind of push or kick or the like. Now, each of those can be paired off with an 'echo' of it in Destroy—by which I mean a proposition which is very like it except that its truth would not rescue the vehicle. For instance, if Survive contains a proposition attributing to Agent a certain kind of movement with his left foot, an echo of that might attribute to him a similar movement of that foot but angled so that the foot misses the rock. In general, for each little proposition in Survive, let its echo be one whose truth would make it look as though Agent were trying but failing to interpose the rock. (The 'echo' propositions must be pairwise

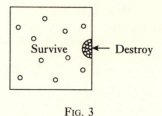

F‌ɪɢ. 3

contraries so that their regions do not overlap.) *Each 'echo' proposition will be exactly as specific as the proposition of which it is an echo*, so that the situation will be the one shown in Figure 3. The pockmarks in Destroy represent the echoes. My 'degree of specificity' criterion secures that their combined area is the same as that of Survive; and clearly they take up only a tiny proportion of Destroy. I do not base that on how the circles are drawn, but on considerations of specificity. Each of the little propositions in Survive has *many* echoes in Destroy; we assign just *one* echo to each, and all the remaining echoes take up further space in Destroy. That region also contains countless propositions that do not echo anything in Survive—that is, countless ways in which Agent could move without coming close to interposing the rock—and millions of those will also be comparable for specificity with the echoes. The result is that, according to my criterion, the vehicle-rescuing part of Agent's behaviour space in Stayback is vastly smaller than the vehicle-is-destroyed part of it; which is to say that Figure 2 is correct for Stayback except that it understates the disparity in size between the two regions. All this applies equally, *mutatis mutandis*, to Push and Figure 1.

That is why Agent's conduct in Push is positively relevant to the vehicle's being destroyed, and why in Stayback it is negatively relevant to this. In Stayback, the truth of any proposition in Destroy would suffice to complete the causal explanation for the disaster, but relevance is defined in terms of the weakest proposition that would suffice for this; that is the disjunction of all the propositions that would suffice, i.e. the proposition represented by the whole of Destroy.

32. The Immobility Objection

My account implies that *He moves* is negative, and that *He does not move* is positive. I have never seen any argument against the thesis that *He moves* is negative, but Leibniz has argued against my other counter-intuitive thesis, namely that *He does not move* is positive. This was put forward by Locke, who questioned whether 'rest be any more a privation than motion', to which Leibniz replied:

> I had never thought there could be any reason to doubt the privative [= negative] nature of rest. All it involves is a denial of motion in the body. For motion, on the other hand, it is not enough to deny rest; something else must be added to determine the degree of motion, for motion is essentially a matter of more and less, whereas all states of rest are equal.[12]

On the contrary, denying rest *is* sufficient for affirming motion. Presumably Leibniz misexpressed himself, and meant to write not of what is 'enough for motion' but rather of what suffices for a determinate way of moving. That would make him right about *He is at rest*: merely by denying that, you do not say how he moves. The same is true, however, of *He is drifting NNE at 5 m.p.h.*—by denying *that* you do not say how he moves either—yet Leibniz would presumably not classify it as negative! His whole point comes down to the fact that *He is at rest* is highly specific, so that denying it does not say much. According to me, this is a reason for classifying not *He is at rest* but *He is moving* as negative. It is bewildering that Leibniz thinks it is a reason for the reverse conclusion.

What can I say on the other side? Well, look at it this way: We have a square divided into tiny subregions, each representing some fairly specific way in which Agent could conduct himself with respect to motion and rest; and the proposition that he moves puts a finger on one point and says *Not that one*. Really, though, it does not matter. I call my distinction 'positive/negative', and freely use those words in expounding it; if the words are wrong, I shall drop them and retain the distinction. What matters is whether the line it draws is plausible as an analysis of the making/allowing distinction which is common property.

The status of *He moves* comes into that question too, but not through a sterile debate about whether it is negative. To see how, consider the following story:

> Henry is in a sealed room where there is fine metallic dust suspended in the air. If he keeps stock still for two minutes, some dust will settle in such a way as to close a tiny electric circuit which will

---

[12] G. W. Leibniz, *New Essays on Human Understanding*, 130. See John Locke, *An Essay Concerning Human Understanding*, II. viii. 6.

lead to some notable upshot U. Thus, any movement from Henry, and U will not obtain; perfect immobility, and we shall get U.

My analysis says that if Henry keeps still he *makes* U obtain, whereas if he moves he *allows* U not to obtain. This story is an instance of the solitary kind of 'counter-example' that has been brought against my analysis by people who contend that if Henry keeps still his conduct relates to the upshot U in the allowing rather than the making way.[13] Either of two things might be going on here: Henry's stillness might be put on the allowing-U side of the line (1) simply because it is an instance of immobility, or (2) because no physical forces run from Henry to U. A proponent of (2) will put some immobilities on the making-U side of the line. For example: After an earthquake Agent finds himself sitting on Patient's chest: she will survive if he moves, but otherwise she will suffocate. According to (2), if Agent stays still in this situation he makes Patient die,[14] with which a proponent of (1) will not agree. I shall discuss (2) in Sections 41–3 below; my present topic is (1).

I don't dispute that in keeping still Henry *allows* the dust to fall; but that is just one example of how the detailed meaning of 'allow' is a poor guide in our present problem area. It would lead us astray about Henry as it would over the Kick scenario which I presented in Section 21 above.

(Although it does not matter for my main line of thought, it would be good to understand why 'let' and 'allow' behave like this. In an earlier writing, I offered an account of this which copes nicely with Kick.[15] The causal chain from behaviour to upshot in Kick involves a negative proposition somewhere down the line. A complete but non-redundant causal explanation of the disaster requires a positive proposition about how Agent moved, but only a negative one about where the rock came to be—namely not in the path of the vehicle, which counts as negative through a natural extension of my earlier account of negativeness. That, I suggested, is what brings 'let' and 'allow' into play: negativeness *somewhere* in the causal chain from conduct to upshot. There may be some-

---

[13] The 'counter-example' was first presented by Daniel Dinello, 'On Killing and Letting Die'. Among the many who have accepted it without discussion are Don Locke, 'The Choice between Lives', 463, and Warren S. Quinn, 'Actions, Intentions, and Consequences: The Doctrine of Doing and Allowing', 295 f.

[14] It is not enough that he will be said to *kill* Patient, for that might be an instance of the bubble phenomenon (see Section 22), and thus irrelevant to the making/allowing distinction.

[15] Jonathan Bennett, *Events and their Names*, 219.

thing in this, but it does not fit the story about Henry's immobility. A full causal explanation of that upshot runs from Henry's keeping perfectly still to the air's becoming still, thence to the metallic dust's falling into the switch, finally to the switch's closing. These are all positive by my standards (or a natural extension of them); so I need a fresh account of why it seems natural to say that Henry 'lets' the dust fall. I think it comes from an intuitive sense that for the dust to fall is *natural*, that in a sense the dust is trying to fall and that in keeping still Henry is giving it its way. Further comment on this would be better given against the background of Donagan's analysis of making/allowing.)

If the immobility objection does not rest purely on facts about 'let' and 'allow', what support does it have? What else would make people so sure that if Henry keeps still his conduct relates to upshot U in a right-of-the-line or allowing way? Here is a guess about that. In most actual states of affairs, relative to most values of U, immobility *would* belong on the roomy side of the U line. When in Stayback Agent does not interpose the rock, he may do something else instead, but his staying still would have had the same effect on the vehicle's fate. It takes work to rig things so that keeping still is almost the only route to some interesting upshot. Perhaps that is why, when people confront a result that is produced by Agent's immobility, they immediately and invalidly infer that this is a case of allowing.

To evoke intuitions on my side, suppose that it is almost impossible for Henry to be still for long, and he sweats and strains to do so because he wants U to obtain. If he succeeds, doesn't this feel like a 'making'? If he fails—gives up trying because the effort is too great, relaxes, and lets his body shift a little—doesn't that feel like an 'allowing'?

'What would it take for you to accept defeat?' someone asked me once. He could have continued like this: 'Hardly anybody agrees with you that if Henry keeps still he makes U obtain. Even if you bring people around to accepting your view, that will be by changing how they think about making and allowing. Considered as an analysis of the making/allowing distinction that we actually have, yours is wrong. It would be more graceful if you were to admit it.' This deserves an answer.

How people use the words 'make' and 'allow' is a pointer to my concerns, but it does not define them. Let us distinguish three ways things might stand. (1) The ordinary uses of 'make' and 'allow', and of the other expressions in my introductory locutions, reflect an underlying jumble with no systematic core. (2) People use those locutions to express a single clean, systematic distinction, and I have failed to describe it. (3) In their uses of the locutions in question, people are guided by a clean, deep concept, but only imperfectly, because they sometimes drift away from it and use the terminology of making/allowing in ways that have no solid conceptual support.

If (1) is true, then there is no such thing as 'the making/allowing distinction' and this part of my analytic project is doomed. I cannot prove that this is wrong, but it is implausible, and I have seen no strong case for it. The friends of the immobility objection do not say 'You purport to describe a distinction that doesn't exist'; rather, they hold that the distinction exists and that I have misdescribed it. That is to assert (2). I cannot disprove that either, but I have seen no convincing evidence for it: an intuition that goes against my analysis is not the same as a rival to it. The most noteworthy rival, Donagan's, does not make a big issue of stillness as such, and in effect comes down on my side against the immobility objection. The facts seem to fit best with (3): our thought and talk about how conduct relates to its upshots do reflect a decently grounded making/allowing distinction, from which we sometimes drift away. It is in that spirit that I stand my ground.

The immobility objection is always presented naked and alone, and never as one counter-example among many. Its friends seem to assume that immobility is special in some way that gives it a unique power to refute my analysis. If they were right about that, I could still preserve most of the analysis by keeping immobility out of it. That is easy to do: simply omit the immobility point from the behaviour square; define the positive/negative line in terms of numbers of ways of *moving*, with not-moving left out of the story. Then cases like Henry's could be dealt with in some other way, suitably to the supposed uniqueness of immobility.

33. Doubts about the Metric

If my analysis is wrong in some matter of detail, I think I know what that must be. The use of 'negative fact' to define 'negatively relevant' seems secure, as does the analysis of negativeness of facts or propositions in terms of an uneven division of a space of possibilities. My way of measuring that space is vulnerable, however: I could be using the wrong ruler.

Of two ways of criticizing it, the more radical says that 'degree of specificity' has no place in this story. Alternatives to it suggest themselves. The link between 'negative' and 'uninformative' suggests that instead of my *specificity* metric we might have a *probability* metric. As before, let each point in the behaviour space represent one specific way of behaving (or of moving), and let regions of the square represent less specific propositions. Then let the size of a region be measured, relative to Speaker, by how likely Speaker thinks the proposition to be: the higher his subjective probability for it, the larger its region. Some of our intuitions about negativeness may well come from this source, but it cannot help us to analyse the idioms of making and allowing, which are plainly not speaker-relative.

We might try a *difficulty* metric, assigning equal areas to two propositions if they would be equally hard for Agent to make true. Frances Howard-Snyder, who suggested this, offers a rationale for it. Consider the ways of moving that are not in Agent's behaviour space because he cannot make them. These are out of his reach because they are in one way or another too difficult for him; so a too-difficult way of moving is assigned no region in the behaviour space. Consonant with that we might assign an almost-too-difficult movement a tiny region, a fairly hard one a somewhat larger region, and so on. Continued right across the board, this yields a difficulty metric.

According to my specificity metric, it is in general harder to make a positive proposition true than to make a negative one true; but that metric does not attend to difficulty as such, and it will sometimes happen that when ϕing is positive and not-ϕing negative according to my metric, ϕing is easy and not-ϕing is hard. For example, Agent has an arthritic condition in which he can alleviate severe pain only by making one fairly specific kind of movement with his left arm while keeping the rest of himself still; anything else brings agony. Put him in a situation where that movement is just what is needed to produce a significant upshot, and you have a case where the relevance of behaviour to upshot is on the left of my line and the right of the one suggested by Howard-Snyder.

If we do equate making/allowing with positive/negative, and base that solely on the difficulty metric, that guarantees a place in basic morality for making/allowing, because difficulty of avoidance has a secure place there. Drawing the positive/negative line on the basis of my specificity-of-fact-about-movement metric, I said that we should consider the moral significance of that difference just in itself, abstracted from other differences such as that of *cost*. If we move to a difficulty metric, that abstraction can no longer be performed, because difficulty is a kind of cost.

Some think that difficulty of avoidance belongs only in second-order morality, providing excuses which are barriers to blame, but not affecting what it is right or wrong to do. On some moral views, however, including one to be discussed in Section 48 below, 'difficulty' in a broad sense of the term does figure in first-order morality. However, I cannot believe that difficulty is what mainly powers our ordinary informal thoughts about making and allowing; the difficulty metric cannot do the work on its own. It was worth mentioning just as another example of what a metric for the behaviour space might look like.

The truth may involve a mixture of metrics. When we classify facts about behaviour as positive or negative, we may be steering by something that involves specificity and probability and difficulty, and who knows what else. Or perhaps no one metric is right, and we carve up the space varyingly according to context. If that is so, it might be that the making/allowing distinction has moral significance sometimes but not always (see Section 27). I have tried in vain to put flesh on these speculative bones.

The less radical criticism retains specificity but uses it differently, rejecting my proposal to define the metric for a space of ways of *behaving* in terms of propositions about ways of *moving*. That is indeed open to two criticisms, of which I accept one and am troubled by the other. (i) An item of behaviour might consist not in moving but rather in directing one's thought in a certain way (see Section 11 above). In practice this matters little, because such non-movement behaviour plays only a small part in our lives; still, it is a defect in my analysis that it is silent on this matter, and I cannot see how to make it speak up. (ii) My metric covers the rest of human behaviour, but not in the terms that interest us: it attends to hand gestures, arm-swings, foot-shoves, and tremblings of the larynx, rather than to morally interesting kinds of behaviour: giving up, betraying, keeping the faith, sharing, and hoarding. These, I repeat, are all covered. To say that he kept the faith with her is to attribute a certain relational property to how he moved; similarly with 'He gave up the project' and 'She shared her food with them' and all the rest. Still, it is a suspicious fact about the metric that it uses none of the relational concepts that give importance to human conduct.

There may be a good deal hanging on this. The positive/negative distinction that I have defined *obviously* has no basic moral significance: if someone moves in a way that causes or makes probable some bad upshot, nobody would think that the moral status of his conduct depends on how many other movements by him would have done the same. Perhaps the obviousness of that is due to my choice of metric; with a different way of measuring the behaviour space the claim might be less compelling.

When I first presented a version of my positive/negative distinction, I said that it does not matter what metric is used provided it is the same one throughout. I thought it was safe to equate 'P is positive and its complement negative' with this: Every uniform finite way of counting possibilities makes P consistent with many fewer possibilities than its complement is consistent with. That, I now see, was too optimistic. There may well be no complementary pair of propositions such that *every* uniform metric has them dividing their space very unequally. When I wrote that, I was thinking only of the different ways of implementing the specificity of movement metric; it did not occur to me that one might measure the behaviour space in other terms altogether. If I had thought about that, I would not have been so sure that positive/negative is morally neutral.

There are various loose, intuitive ways of revising the metric. Consider these three stories:

> *Suit*: An African village is in need. I launch a lawsuit that deprives them of a thousand dollars they would otherwise have had.
>
> *Cancel*: Same village, same everything, but this time I learn that my accountant thinks he is supposed to sign away a thousand of my dollars to the village, and I tell him not to.
>
> *No-help*: Same village, etc. This time I could but do not give the villagers a thousand dollars.

My positive/negative line has Suit and Cancel on the left and No-help on the right. One might hope for a line having Suit on the left and the other two on the right: Cancel and No-help, one might think, are just two ways of *not giving money to the village*, and it does not matter that one does and the other doesn't require a fairly specific kind of movement. This view of the cases requires a behaviour space that represents not *ways I could move* but rather *things I could do with my money*, with these (perhaps) dividing into such equal-sized kinds as investing it in bonds, giving it to my children, spending it on a swimming-pool for myself, donating it to Oxfam, and giving it to that African village. On this account, *giving it to the village* would just be so *conducting myself that it gets to the village*, with no special attention being paid to what movements are needed for this to happen, and thus with no regard to whether I would be signing a document or not blocking my accountant's signing it. That would put No-help and Cancel on a par because in each the weakest proposition that about my conduct that suffices to complete the explanation of the village's continuing misfortune is *I do not give money to the village*.

That sounds natural, but it is tailored to fit that trio of cases; it is no use until we can generalize it, and I cannot see how to do that. Furthermore, I suspect that its plausibility comes from seeing the different ways of not giving money to the village as morally on a par. So indeed they are, but if moral judgements are to dictate the metric, this whole approach fails. Its purpose was to get clear about the difference between making and allowing, in order to assess its role in the *basis* for moral judgements. In the mean time, I see no alternative to staying with the metric based on specificity of propositions about how Agent moves.

7

ACTIVE/PASSIVE

34. Agency and 'the Course of Nature'

The other analysis of the making/allowing distinction that I propose to consider in detail was propounded by Alan Donagan. It is not clear why he took the trouble to do so, as he seems to have had no use for this analysis. (The pages of his book that contain it are ignored in the index.) Whereas the positive/negative distinction which I have equated with making/allowing is *obviously* morally neutral, the same is not true of Donagan's analysans for making/allowing; yet we never find him making that point, let alone arguing that making/allowing on his account of it really does have basic moral significance. I think I know why.

The 'traditional morality' which Donagan defends includes something close to absolutism. For some values of ϕ it enjoins *Do not* ϕ in almost every conceivable situation, though such injunctions may be breakable if the alternative is the death of mankind. Now, here are two ways in which this position might be reached. (1) We might start with the thesis that making/allowing carries a lot of moral weight. We put into one pan of the balance the bad upshots U_m that Agent would make occur by ϕing, and into the other the bad upshots U_a that he would allow to occur if he did not ϕ; then we add to the first pan the extra weight that comes from making. Usually that together with U_m will outweigh U_a, but if U_a is enormously heavy—as is the extinction of mankind—then the second pan of the balance may swing downwards, overcoming the combined weight of U_m and making. (2) We might refuse to look at things in that way, declining to think of torturing someone (for instance) as behaving in a way that makes the person suffer extreme pain. As soon as we see torture in that way, we might think, it becomes too easy for us to envisage situations where it would be right to torture someone because the alternatives would be worse by an amount that could not be overcome by any mere moral weight attached to making. To get straight about the morality of torture, according to this line of thought, we must not think of it as analysed in terms of 'making' and 'consequential pain': that assigns it to the wrong part of morality, as though crises involving it were on a par with triage problems. To get morally straight about torture, we must look at it whole and unified—as *torture*.

Donagan's procedure was more like (2) than like (1), I am sure. He accorded to the making/allowing distinction a moral significance that he did not regard as defeasible by analysis. That would explain his not using his analysis of making/allowing in defence of his morality. Defending moral absolutism against an attack of mine, he could have said this: 'The attack requires the thesis that the making/allowing distinction is neutral, which Bennett derives from his positive/negative analysis of it. If that is replaced by my analysis, the neutrality of making/allowing is no longer so obvious.' In fact he says no such thing. Indeed, his defence of near-absolutism looks notably weak.[1] Still, his handling of this matter is, I now think, faithful to his assumption—which all near-absolutists seem to need—that making/allowing lies so deep in morality as to be beyond the reach of analytic criticism.

Anyway, Donagan's way of understanding the making/allowing distinction, whatever he thought about its usefulness, is worth studying. In this chapter I shall present a version of it, which I shall call the 'active/passive' analysis of making/allowing, and which I shall compare with my own positive/negative analysis. A quick, rough statement can be given in terms of Push, where a vehicle rolls over a cliff top because Agent gives it a push which starts it rolling, and Stayback, where the vehicle is already rolling and where Agent could but does not interpose a rock which would bring it to a halt. On the active/passive account, the crucial difference is that in Push but not in Stayback the vehicle is destroyed because Agent *intervenes in the course of nature*—that is, exercises his agency so that what happens is different from what would have happened in the course of nature.

There is here an ominous hint that human agency can indeed thwart nature's laws. This is the view of those who—in Spinoza's memorable words—'consider man in nature as a kingdom within a kingdom' and 'believe that man disturbs rather than follows nature's order'.[2] In his use of 'course of nature', and in other ways, Donagan seems to flirt with this view, if not to espouse it; but it is not needed for the active/passive account of making/allowing to go through. For purposes of that analysis, we can stipulatively define 'the course of nature' to mean 'what

---

[1] Alan Donagan, *The Theory of Morality*, 157 f.

[2] Benedict Spinoza, *Ethics Demonstrated in Geometrical Order*, first para. of pt. 3.

happens unaffected by human agency'. Then the analysis says that in Push (but not in Stayback) Agent so exercises his agency that what happens is different from what would have happened if human agency had not been engaged.

To discuss this properly, we must first grasp the three ways in which a person's agency can relate to the world. *Intervention*: She exercises her agency so as to make a difference to what happens. She raises her arm to wave to a friend. *Abstention*: She exercises her agency so as to make no difference to what happens. Feeling the onset of a suppressible sneeze, she decides to let it happen. *Quiescence*: Agency is uninvolved, not at work, not engaged, e.g. because she is asleep or day-dreaming or in a trance, or subject to something over which she has no control. She hears a sudden loud noise and starts involuntarily.

If Stayback involved Agent's quiescence, his behaviour would play no part in the disaster; that is not a case that I want to consider. I have been taking Stayback to be a case where Agent voluntarily behaves so that the rock stays out of the vehicle's path, as it *would* also have done *if* no agency had been at work. So we should set quiescence aside, and look at Push and Stayback in the light of the difference between intervening in the course of nature and abstaining from doing so. Here is Donagan saying some of that:

Should he be deprived of all power of action, the situation, including his own bodily and mental states, would change according to the laws of nature. His deeds as an agent are either interventions in that natural process or abstentions from interventions. When he intervenes, he [causes] whatever would not have occurred had he abstained; and when he abstains, [he allows] to happen whatever would not have happened had he intervened. Hence, from the point of view of action, the situation is conceived as passive, and the agent, *qua* agent, as external to it. He is like a *deus ex machina* whose interventions make a difference to what otherwise would naturally come about without them.[3]

Never mind the suggestion—embodied in Donagan's use of 'naturally' and of 'the laws of nature'—that human agency is contra-causal; we can resist that without losing the main thrust of the analysis.

A different flaw in Donagan's handling of his own ideas has to be corrected. The quoted passage implies that what you allow is what happens because you abstain from intervening in the course of nature. Later, Donagan says as much: 'What an agent causes [= makes] or

---

[3] Donagan, *The Theory of Morality*, 42 f, lightly edited. This account of allowing is 'roughly' adumbrated in Don Locke, 'The Choice between Lives', 464.

allows to happen follows in the course of nature from his intervention or abstention.'[4] It is a mistake thus to equate *allowing* with *abstaining from intervening in the course of nature*. Allowings are as common as blackberries, whereas abstention from intervening etc. is a rare performance: one could get through life without ever exercising one's agency in such a way that the rest of the world runs as it would have done had one been asleep or on auto-pilot. If in Stayback Agent is making a daisy-chain (or shuffling his feet, or whistling) at the moment when he could interpose the rock, he is intervening in the course of nature; yet he still counts as allowing the vehicle to go over the cliff.

We can turn the active/passive analysis into something in which allowing is related to, but not outright identified with, abstaining from intervening etc. To do that we must drop the monadic question about his behaviour 'Did he abstain from intervening in the course of nature?' in favour of this dyadic one about how his behaviour relates to an upshot U, 'Would U have come about if he had abstained from intervening etc.?' Perhaps in Stayback Agent was making a daisy-chain or blowing smoke-rings, but the vehicle would still have been destroyed if he had abstained altogether from intervening in the course of nature. That is what puts it on the right of the making/allowing line.

(Although Donagan's preferred terminology for making/allowing is that of 'causing/allowing', his analysis like mine applies also to non-causal consequences. Reverting to the examples I used in Section 30 above: If she *puts someone in danger* by removing a warning sign, the active/passive analysis can say that the danger existed only because her agency was exercised; if she *leaves someone in danger* by not replacing a warning sign, the analysis can say that the danger would still have existed if her agency had not been exercised.)

Here is the story again, told in terms that will help us to compare the active/passive distinction with my positive/negative one. Wanting to decide whether Agent's behaviour relates to upshot U actively or passively, we form the square representing all the ways he could have moved at that time; we divide it into the U subspace, each of whose points satisfies this: *If he had behaved in that way, U would have ensued*, and the non-U subspace, each of whose points satisfies this: *If he had behaved in that way, U would not have ensued.*[5] This is also the frame needed for positive/negative, but now the two part company. My dis-

[4] Donagan, *The Theory of Morality*, 50.

[5] For simplicity's sake, I assume again that Agent could not have given U a probability between 0 and 1.

tinction asks: Is the U subspace vastly larger than the non-U one? The active/passive one asks instead: Does the U subspace contain the abstention point? That is to ask: Would U have ensued even if the Agent's agency had been so exercised as to make no difference to the rest of the world?

The abstention point represents Agent's voluntarily moving as he would have moved if his agency had not been engaged. That is something he could do, so it is represented on the square of possibilities; but we are not asking whether he *did* abstain from intervening in the course of nature. The question 'Was his conduct passively relevant to upshot U?' does not ask whether his conduct was at the abstention point; rather it asks whether the U space, which contains the point representing his conduct, also contains the abstention point.

(Abstaining is something he could do, I have said, but perhaps sometimes it is not. It could in theory happen that some subtle sequence of movements which he cannot make voluntarily are exactly those his body would make if his agency were entirely disengaged. Then there would be no abstention point in his square of possible ways of behaving: the movements that would occur if his agency were not engaged are not ones that he could make voluntarily. For that reason, and also because (I find) some people are vaguely but strongly bothered by the concept of abstention, we might prefer to remove it from the story. We can do this by adding to the square of Agent's possible ways of behaving a further point representing his *not* behaving, not exercising his agency at all. Then we can construe the question 'Was his conduct passively relevant to upshot U?' as asking whether the U space contains this no-agency point. Help yourself to that version if you prefer it.)

Summing up: It is plausible to suppose that if Agent's agency had not been exercised in Push the vehicle would have survived, whereas if it had not been exercised in Stayback the vehicle would have been destroyed. Thus, the active/passive distinction, like mine, puts Push on the left and Stayback on the right of the making/allowing distinction.

35. The Two Distinctions as Collaborators

We have seen that there is a single structure, about which positive/ negative asks one question and active/passive asks another. These utterly different questions tend to have the same answer, because it is usually the case that if *U would have occurred even if the person's agency had not been exercised*, then also *Whatever the person did (with a few exceptions), U would have occurred*, and vice versa. Let us now consider some cases where the two come apart.

In Push a fairly specific kind of movement by Agent—call it a 'shove'—is needed to get the vehicle moving. Now add this detail: Agent feels the onset of an involuntary muscular spasm which, if not checked, will result in his body's making a shove. He could quell this spasm, but he chooses not to and his body does produce the shove which starts the vehicle rolling. For active/passive this is a case of *allowing* the vehicle to roll: the relevance of conduct to upshot is on the right of that line. It remains on the left of positive/negative.

We can also modify Stayback so that active/passive puts it on the left while positive/negative still has it on the right. Agent feels coming over him an involuntary muscular contraction that would get the rock into the path of the vehicle, and he fights it off, so that the rock stays still. In that case, the relevance of his behaviour to the disaster would be on the right of the positive/negative line and on the left of the active/passive one.

Trying to understand better a central feature of our understanding of ourselves, I run into suppressible twitches and spasms! This comic feature of the discussion could not be avoided. If a particular conduct–upshot relation is to fall on the left of positive/negative it must involve some fairly specific kind of movement; for it to fall on the right of active/passive, the movement must be one which would occur in the course of nature. Put the two together and you get *a fairly specific kind of movement which would occur in the course of nature*; which is why I bring in twitches and spasms. Also, since the movement must involve agency, the twitches etc. must be suppressible.

Now that we have seen the two analyses part company, which do you want to follow? In the permitted-spasm version of Push, does Agent make the vehicle go to its destruction (positive/negative) or allow it to do so (active/passive)? In the suppressed-contraction version of Stayback, does he make the vehicle go to its destruction (active/passive) or allow it to do so (positive/negative)? I predict that you will be uncomfortable with every answer; our ordinary making/allowing distinction gets no firm hold on cases like these.

Morally significant upshots are seldom reachable *only* through suppressible twitches, and that could be why these cases reduce us to silence: we are simply not forearmed to deal with anything so rare and peculiar. The real reason, however, seems to be different. We hesitate to apply the making/allowing distinction to the 'spasm' cases, I suggest, just because in them positive/negative does not coincide with active/passive. We confidently apply the notion of allowing, I am maintaining, only when the negativeness thought and the abstention thought both favour our doing so. It follows that a decision between the two analyses is blocked by the very feature of the cases that was supposed to give the decision something to feed on.

Both accounts of making/allowing are right, I submit. When people use the making/allowing locutions, they may be guided by the abstention thought or by the negativeness thought or by both at once, with neither being always uppermost. In the form in which most people have it, the making/allowing distinction does not equip them to deal with the unusual cases where only one of those thoughts is available. In short, the two analyses share the truth between them.

This is an odd result. The two distinctions are so unalike in their formal aspects that one would hardly expect them to collaborate, or to operate interchangeably, in our thinking. I shall sketch that contrast, which I find too interesting to pass up. Assume throughout that a person behaves in a certain way which is relevant to an upshot U. We have the person's behaviour space, with the U line drawn through it.

(1) Active/passive identifies one particular point in the person's behaviour space, namely the abstention point; positive/negative does not in that way pick out any one absolutely specific way of behaving.

(2) Active/passive identifies that particular way of behaving by means of a monadic predicate: . . . *is an abstention from intervening in the course of nature.* All the other possible ways of behaving fall under another monadic description: . . . *is an intervention in the course of nature.* Positive/negative does not monadically describe behaviour; all its descriptions are relatings of the behaviour to a particular upshot.

(3) Active/passive's central question about the U line is: On which side of it does the abstention point lie? It does not ask about the relative sizes of the two regions, and the question it does ask must have an answer (vagueness apart). Positive/negative's question about the regions that are separated by the U line is: Which, if either, is by far the larger? It does not ask what movements each region contains, only how many. Also, if neither region is much larger than the other, the question has no answer.

(4) I explained at the end of Section 30 above why it is apt to be easier to pursue a plan or obey a command if it is negative than if it is

positive. That explanation, depending as it did on the size difference between two regions of the behaviour space, could not work for active/passive. One might think: 'Active/passive has another route to the same conclusion. Whatever its size, the region in which the person allows U to happen always contains the abstention point, which represents a costless way of behaving. It cannot be hard to slump into inactivity for a while, thus refraining from intervening in the course of nature in *any* way.' This implies that the two distinctions share a certain feature but for different reasons. That would be enjoyable, but it is not right. Even if abstaining from intervening etc. were always easy (and I have pointed out that it might sometimes be impossible), it can still be costly in other ways: painful, morally repugnant, mentally demanding, a damaging departure from current projects. Active/passive does tend to resemble positive/negative in respect of cost, but that is because it borrows from the latter. The two distinctions usually coincide: in most cases a significant upshot U is reachable through abstention etc. only if it is reachable also through most things that the agent might do; so usually the region containing the abstention point is the larger of the two, and therefore the less costly to be confined to.

36. Immobility Again

The active/passive distinction makes no more of immobility than mine does. In most behaviour spaces, relative to most upshots, the immobility point will be in the region that contains the abstention point, and thus also in the larger of the two regions; which is why, in most cases where U would have ensued if the person had remained still, his conduct's relevance to U will be on the right of both lines. But neither line employs the concept of stasis: neither asks what would have happened if the person had remained still. Donagan is explicit about this. In the natural course of events, he says in the passage I quoted early in Section 34, the person's 'bodily and mental states *change* according to the laws of nature'—and the changes could include movements. Thus, two considerable analytic treatments of our topic are silent about immobility. If they are both wrong, and stillness deserves a special emphasis, I would like to hear the reasons for this.

We encountered the immobility objection in a case where U will occur if Henry moves, and not otherwise. Now consider two ways in which that story could unfold:

(1) Henry sits completely still, *slack and comfortable*; U ensues, and would not have done so if Henry had moved.

(2) Henry sits completely still, *heroically enduring a terrible itch*; U ensues, and would not have done so if Henry had moved.

The positive/negative distinction ignores the emphasized phrases, and classifies Henry's conduct as positively relevant to U both times. But if Henry's itch means that in the course of nature he would move, so that his stillness is an intervention, then the active/passive analysis counts Henry's behaviour as relevant passively in (1) and actively in (2). Case (2) is the one I appealed to when I first introduced Henry: I was trying to shift your intuitions about stillness my way, by bringing them up against a case where *both* analyses were against them. Mine without help from active/passive is less powerful than are both together.

That is what we should expect if I am right in holding that thoughts about negativity *and* about abstention feed our making/allowing intuitions. I illustrated that by looking at cases where the two distinctions come apart. Those cases involved spasms and twitches; but now I should acknowledge that the two also part company in some cases involving stillness. We have just looked at one—comfortable Henry— where only my distinction is available to dislodge the intuition that immobility matters, and then another—itching Henry—where the two distinctions work together. I think that in most people's minds the intu- ition about stillness would begin to yield in the latter case.

What happens to the immobility intuition when it is confronted by the active/passive distinction without the positive/negative one? Well, consider this case:

(1) An alarm will sound if a certain button is pushed, and Henry is standing close to it. He keeps still; the button is not pushed, and the alarm does not go off. (2) One fairly specific kind of movement was needed if he was to press the button; most movements he could have made would have resulted in its not being pushed, as did his keeping still. (3) At that time, Henry was subject to a barely controllable muscular spasm which, if allowed to run its course, would have jerked his hand on to the button so that the circuit was closed and the alarm set going; Henry kept still by voluntarily fighting this spasm.

Parts (1) and (2) entail that Henry's behaviour is negatively relevant to the alarm's silence, while (1) and (3) entail that his behaviour is actively relevant to it. Positive/negative doesn't care about (3); active/passive doesn't care about (2). I believe that untutored intuition will be unhappy with what the active/passive analysis implies about this case, where it is not supported by positive/negative.

I have confronted the immobility intuition with positive/negative alone, with active/passive alone, and with the two together. The main purpose of this was to explore further how the two distinctions are related, not to argue against the intuition about stillness. The latter is significant only as a matter of epidemiology: *There's a lot of it about.* There are people out there who have strong, confident ideas about the import of someone's keeping still, and in argument this has to be reckoned with. I have offered two ways of explaining these ideas away, and nobody has said a word in their defence. Until someone speaks up on their behalf, I do not see why the immobility intuition should be counted as a serious obstacle to either analysis.

37. What is 'the Course of Nature'?

The active/passive analysis starts with the general idea that what happens in the course of nature is what happens without help from human agency. Two questions arise: *Whose* agency? and *Where* in the causal chain? I plunged straight into a version of the analysis which focuses on what would have ensued at T_2 if our protagonist's agency had not been exercised at T_1—thus attending to one person's agency at one time. This yields the best understanding of active/passive that I can find (and the one that is most easily contrasted with positive/negative); but it could be interpreted in other ways, and I want now to turn back and explore some of the roads not taken. Let us start with the 'Where in the causal chain?' question.

We could take 'U would have obtained in the course of nature' to mean that it would have obtained even if no human agency had ever been at work. But if we thus confine nature to aspects of the world that have no agency anywhere in their origins, the concept will be almost idle, because most significant aspects of our planet already bear the marks of human intervention. We might try to get around this by making 'naturalness' a matter of degree. A state of affairs with no human agency in its aetiology is perfectly natural, while others are more or less so according to how remote the nearest relevant agency is, and/or on how big a difference it made. This would turn the active/passive distinction also into a matter of degree, thereby—if the active/passive analysis is right—doing the same for making/allowing. It would yield results like this: Suppose that in Stayback the vehicle was set rolling two seconds ago by someone else's pushing it; in that case, Agent, in not interposing the rock, is only to a slight degree allowing the vehicle to go over the cliff. And is to a greater degree *making* it go over? No, that would be absurd, and the present line of thought need not say anything so silly. But I shan't bother with the details of what it might say instead, because in any case this approach is nowhere near to the making/allowing distinction as we ordinarily understand it.

There has been much discussion of *making/allowing dilemmas*—situations where it is only by φing (which is atrocious) that Agent can prevent the occurrence of U (which is even worse). Some moralists think that the case for φing is weakened if the entire dilemma has been malignantly contrived by a human being; and that might seem to bring back the idea that I have just banished. The thought might be that because human agency would be involved in U's occurring, it would not obtain in the course of nature, and so Agent would not count as having 'allowed' it to obtain. This is all wrong, though. In the dilemmas in question, the apparent moral sting comes from the fact that the scene has been set with malice aforethought by someone wanting to give Agent trouble. That goes far beyond its merely being the case that the situation is a product of human agency.

Attention is also paid to cases like this: At T_1 Agent gives Patient some poison; at T_2 he could give her an effective antidote, but he does not do so; at T_3 she dies. It is sometimes thought that Agent's conduct at T_1 affects the status of his conduct at T_2, perhaps by implying that at T_2 Agent does more than merely *allow* Patient to die. This is another apparent use of the idea that prior agency is relevant to the making/allowing distinction. This is all wrong. One naturally thinks that Agent is specially obliged to block a dangerous causal chain if it was he who set it going, and one may reasonably say that at T_1 he killed Patient; but specifically at T_2 what he did was to allow her to die.[6]

Let us drop the comprehensive answer to the 'Where in the causal chain?' question. I shall now assume that when the active/passive distinction classifies the way in which Agent's φing at T_1 relates to U's obtaining at T_2, it does so on the basis of what would have happened if no human agency had been at work from T_1 through to T_2. The

---

[6] He killed her and then *later* let her die? Yes indeed; you can kill a person long before he or she dies. See my 'Shooting, Killing, Dying'.

distinction is now to be thought of as inquiring only into the role of agency between the conduct and the upshot whose linking is in question, not the role of agency at earlier times.

Now we can confront the question 'Whose agency?' Consider this scenario: *You are planning to strike a match and throw it, burning, into some gasoline. I could prevent you by knocking the match out of your hand before it is lit, and I consider doing so but decide not to. You go ahead and start the fire.* Although in this case my conduct is relevant to the fire's starting, Donagan says that I neither cause nor allow it to start.[7] I do not cause it, because it would have started even if I hadn't exercised my agency; and I do not allow it, because the causal chain leading to it involves human agency (yours), and so is not part of 'the course of nature'. This presupposes that the relevant causal chain must be free of everybody's agency, not just mine, which is to say that it must be direct rather than mediated (in the sense of those terms introduced in Section 2 above).

Although there may be something to be said for this (see Section 45 below), it is not a good way to go. It seems to be intended to produce a scale of moral relevance: (1) I throw a match on to the leaves, causing a fire through intervention in the course of nature; (2) I do not extinguish the fire which lightning has started in the leaves, allowing a fire to happen in the course of nature; (3) I do not prevent you from igniting the leaves, so that there is a fire but not one that is part of the course of nature. In Donagan's view, I think, I am most on the moral hook in (1), less so in (2), and less again in (3). I disagree with these judgements, for reasons I shall give in due course. My present point concerns method, not substance. The moral contrast between (1) and (2), I submit, is an utterly different affair from that between (2) and (3). Indeed, we ought really to consider first the difference of (1) from both (2) and (3), and then come to the difference of (2) from (3). For that purpose, it is convenient to use 'allow' to cover (3) as well as (2); no good purpose is served by confining it to (2) alone.

Let us therefore work with a version of active/passive in which 'the course of nature' is understood in a person-relative or subjective manner: What happens in the course of nature relative to Agent is what would have happened if *he* had not intervened, that is, if *his* agency had been activated either not at all or only in abstaining from intervening. That is pretty much how I did understand 'course of nature' until this

---

[7] Donagan, *The Theory of Morality*, 50.

section. I kept quiet about it by sticking with cases where only one agent is involved, and by ignoring their history.

Anyone can use this subjective concept relative to anyone; but its home ground, where it is fundamentally active and important, is in first-person uses when one asks: 'What would have happened if *my* agency had not been exercised?' and 'What will happen if *my* agency is not exercised?' There is a sober reason to emphasize the line between one's own agency and the rest of reality. It may seem grandiose to call it the line around 'nature', but the line is real and, for the person concerned, deeply important. Here is why.

I must relate to my own future behaviour in a way that I cannot to anything else. In relation to other things, including other people, I am a predicting observer: I consider the present state of affairs, and predict on that basis. To some extent I can do that with my own future behaviour, but I also must relate to that in another way. As well as the predictor's question 'How in fact will I behave?', which I answer by predicting, I have the agent's question 'What am I to do?', which I answer by deciding. When I am wondering what to do, you might be predicting what I shall do, and (given determinism) you could in theory predict my decision before I make it. That suggests that it is only because I am ignorant that I can have practical problems and can resolve them. If I knew enough about my present state and about physiology and psychology (the thought goes), I could not have practical problems, only theoretical ones about my own future behaviour: the question 'What am I to do?' presupposes that, for me, at least, it is not yet settled what I shall do; if the gap is closed predictively, then it cannot be open practically. This is a dismal conclusion to come to: my status as a practically deliberating agent, which is the core of any sense I have of my own dignity, is a product of ignorance!

This conclusion is wrong, however. It does not follow, for a reason that I learned from Ryle. Sound predictions need a basis that is not affected by their being made: when I predict tomorrow's weather from today's, the weather I now perceive is not changed by my predictive use of it; but when I predict my own future behaviour from my present state, I alter my state by making predictions. I could take those changes into account as well, but that would be a further intellectual event which might also affect the basis for prediction. I could then take that into account as well . . . but you can see how the story continues: I can no more attend to the *whole* relevant basis for the prediction than I can overtake my shadow.

This is the best reason for Kant's view that even if determinism holds sway throughout the natural world, we not only do but must 'act under the idea of freedom'. He says: 'Reason does not here follow the order of things as they present themselves in appearance, but frames for itself with perfect spontaneity an order of its own according to ideas, to which it adapts the empirical conditions.'[8] The Rylean point explains why 'reason' must proceed in that way, and does not call upon Kant's theory about empirical determinism and noumenal freedom.

There is, therefore, a good sense in which each of us must see him or herself as, in Donagan's phrase, 'like a *deus ex machina*', standing outside nature and deciding when and how to intervene in it. So the first-person subjective concept of nature is reasonable and grounded. It gives to the active/passive distinction its best chance of serving as an analysis of making/allowing, which is why I adopted it at the outset.

38. The Non-intervention Principle

As I have already remarked, when the positive/negative distinction is based on the only workable metric I can find for it, it is obviously without fundamental moral significance. Not so with active/passive. Of no version of that can one say: '*Obviously* it is morally neutral', yet it is not obviously morally significant either. There is, therefore, something to be investigated here.

The basic idea is as follows. We are taking it for granted that if Agent's φing would have a bad consequence U, that fact counts morally against his φing. To this we are invited to add a thesis about how greatly the badness of U counts against Agent's φing, namely:

> It counts significantly less if this holds: *If in this situation Agent had not exercised his agency at all, U would have ensued.*

I call this 'the non-intervention principle', because it is equivalent to this:

> It counts significantly less if this holds: *If Agent φs, U will be a consequence of his behaviour, but not of his intervening in the course of nature.*

The phrase 'significantly less' makes the principle vague. Someone who wanted to accept it and build it into a moral theory would have to

---

[8] Immanuel Kant, *Critique of Pure Reason* B 576. There is a fuller discussion in my *Kant's Dialectic*, sects. 68–70, leaning on Gilbert Ryle, *The Concept of Mind*, 197.

tighten it up; but I shall not go into that. (If 'significantly' were dropped, the principle would no longer be vague but it would be practically empty.) Even when tightened up, the non-intervention principle does not on its own yield any moral judgements on conduct: it implies nothing for morality except when combined with other moral judgements coming from some other source.

I can find no reason to accept the non-intervention principle. When some bad state of affairs U comes about, this implies nothing about the morality of my behaviour if my agency was not involved—e.g. because I was asleep at the time when I might otherwise have made a difference. (If it was wrong of me to be asleep, then my agency must have been involved in my falling asleep and, through that, in the obtaining of U.) There is an unbreakable link between

Wasn't: My agency was not involved in the causation of U,

and 'I did not act wrongly'. The moral force of Wasn't, however, does not carry over to

If-hadn't: U would have obtained even if my agency had not been involved.

Think of the unrolling of the actual world α in terms of a line from which various non-actual possible worlds branch off. At this moment my desk light is actually on; it is off at some worlds that are just like α up to a few moments ago but now differ from it because at them my desk light is now off. Some of those Off worlds diverged from α at nodes dominated by my actually turning on my light; others at nodes dominated by my actually not turning it off again. Now, there are also worlds where the lights now shining in the high-security wing of Wandsworth prison are off; but my agency did not create any of the nodes at which those worlds diverged from α. At no point did my conduct make any difference to whether those lights were off. The latter situation is pointed to by Wasn't, the former by If-hadn't. At T_1 someone turned the light on. At T_2 I could have turned it off, but I did not; so far as the light is concerned, the state of affairs at T_3 is just what it would have been if between T_1 and then I had been asleep or in a coma. But I wasn't! I could have turned the light off. So its remaining on is a consequence of how I exercised my agency. Only muddle could lead anyone to think that 'I could have prevented it, but I did not' is significantly like 'I had nothing to do with it'.

With that muddle set aside, I see no way of finding moral significance in active/passive on our present version of it. This is not to say that it obviously has none, as I do say about positive/negative when that is based on the specificity metric; but I do contend that those who think that it is ever morally significant owe us reasons for saying so. I cannot find that any reasons have been given. The consequences of this, as we shall see in Chapters 9 and 10, are acutely uncomfortable.

8

OTHER ATTEMPTS

39. Changing Conditions

In this chapter I shall look briefly at the most instructive of the other
attempts that have been made to analyse the making/allowing distinction. Taken together, they carry the message that making/allowing is
elusive, and resists being clarified in a quick phrase or two.

One of the earliest proposals was this: What makes conduct relevant
to upshot U in the passive or 'allowing' way is its occurring just after
a time when: *If conditions are not altered, U will come about.*[1] That
sounds right. 'If conditions are not altered, that vehicle will go over the
cliff' sounds like a truth in Stayback just before Agent could interpose
the rock, and it sounds false in Push just before Agent starts the vehicle rolling. Feeling comfortable with the words, however, is not the
same as understanding what is going on. This 'analysis' needs work: we
cannot do anything with it until we know more about what it is supposed to mean.

First, what is its logical form? It could be using 'conditions are
altered' monadically, to mean *Conditions change*, or dyadically, to mean
Somebody changes the conditions. These differ as 'The water boiled' differs from 'Somebody boiled the water'.

(1) On the monadic reading, in which the key concept is that of conditions changing, the analysis implies that *If conditions do not change, the
vehicle will roll over the cliff* is true in Stayback just before the vehicle
draws level with the rock, but false in Push before Agent pushes the
vehicle. What does it mean to say that conditions change? (*a*) It cannot
mean merely that some change occurs, for then the analysis would say
that *If no change occurs, the vehicle will roll over the cliff* is true in
Stayback, whereas really it must always be false. (*b*) 'Conditions change'

[1] Daniel Dinello, 'On Killing and Letting Die', followed in essentials by James Otten,
'Even if One were Letting Another Innocent Person Die', by Bruce Russell, 'On the
Relative Strictness of Negative and Positive Duties', and others.

might mean that some uniform process acquires a discontinuity, but that too makes the analysis come out wrong. On that reading, it says that *If no uniform process becomes jerky, the vehicle will roll over the cliff* is true in Stayback and false in Push. Perhaps that is right; but it fits Stayback only because the vehicle is rolling smoothly down the slope, and that is an accident of the example. Even if in Stayback the vehicle is jerking and stuttering its way down the slope, Agent's not interposing the rock will still be his allowing the disaster to happen. This has nothing to do with what would have happened if a smooth process acquired a bump. I can find no other plausible reading for 'conditions change'.

(2) We had better stop trying to read 'Conditions are [not] altered' in a monadic way. On the dyadic reading, the analysis says that *If nobody changes the conditions, the vehicle will roll over the cliff* is true in Stayback, false in Push. That looks right. It does not say absurdly that in Stayback the vehicle will roll over the cliff if no changes occur, but rather that it will do so if nobody makes any changes occur.

Does this analysis achieve anything? The word 'makes' in the analysans is a danger signal—a hint of circularity. If the analysans is meant to speak of changes that someone could make as distinct from ones he could allow, the analysis says that *If nobody (positively) makes any change occur, the vehicle will go over the cliff* is true in Stayback, false in Push. So indeed it is, but this relies on the distinction that is under analysis. So we had better take the analysans to be invoking the generic relevance (or consequence) relation, rather than the 'making' species of it. Thus understood, it says that *If no change occurs in consequence of someone's behaviour, the vehicle will go to its destruction* is true in Stayback, false in Push. It is false in Push, all right: if in Push no change occurs in consequence of someone's behaviour, the vehicle will stay motionless and thus will not go to its destruction. That, however, is an accident of the example, and not essential to the 'making' side of the line. Vary the story a little:

> *Divert*: The vehicle is slowly rolling towards the top of a long ramp which slopes gently downward; Agent nudges it, changing its path so that it misses the ramp, rolls off the cliff top, and plummets to its destruction.

In Divert, as in Push, the relevance of Agent's behaviour to the vehicle's destruction is clearly of the positive or active or making kind. So the present analysis should be able to distinguish Divert from Stayback on the grounds that *If no change occurs in consequence of someone's behaviour, the vehicle will go to its destruction* is true in Stayback, false in Divert. This is wrong, however. The two scenarios relate to that formula in exactly the same way, namely by being vacuously true: in each it is impossible for the antecedent to be true. In Divert the vehicle must roll in one direction or another, and each would be a consequence of Agent's behaviour, because it is in his power to determine which happens; in Stayback the vehicle must either roll on or stop, and each of these would be a consequence of his behaviour also, for the same reason. At the outset of each scenario, therefore, it is physically necessary that there be a change which is a consequence of Agent's behaviour.

There seems to be no way of turning the 'If conditions are not altered . . .' proposal into a useful analysis of the making/allowing distinction.

40. Threats and Efforts

Frances Kamm has a quite different, four-part, way of drawing the line that we are trying to understand.[2] She introduces it in terms of the difference between 'making' and 'letting', but the line she cares about does not coincide with that one. Her line has some of the 'makings' on one side and, on the other, the rest of the 'makings' and all the 'lettings'. Her four defining features of lettings (and some makings) can be condensed into two, which I present in what I take to be a slightly improved form.

One is based on an idea of Philippa Foot's.[3] It has since been taken up by several others, and it suits me to discuss it in the context of Kamm. If I let you suffer, Kamm says, then before that conduct of mine you were under a threat of suffering; but I might hurt you without your having antecedently been under any such threat. If I let the shed collapse, it must already have been under a threat of collapsing, but this is not necessarily so if I crush it. If I let you recover, you must already have had a prospect of recovering, which may be false if I cure you. (Kamm, thinking of bad upshots, speaks only of being under threats; I use 'having prospects' to bring in good upshots as well.) Here is what this says about my two examples: In Stayback, before the time when Agent could have intervened, the vehicle was already under a threat of

[2] Frances Myrna Kamm, 'Killing and Letting Die: Methodological and Substantive Issues'.
[3] Philippa Foot, 'The Problem of Abortion and the Doctrine of Double Effect', 29.

destruction. In Push it need not have been the case that, before Agent acted, the vehicle was under such a threat.[4]

That is intuitively plausible, but what does it come down to? It might be replied: 'What it comes down to is *itself.* You imply that more needs to be said, but the analysis is complete as it stands. In almost every case, competent speakers will agree about whether x is under a threat of y, for example whether a given person is under a threat of death. That agreement is all we need.' It is enough to bring peace, but not to achieve understanding. We are being invited to split a certain genus of morally significant states of affairs into two species, according to whether most people are willing to describe them in terms of 'threats' or 'prospects'. Suppose there were broad agreement about this—what would that show? Agreement may stop our questions, but not by bringing answers.

Judith Thomson has done work using the notion of behaviour that introduces a new threat; so she has to be able to distinguish threats from one another. She is not concerned with the making/allowing distinction, but this comment of hers bears on my topic:

> What marks one threat off from another? . . . It is surely a mistake to look for precision in the concepts brought to bear to solve this problem: There isn't any to be had. It would be enough if cases in which it seems to us unclear whether to say 'same threat' . . . also seemed to us to be cases in which it is unclear whether the agent may or may not proceed; and if also coming to see a case as one to which ['same threat'] does (or does not) apply involves coming to see the case as one in which the agent may (or may not) proceed.[5]

That implicitly challenges the line I am taking throughout this book, but I am not yet moved by it. I don't see why we should be satisfied with the result that Thomson says 'would be enough'. It would tell us that the change in moral judgement was accompanied by a change in disposition to apply a certain phrase; but what real problem does this solve? It seems to me interesting only as a start, not as an end. Without answering any questions that were troubling us, it raises several. What is going on here? What is our investment in this phrase 'same threat'? Why do we allow it to affect our moral judgements, and should we continue to do so? Any analysis must start somewhere, I agree; but I invite you to agree with me that 'threat' marks a bad place to start.

I ask again, therefore: what does 'under a threat' come down to?

---

[4] A similar use of the concept of 'being under a threat' dominates Richard Brook's 'Agency and Morality', and is a theme in Jeff McMahan, 'Killing, Letting Die, and Withdrawing Aid'.

[5] Judith Jarvis Thomson, 'The Trolley Problem', 113.

Kamm says nothing about this, so we must do the work for ourselves. For the rest of this section, I shall use 'is under a threat' as short for 'is under a threat or has a prospect'.

We might think that 'x is under a threat of y' means that x is so situated that it is highly likely that y will befall x. It is easy to develop Push so that in it the vehicle was likely to be destroyed even before Agent pushed it; but that does not refute Kamm, because she is trying only to describe a feature that all allowings must have, acknowledging that some makings have it also. However, the present proposal would commit her to holding that in Stayback there was a high likelihood of disaster at the moment when Agent could have interposed the rock. That need not be so. It might be that until the very last moment Agent is firmly resolved to interpose the rock, and with a tenth of a second to spare he improbably changes his mind. We have to say that up to that moment the vehicle was not under a threat of destruction, so that by Kamm's analysis it does not count as an 'allowing'.

Objection: 'That misses the spirit of proposal, which does not concern the probability *all* things considered of y's befalling x, but rather its probability relative to the state of the world apart from the agency of the protagonist'. This implies that 'threats' are just a matter of objective probabilities except when a human agent might avert a threat; and then the threat is defined by the probabilities established by all the facts except those about the dispositions of that agent. This amounts to saying that *There is a threat that U will occur* means *U's occurrence is probable relative to (i) the facts of the non-human situation conjoined with (ii) the proposition that the agent will not exercise his agency.* (There could of course be more than one agent. Also, the probability could be a certainty.) All my attempts to clarify 'under a threat' have led to this same point, which I must suppose is the best that can be done.

Thus understood, Kamm's account draws the line in what may be the right place, doing so in terms that are fairly clear and well grounded. What I have done, however, is to use her *word* 'threat' as a lead into a complex idea which is not presented by any of the friends of the threat approach. You will recognize it, of course, as the core idea in the active/passive analysis of the making/allowing distinction.

Kamm's second main proposal concerns what would have happened if the 'letting' had not occurred. The alternative to my letting you lose something is your retaining it *via* me, or *through my efforts*, Kamm says, whereas sometimes the alternative to my depriving you of something is not your retaining it via me or through my efforts. This too fits my examples on a natural understanding of them. If in Push Agent had left the vehicle alone, it would not have received its extra lifespan via Agent or through his efforts, whereas that would have been the case if, in Stayback, he had interposed the rock. Here again, though, more must be said if we are properly to grasp what is going on.

Furthermore, this analysans taken literally does not always give the right answer. Add this detail to Stayback: Agent is under great psychological pressure—a mixture of threats and bribes—to interpose the rock; not interposing it is the hardest thing he has ever done. In that case, it will not be true that *If the vehicle had survived this occasion, it would have owed its further life-span to Agent's efforts*, if this is taken in its plain meaning. Yet it will still be true that Agent's conduct relates to the vehicle's destruction in a negative or passive or allowing fashion. To get this analysis of Kamm's to fit the cases properly is to construe 'through *x*'s efforts' or 'via *x*' as meaning 'as a result of what *x* actively or positively did or made happen'. So this analysans succeeds only when helped by the distinction that is supposed to be analysed.

41. Making and Causing

It is natural to associate 'cause' with the left- and not with the right-hand side of the making/allowing distinction. Donagan, indeed, called it the causing/allowing distinction, and one of my introductory idioms in Section 20 used 'cause' on the left. I have encountered—though not in print—the view that this is all the analysis we need. On the left of the line is behaviour that causes U to obtain, while behaviour on the right, though it is in my sense 'relevant' to U, does not cause it. The only proper use of 'cause' on the right of the line is in saying that Agent could but does not cause U not to obtain. So it is said.

The mere fact that most people use 'cause' and 'make' almost interchangeably is negligible: it offers no promise of casting light in any direction. The line of thought I want to discuss holds that the real making/allowing distinction which I have been pursuing can be genuinely analysed (clarified) by an account in which the concept of cause plays a part on the left of the line and not on the right.

The ongoing fight about what causality is makes one hesitate to say that this is a *clear* concept. Still, we don't doubt that it is, somehow, solid and well grounded. It enters into many important thoughts, including these:

It can be causally inevitable that if S_1 obtains at T_1, S_2 will obtain at T_2.

Our knowledge of the world comes from its acting causally upon us.

A present mental state is a memory of a past event only if it was caused to obtain by it.

Some true general propositions express causal laws while others do not.

A *de re* thought about a particular must be causally related to it.

Such statements as these, even if there is a puzzle at the dark heart of them, are bone and sinew in our understanding of the world and our place in it; they are not fuzzy or cluttered or superficial. If the causal concept that runs through them can be used to explain the difference between making and allowing, that will be progress.

The simplest idea one might have about how 'cause' could be used to explain making/allowing is this:

(1) Agent's φing relates in a making way to U's obtaining if Agent's φing causes U to obtain

(which I equate with its being a cause of U's obtaining; we have no serious theoretical use for the notion of *the* cause of something). Before coming to (1), which will be my topic for most of three sections, we should look first at a potentially fatal problem of scope with which it is confronted.

It comes from the fact that (1) leaves untouched the making/allowing distinction as it applies to non-causal consequences, especially the creating of dangers. The contrast between 'She put them in danger by reporting them to the Gestapo' and 'She left them in danger by not lying to the Gestapo about where they were hiding' cannot be elucidated with help from (1), because in each case the stated fact about her conduct relates in a purely non-causal way to their peril: added to already obtaining facts, it brings to completion their being in danger (see Section 12 above). Her conduct related causally to their being arrested, but not to their being in danger; their danger, which is a probabilistic state of affairs, obtained at the instant the Gestapo were told, indeed at the instant when she moved her larynx in those ways. When movements make dangers exist, they often do so immediately, non-causally. Not always, as witness the contrived story with which I ended Section 17, where Agent's movements led to danger only through an unrolling causal chain. Still, a great deal of risk-making, including much of what morally matters, is non-causal.

If the attempt to elucidate making with help from 'cause' is to survive this point, it must widen its scope, adding some further condition (2) which also suffices for the truth of 'In φing Agent makes U obtain'. It will have to apply to the non-causal creating of risk, though the friends of (1) will presumably want it to make some use of the concept of cause, so as to keep it in the spirit of (1). A satisfactory (2) should also be such that (1) and (2) both follow from some more general principle; otherwise the (1)–(2) account will be broken-backed, in contrast to the unity of the active/passive and positive/negative analyses. The prospects for rescuing (1) from its scope trouble look dim to my eye, but the friends of (1) may succeed where I have failed. So far, they have not tried. They have been unaware of the difficulty about scope, this being part of the general neglect of the vitally important concept of *non-causal consequence*, which covers so much of the moral terrain, especially in connection with risk-making.

The *causing* approach to making faces other problems as well, and I shall now attend to them. From now on, let us focus on how behaviour relates to what actually does ensue from it, setting probabilities aside and taking (1) to be offered as the whole truth about making. The claim to be investigated, then, is that Agent's pushing the vehicle causes the disaster in Push, whereas his not interposing the rock does not cause the disaster in Stayback, and that this explains why the making/allowing distinction falls as it does between the two cases.

I reject this on the ground that Agent's not interposing the rock in Stayback is indeed a cause of the vehicle's destruction. Here is why. If you are trying to describe the state of affairs at T_1, the last moment when Agent could stop the vehicle with the rock, including causally sufficient conditions for the vehicle's going over the cliff at T_3, you must mention the fact that Agent does not move in a certain way (or something that causally requires it, e.g. the rock's not moving in a certain way). That fact is essential to the causal story; if it is omitted, the disaster has not been fully causally explained. From the fact that at T_1 the slope is thus, the vehicle is rolling so, there is no obstacle in its path, and so on, it does not causally follow that it *will* go over the cliff at T_3 if there is time before then for an obstacle to be imposed. We can get causally sufficient conditions by describing the state of affairs at T_2, the moment when the vehicle has passed the rock but not yet reached the cliff top; but if we go back to a point where there is time for Agent to make a difference, the fact that he does not interpose the rock is a vital part of the story. That, I submit, makes it a cause of the vehicle's going over the cliff.

I am relying here on the thesis that *If P's being the case at T is a necessary part of every T-dated causally sufficient condition of Q's being the case later, then P's being the case is a cause of Q's being the case.* That expresses the clearest idea we have of what it is for one item to be a cause of another.[6] Of course, no significant philosophical story is as short as that, and I mention here three corners that I have cut. (1) The formula is not right if 'conditions' can include things like *Either Agent did not interpose the rock or a nearby volcano erupted.*[7] Adapting John Pollock's solution to a different problem, we can exclude all such damaging disjunctions on the grounds that they are not 'simple', in this sense: A simple proposition is one whose truth one can know noninductively without first coming to know the truth of some proposition which entails it.[8] (2) Because '. . . is a cause of . . .' is transitive, the following also suffices for P_1 to be a cause of Q: There is a chain of items P_1, ..., P_n, Q in which each P_i is a cause of its immediate successor. This can safely be ignored in our present context. (3) At our indeterministic world, 'sufficient condition' should be understood probabilistically. For simplicity's sake I shall ignore that too.

I have partly elucidated 'P's being the case is a cause of Q's being the case' in terms that include '*causally* sufficient condition'. That is not circular, because what I am offering to analyse is not the whole concept of causation, but only the restricted notion of one fact's being 'a cause of' another. I do this with help from 'causally sufficient condition', which I can elucidate in its turn, with help from 'causal law': R is a causally sufficient condition of S if and only if there are causal laws L such that S is entailed by the conjunction of R and L and not by either alone. The frog at the bottom of the beer mug—the concept of causal law—is a topic for another book.

To be on the safe side, I should explain that my account quantifies only over conditions that actually obtain. It is irrelevant that P is not a part of some states of affairs which, if they did obtain at T_1, would causally suffice for Q's obtaining at T_2.

My account of causation makes it impressively weak. It implies that

---

[6] I partly follow J. L. Mackie, 'Causes and Conditions'.

[7] For evidence that this is so, see David H. Sanford, 'Symposium Contribution on *Events and their Names* by Jonathan Bennett'.

[8] John L. Pollock, *Subjunctive Reasoning*, 91–3; see also 73–5.

in Stayback the causes of the vehicle's demise include its momentum, the slope of the ground, the presence of the cliff, the stillness of the ground, and *Agent's not moving in a certain way*. That is the crux: Agent's not interposing the rock is a cause of the vehicle's destruction; so the causal analysis of our distinction fails.

Agent's not moving thus and so is not an event or an act, but that does not stop it from being a cause. As I argued in Section 13, many kinds of fact can be causally related, not merely ones about events. We should not try to cram all the news about causal links into statements about which events cause which others, any more than we should confine our descriptions of behaviour to facts about what acts are performed.

Eric Mack, understandably finding this account of causation 'peculiar', makes it look worse than it is by implying that it includes among the causes of the vehicle's destruction the fact that the rock was not interposed by Absent, who was a thousand miles away at the time.[9] He easily shoots down the anticipated reply: 'Absent's not interposing the rock is not a cause of the disaster, because the circumstances make it inevitable.' But he does not mention the right reply, which is that at the relevant time no sufficient conditions for the disaster owed their sufficiency to their including Absent's not interposing the rock. A description of the environment can be given which automatically excludes billions of such facts by excluding from the scene billions of people and things that might otherwise have intervened; it is just a mistake to think that each of these non-interventions is a required ingredient in the sufficient conditions.

42. A Short Lecture on Pragmatics

What I have been saying implies that countless 'cause'-using statements that would seem daft for anyone to utter are nevertheless true. That is some evidence that I have gone wrong. Indeed, it seems to be the only evidence: facts about how it would be sensible, natural, intuitive, not 'peculiar', to use the word 'cause' apparently provide all the case there is for saying that the meaning of 'cause' is stronger than I make it out to be. Those facts, however, when properly understood, have no such power.

---

[9] Eric Mack, 'Bad Samaritanism and the Causation of Harm', 252.

Suppose that my friend gives me a shirt, and I report (R) 'She gave me something that was smaller than a Cadillac'. This would ordinarily be an idiotic thing to say in the circumstances, but is that because it would be false? If so, then how can we re-express the meaning of R so as to make its falsity manifest? Well, perhaps in that context R means what would ordinarily be meant by 'My friend gave me a gift that occupied a little less space than a Cadillac does'—and this is indeed what most hearers would infer from hearing it. Yet we cannot say that 'smaller than' always means 'occupying a little less space than', for that would knock out such elementary truths as this: if x is smaller than something that is smaller than y, then x is smaller than y. So we shall have to say that 'smaller than' means something special in R that it does not always mean; and then we must assign other special meanings to it for other contexts where sentences of the form 'x is smaller than y' are idiotic things to say although y is neither larger than x nor the same size as it, and must explain how we know which of its many meanings is activated in a given context. A horrifying prospect of multiple ambiguity looms before us, and it is repeated for virtually every general term in the language. We need some way of explaining how R could be idiotic yet not false.

Work pioneered by the late Paul Grice and developed by others under the name of 'pragmatics' has shown us how to do this.[10] What have to be explained are facts about what is 'unassertible' or silly-to-say—facts that involve tens of thousands of words. Rather than giving a complicated account of the meaning of each word, the pragmatic approach allows each word a relatively simple meaning, and explains the unassertibility data through a few general principles governing language use generally.

One of these might be called the news principle: Give as much probably useful news as you easily can without being prolix. Someone who knows that the gift was a shirt, or who knows that it occupied less than a cubic foot, could briefly and easily be much more informative about it than R is; so R is a poor thing to say if one knows more about the size of the gift. For a speaker who knows only that the gift was brought in a Cadillac, or for one whose hearer's only interest is in how the gift's size relates to a Cadillac's, R is a sensible thing to say and is not condemned by the news principle.

---

[10] See H. P. Grice, *Studies in the Way of Words*, chs. 1–4. For developments by many writers, see e.g. Peter Cole (ed.), *Radical Pragmatics*, and Steven Davis (ed.), *Pragmatics*.

Most hearers of R would infer that the gift was only slightly smaller than a Cadillac, and Gricean principles explain why. Those hearers would be assuming that the speaker was not flouting the news principle, and that the speaker knew fairly precisely how big the gift was. From these two natural assumptions, together with the assertive uttering of R, it follows that the gift was a little smaller than a Cadillac. QED. This also explains why, to a hearer who knows what the gift was, R may seem to be false though really it is true.

This way of explaining the data combines a simple account of the meaning of 'smaller' with a principle of conversational rectitude that holds good generally, and can be used to explain similar data that don't involve 'smaller' at all. With help from a few such principles we can explain countless facts about truths that it would be odd or unsatisfactory or stupid to assert, and about how utterances can imply more than they mean.

Another example: If I say 'After you had supposedly cleared out your desk, I found something in one of the drawers', you will naturally infer that I have found something more than mere dust, though dust would make my statement true. (There is no dust-excluding meaning for the word 'something'.) In making that inference you will be taking me to have conformed to what I'll call the salience principle: Don't say things that have no chance of being notable, interesting, useful, surprising, etc. That explains the fatuous nature of countless true assertions—e.g. 'Schweitzer resembled Hitler in many ways', which is misleading yet true: they both spoke German, liked music, had two hands and ten toes, lived for more than fifty years, were born in the nineteenth century and died in the twentieth, had moustaches, and were famous.

We must choose between two ways of explaining certain data. The semantic one says that various sentences are unassertible in certain contexts because they are false there; and it has to explain how the contexts vary the meanings and thus produce the falsity. If this last part of the story were worked out in detail, it would be horribly long and complex.[11] The pragmatic one allows the words of our language their ordinary, fairly uniform meanings, and explains the facts about unassertibility on the strength of a few general principles of discourse.

[11] In the 1950s some philosophers tried to carry parts of this programme through, exploring the 'uses' of various words through patiently detailed inquiries into what it would be 'odd to say'. When Grice explained how it can be 'odd' yet true to say 'That appears to be a house' when you can see clearly that it is a house, this way of doing philosophy began to collapse, and not a moment too soon. H. P. Grice, 'The Causal Theory of Perception'.

The latter explanation is obviously simpler and more efficient, which gives it a better claim to be accepted: of two unrefuted theories, the simpler and more manageable is the better. Objection: 'It isn't better unless it is true, or truer, or more probable. What leads us from simplicity to truth?' I am not equipped to plumb this question in the philosophy of science, and I do not need to here. No one who grasps how the purely semantic treatment differs from the partly pragmatic one could doubt that the latter, over an enormous range of cases, is true and the former false.

This lesson from pragmatics can be applied to the verb and noun 'cause'. I have offered a partial analysis of causal statements which ran thus: *If P's being the case at T is a necessary part of every T-dated sufficient condition of Q's being the case later, then P's being the case is a cause of* [*or: causes*] *Q's being the case.* That makes 'cause', whether noun or verb, impressively weak, and transitivity makes it weaker still—so weak as to make it likely, as David Lewis has remarked, that one's own behaviour will be among the causes of each human death that occurs in the twenty-first century or later. That sounds spectacularly false, but I contend that really what it lacks is not truth but assertibility. In general, truths about causes will be assertible only if they report causes that are *salient*—that is, stand out as notably significant, surprising, or the like—because discourse generally is governed by the salience principle.

The weakness of '*x* causes *y*' need not get us into much trouble: we have good noses for what is worth saying among all the things that are merely true. This general skill of ours can be brought to bear on our uses of 'cause', as on our uses of 'something', 'resembles', and countless other expressions.

When in introducing the making/allowing distinction I used 'cause' on the left of the line and not on the right, that was just to launch the discussion. I got away with it because statements to the effect that a person or his behaviour caused some upshot are much more likely to be assertible—to be natural, reasonable, sensible, unmisleading things to say—when the conduct was positively or 'makingly' relevant to the upshot than when it was negatively or 'allowingly' so. (Reasons for this can be given in terms of active/passive or of positive/negative.) Such statements, though, have as good a chance of being *true* on the right of the making/allowing line as on the left, which means that the making/allowing distinction cannot be elucidated by associating one side and not the other with 'cause'.

43. *Tighter Meanings for 'Cause'?*

Those who want 'cause' to help with making/allowing must mean to be using the word in a narrower sense than the one I have defended; so if I am right they are misusing it. What a tiny point that is! The big question, the one that matters, is whether what they mean is true, not whether they have worded it correctly. To answer the big question, however, we must know what they do mean by 'cause'; and since they do not tell us we must canvass the options for ourselves.

The most likely guess is that they mean 'cause' to carry in its meaning the implications that I say come from pragmatics. That would make 'cause' in their sense of it roughly coextensive with 'salient cause' in my (correct) sense of that phrase, so that the only items they will call causes of a given state of affairs will be causes that are large or conspicuous or surprising or otherwise notable. That might make 'Agent's conduct is a cause of the disaster' outright false in Stayback yet still true in Push, which is what is wanted. In discussing this idea, I shall use 'condition' to mean what I think is properly meant by 'cause'. This is a temporary device, to be discarded after the present section. The proposal, then, is to give 'cause' a meaning which makes it coextensive with 'salient condition'. There are two ways of achieving this.

(1) We could make 'x causes y' mean about the same as 'x is a highly salient condition of y'. In this strengthened meaning, '. . . causes . . .' will no longer be unrestrictedly transitive: a salient condition of a salient condition of y need not itself be a salient condition of y. As causal chains run on in time, and different ones come together in various ways, salience dies out. Yet we do sometimes avail ourselves of a sort of transitivity, inferring that one thing caused another from its causing a cause of it. The proposed strengthening offers a way in which some such inferences could be preserved, allowing us to retain some transitivity, while keeping it on a leash. If we had a measure of *how* salient various conditions are, expressing that on a scale from 0 to 1, our present proposal could take this form: x *causes* y *if and only if* x *is a 0.5 salient condition of* y, in which you can replace 0.5 by any proper fraction you like. Then limited transitivity can be secured by this: *If* x *is an* n *salient condition of* y, *which is an* m *salient condition of* z, *then* x *is an* n.m *salient condition of* z. In this, *n.m* is the product of *n* and *m*; it will be lower than each except when one of them is 1. Sometimes they will be high

enough for their product $n.m$ to be high enough to satisfy the definition of 'cause', and then the transitivity argument will go through; not otherwise. That form of argument will hold for short causal chains with fairly high salience at each link, but where the salience is lower or the chain longer, a conclusion about causes—as distinct from conditions—will not be derivable. This is intuitively agreeable, and it may correspond to some of our ways of talking and thinking. Whether it could be firmly based on a real metric for salience is another question.

(2) The second proposal is to make 'x causes y' mean that x is a condition of y which is surprising or conspicuous or a large part of the total conditions of y that obtained at that time or illegal or done maliciously by someone who expected y to ensue or done in breach of a previously made promise or . . . and so on. Where (1) puts the concept of salience into the meaning of 'cause', (2) includes, disjunctively, the elements that can make a condition salient. It provides no basis for any transitivity, however restricted; it also gives to 'causes' a more complex and jumbled meaning than (1) gives it.

It is clear why neither of these is a good meaning for 'cause' to carry: (2) is a jumbled mess; and (1) amounts to letting 'cause' mean 'condition worth mentioning', which opens a Pandora's box of bad semantics: Let 'book' mean what we now mean by 'book worth mentioning', 'distance' mean 'distance worth mentioning', and so on through thousands of others. That, however, is not the question before us. Granted that neither (1) nor (2) captures what 'cause' does mean, and that neither is a good proposal for a new meaning for it, our question is: If the friends of the causal analysis of making/allowing are using 'cause' in accordance with (1) or (2), is their analysis true and helpful?

Well, it is not conservatively true, just as it stands. Neither proposal draws the line in the same place as my introductory locutions in Section 20 above. Although salience of conditions is found more on the 'making' than on the 'allowing' side of the line, there are non-salient conditions on the former side and salient ones on the latter. So the proposal had better be meant as revisionary, or as a rescue operation: it is to pluck out of the making/allowing mess a distinction that tends to accompany making/allowing and that *is* worth a place in moral theory.

The most likely place that will be claimed for it is that of a distinction carrying moral weight. When someone says that Agent's conduct in Push causes the vehicle to be destroyed while in Stayback it does not, expect him to infer from this that the difference matters morally. When you just take the unexamined sentence 'In Push he causes the disaster, in Stayback he doesn't', that sounds weighty indeed; but if all it means is either (1) *In Push his contribution to the disaster is salient; in Stayback it is not*, or (2) *In Push his contribution to the disaster is illegal or conspicuous or unusual or . . .; in Stayback it is not*, the appearance changes because neither of those sounds remotely plausible as a basis for a fundamental moral judgement. No one would think that (1) points to a morally significant difference. Salience is a matter of what is conspicuous to us, and it would be a strange morality that accorded basic moral significance to that. It might sometimes bear on policy: Because his conduct was not a salient condition of the catastrophe, our ignoring it will not have a bad effect on the populace at large. What we are discussing, though, is *basic* moral significance. Nor could basic moral judgements involve the sort of disjunctive clutter that occurs in (2). Nobody could put his hand on his heart and say 'Yes, *that* makes a fundamental moral difference' as one might about the difference between what does and what does not cause suffering, or satisfy desires, or obstruct love between people.

The nearest one can come to getting moral significance out of the present proposals is through the fact that a condition may be salient because of an adverse moral judgement that we make on it. Even behaviour that 'allows' U to obtain may be described as a 'cause' of U by those who frown on it. Although most people would hesitate to say that Agent's behaviour in Stayback 'caused the crash', many would be willing to say this if (for example) Agent maliciously didn't interpose the rock, though he knew that when Mary started the vehicle rolling she was relying on him to do so.[12] It is in the spirit of the two proposals that this too should be reflected in the meaning of 'cause', but if it is, then we are being given a distinction that does not cleanly belong to the non-moral facts. We have been trying to clarify facts about human conduct upon which moral judgements can be based, through principles of the form 'If [non-moral] then [moral]'. We have been edging towards the question: 'Does making/allowing have a place in the antecedent of any acceptable principle of that kind?' If the distinction is itself conceptually tinged with morality, so that it is applied on the basis of prior moral judgements, then it cannot appear in any such principle: and our question has been brushed aside without our getting any insight into the matter we have been wrestling with.

[12] This fact about usage is explained by considerations of salience. It is not an instance of the bubble phenomenon discussed in Section 22, and does not fit the explanation I gave of that.

Objection: 'Perhaps the only common thread running through all your introductory idioms is a distinction that *does* rest on moral judgements. It may be that when ordinary people use the language of "do"/"let", "make"/"allow", "active"/"passive", etc., they are in part expressing some prior moral judgement. If that annihilates your inquiry, so much the worse for it.' I cannot disprove this. Both sides in the debate about the moral significance of making/allowing have thought they were discussing the moral import of something that does not rest on any prior moral judgement; if they were wrong about that, the issue dies; I shall continue to assume that they were right.

(3) A cleaner and more manageable way of tightening the meaning of 'cause', though it does not build salience into it, does yield the result that Agent's behaviour causes the disaster in Push and not in Stayback. Still using 'condition' to mean what I think 'cause' really means, this third proposal equates 'P's obtaining is a cause of Q's obtaining' with *P is a condition of Q, and P entails that some change occurs*, where change includes movement. Then Agent's shoving the vehicle in Push is a cause of the calamity, unlike his not interposing the rock in Stayback. Perhaps Agent changes at the crucial time in Stayback—shaking his head or dancing a jig—but the causing fact, namely that he does not interpose the rock, does not entail that he changes.

This draws a clean line, and it aligns those two examples—and millions of others—in the right way. It also restores unrestricted transitivity to '. . . is a cause of . . .', thereby making 'cause' very weak, though not as weak as my account of it does. The question remains as to why we should use this in analysing the difference between the two kinds of relevance. What we have here is first cousin to the immobility objection to active/passive and positive/negative analyses of the making/allowing distinction (Sections 32, 36). As there, so here some *reason* should be given for making so much of the difference between movement and immobility.

44. Other Attempted Analyses

(1) It has been proposed that you allow P to obtain if you could have acted so that P did not obtain and P would have obtained even if you had been absent from the scene—or, in an extravagant version that Shelly Kagan discussed at length, if you had never existed.[13] This does

---

[13] Shelly Kagan, *The Limits of Morality*, 94 ff.

not draw the line in the right place, because sometimes the person's being absent would have altered the whole structure of the situation. For example: *As things stand, Agent must ϕ or else allow something still worse to happen, but this is so because a second person makes this so in order to torment him. If Agent were off the scene, the 'allowed' upshot would not occur.* Still, we might rescue this account of making/allowing by taking it to speak of what would have happened if Agent had been absent *qua* agent, that is, if he had not exercised his agency. That brings us back to the idea of what would have happened 'in the course of nature' with this understood in Donagan's way, or rather my variant on it.

(2) This same idea may lie some distance behind Bentham's definition of 'negative acts' as 'such as consist in . . . forbearing to move or exert oneself'.[14] The immobility aspect of this is indefensible, but 'forbearing to exert oneself' is better. It might be a gesture towards this: Negatively relevant conduct is behaviour that bears on the given upshot in the same way as would the person's not exerting himself, i.e. his agency's not being engaged. Active/passive again.

(3) Again, when philosophers offer to explain our distinction—as Warren Quinn did—in terms of 'the distinction between action and inaction', they have clearly gone wrong.[15] When Agent allows something to happen he need not be in any reasonable sense 'inactive' at that time. Perhaps these philosophers mean to be talking about what would have happened if the person had been inactive; in which case they too are rescued through reinterpretation and the active/passive analysis.

(4) Some of the informal locutions that express making/allowing—and some of the analytic assaults on it—use the language of the contrast between positive and negative or between 'did' and 'didn't'. One of these, too, occurs in Quinn's paper where he writes that 'harmful negative agency' involves 'harm occurring because of . . . the noninstantiation of some kind of action that [the person] might have performed'.[16] Quinn used 'positive' and 'negative', as I do 'making' and 'allowing', merely to label the analysandum; evidently he thought he did not need these terms in his analysans and so did not have to get them clear. In fact, though, he *did* need to make theoretical use of them to solve a problem which he apparently overlooked—namely, that of setting lim-

---

[14] Jeremy Bentham, *An Introduction to the Principles of Morals and Legislation*, 72 (ch. 7, sect. 8).

[15] Warren S. Quinn, 'Actions, Intentions, and Consequences: The Doctrine of Doing and Allowing', *passim*.

[16] Ibid. 361.

its to what kinds of act(ion)s there are. If no limits are set, we are free to say that *not*-pushing-a-vehicle is a kind of act; then in Push the disaster occurs because of the *non*-instantiation of that kind of act, which puts the Push scenario on the allowing side of the line. Quinn would reject this, no doubt, protesting that not-pushing-the-vehicle is not a kind of act. Then he should explain why; and that should force him to engage seriously with the notion of negativeness.

(5) Here is an idea about the making/allowing distinction. It might be suggested that *Agent's conduct at T related to U in an allowing rather than a making way* is equivalent to *Agent could at T have prevented U from ensuing, and did not do so* perhaps with a further clause saying that this is the whole relevance of Agent's behaviour to U's obtaining. I showed in Section 21 that this does not accurately track the ordinary meaning of 'allow', because we also say that Agent 'allowed' U to occur when he could have so acted that something else prevented it from occurring. Having separated the making/allowing distinction from the niceties of the meaning of 'allow', however, we still have to consider whether the distinction can be elucidated in terms of 'prevent' in the suggested manner.

It cannot. In fact, 'prevent' itself needs to be explained. We might try this: To prevent U from occurring is so to behave that U does not occur, when one could have so behaved that U did occur. That is neat and clean, but it is wrong, because it covers every kind of relevance of conduct to upshot, sprawling across both sides of the making/allowing line. The only improvement I can think of is this: Agent *prevents* U from occurring if (i) he so behaves that U does not occur, and (ii) U would have occurred if he had not intervened. I do not insist on 'intervene', but I do say that the meaning of 'prevent' includes the notion of what would happen if some person's agency had not been at work. If that is right, then this approach through 'prevent' is just a disguised version of the active/passive analysis.

45. The Neutrality of Making/Allowing

I conclude that of all the attempts to clarify the making/allowing distinction, the ones that have most success are the active/passive and positive/negative accounts. Since each supports the view that the difference between making and allowing is morally neutral, I reluctantly accept that. The analyses support the neutrality thesis with help from moral intuition: Making/allowing just seems to be undeniably without basic moral significance when seen in the clearest analytic light I can throw on it. Described in realist terms, I have tried to create optimal viewing conditions and have then looked to see whether making/allowing carries moral weight. In terms of the non-realism which I actually believe: having cleared away the clutter and seen what is really at stake, I find myself altogether unwilling to put weight on making/allowing in my fundamental morality.

Some moral philosophers will be untouched by all this because they are not willing to come at these matters analytically. The making/allowing distinction enters into their moral thinking at such depth, and with such force, that they are unwilling to subject it to scrutiny under analysis, raising the question whether it ought to have the moral significance that they accord to it.

Others will disown my line of thought because of its appeal to moral intuition. Let us glance at some of these. (1) If Hare's a priori proof of utilitarianism is sound, there should be no appeal to intuitions in fundamental moral theory; and this would undermine the procedure I have followed. Lacking my route to my conclusion, however, Hare would have his own. His proof of utilitarianism arrives at moral conclusions from premisses about what unfanatical people prefer. These preferences are not in themselves moral: to launch Hare's proof I have to consider what I now prefer should happen to me on the supposition that I am in this man's shoes, then that woman's, then that child's . . . Everyone's preferences of this sort are, I should think, symmetrical along the making/allowing axis. My preference for getting food on the supposition that I am starving is no stronger in cases where the food would be allowed to reach me than in those where it would be positively given to me. This symmetry in the input of preferences will make the moral output symmetrical also; which means that the basic morality yielded by Hare's proof of utilitarianism will be making/allowing symmetrical. (2) Some hold that the will of God is the ultimate source of morality. They will tackle the question 'Is it worse to hurt someone than to let him or her suffer?' by consulting the divine commands, not by analysing the making/allowing distinction. That holds, however, only for those who depend entirely on revelation for their moral theology. My kind of project should not be evaded by moral theologians whose beliefs about what God wants depend partly on what they think a wise and good God *would* want. (3) For others, judgements on behaviour come through beliefs about how a virtuous person would behave. They might want to replace my analytic endeavours by an inquiry into how the making/allowing distinction figures in the virtues. This might involve appealing to our sense of what goes into the virtues that are conventionally recognized and named, making such points as that killing one person to save several would not count as benevolent (see Section 56 below). That, however, would be a weak and unpersuasive basis for a whole morality. A less shallow and limited one might come from looking beyond the conventional catalogue of virtues, asking (for instance) whether the making/allowing dual of benevolence is also a virtue, though not so far a named one. That approach, however, requires independent moral thought about the making/allowing distinction; it is not a substitute for it.

Most of us, anyway, do allow moral intuitions at the foundation of our moral views, and must therefore face the challenge posed by the apparent moral weightlessness of making/allowing. The next two chapters will explore some upshots of the thesis that the making/allowing distinction has no basic moral significance. This will involve using the notion of a *making/allowing dual*—a concept I introduced in Section 27, have just used again, and must now explain more fully.

Here is what it is for Agent to hurt Patient: (1) he behaves in such a way that Patient suffers in consequence, (2) the relevance of the conduct to the suffering is of the making rather than of the allowing sort, (3) the causal chain from the behaviour to the suffering is direct rather than mediated, and (4) the causal chain is stable.[17] Condition (3) implies that I don't hurt Patient if all I do is to induce you to throw a stone at her; it does not touch the case where you throw a stone that would have missed her and I alter its trajectory so that it hits her. Whether I hurt her depends on whether the causal chain from my conduct to her hurt runs wholly through your will.

What I shall call dual-hurting is defined by the same formula except that in it 'making' and 'allowing' are interchanged. Roughly speaking, dual-hurting is avoidably not preventing someone from being made to suffer. More precisely: If I could but do not dissuade you from throwing a stone at her, that does not mean that I dual-hurt her; but I do dual-hurt her if I could but do not deflect from her a stone that you have already thrown. The difference between those two may not matter much in basic morality; but I separate them because I want

---

[17] See Section 2 above for reminders of 'direct', 'mediated', and 'stable'. As there, so here, I conscientiously mention the stability condition only to drop it from the ensuing discussion.

dual-hurting to differ from hurting *only* through the making/allowing switch. In this respect my 'dual-hurting her' resembles Donagan's 'allowing her to suffer'—ruled out if someone else's agency intervenes. When Donagan handled allowing in that way, he was probably influenced by a duality thought (see Section 37).

Having so far used 'φ' to stand for any verb phrase that could fit you because of how you behave, I shall now use it only for verb phrases that belong on the making side of the line. Roughly speaking, φing will be making something be the case (not through someone else's agency), while dual-φing will be allowing that same thing to be the case (not through someone else's agency). This is mere terminology: it does not embody doctrine.

Our concern, then, is with the thesis that φing is no better or worse, *ceteris paribus*, than dual-φing. For many values of φ, we are intuitively inclined to think that φing is more wrong, or more easily or often wrong, than dual-φing is: for example, that one is more likely to act wrongly in hurting someone than in dual-hurting someone. Some reasons for this are compatible with the neutrality of making/allowing. For example, it is often easier to avoid φing than it would be to avoid dual-φing, and it is easier to know that one is φing than to know that one is dual-φing; and these differences affect right and wrong. But they are merely frequent companions of making/allowing, and are not of its essence. They cannot explain all our intuitive moral discriminations between making something bad happen and allowing it to happen.

The thesis that making/allowing is morally weightless even-handedly condemns many moral judgements that we are inclined to accept. It attacks judgements of the form 'φing would be wrong, while dual-φing would be right', telling us that we must relinquish one—either one—conjunct. The thesis can lead us in either of two directions: we can become more severe about dual-φing, or less so about φing; more prone to condemn allowing innocent people to die prematurely, or less prone to condemn killing them. At this T-junction, we must turn right or left. In the next two chapters I shall peer along the road in each direction.

9

DEMANDS

46. Morality as too Demanding: Tight Reins

If we cannot attach moral weight to making/allowing, it is often said, morality will be too demanding. This could mean either of two things— it could concern (1) how many demands morality makes, or (2) what its demands are. (1) A morality that makes too many demands keeps us on too tight a rein, not leaving enough practical decisions to be made on non-moral grounds. The tightest rein would be that of a morality which answered every practical question, requiring or forbidding each possi- ble course of action and thus putting non-moral reasons out of work entirely. (2) A morality that is demanding in quality, rather than quan- tity, is one that thwarts (too) many of our natural desires—that is, desires that we have independently of our moral beliefs or attitudes. However tight the reins are, it does not follow that morality thwarts our natural desires. A morality that never lets go might often tell us to do what we would have wanted to do anyway. Nor does thwarting entail tight reins; though the more of our natural desires that a morality thwarts, the less value will we find in any elbow-room that it leaves us. Anyway, the two should be considered separately. I shall start with tight reins.

On its own, of course, the thesis of the moral neutrality of making/allowing issues no marching orders; but if we already have a morality, its demands can be greatly strengthened if that thesis is added to it. Here is one way this could happen. Start with a morality that absolutely forbids harming people—that is, positively making their level of well-being lower than it could have been. Add the neutrality of making/allowing, and you have a morality that absolutely requires help- ing people—that is, not allowing their level of well-being to be lower than you could have made it. The resulting morality always gives con- flicting instructions, for we can never help someone except by not help- ing others whom we could have helped. The natural way to iron out these conflicts is the quantitative one, according to which lesser failures to help (and indeed lesser harms) are permitted if they are needed for greater helps. This leaves us with a kind of utilitarianism, according to which one acts wrongly unless one acts in the way that will leave people overall as well off as one is capable of doing.[1] I shall abbreviate this to '. . . that will create the best accessible world'.

For reasons given in Chapter 3, the actual consequences of behaviour have nothing to do with its moral quality. We need some way of combining the general idea behind utilitarianism with the probability principle, which says that behaviour is to be judged by its probable rather than its actual consequences. The simplest device is to say that the right way to behave is always the one that is most likely to lead to the best accessible world. That has the advantage that it requires us only to rank-order the worlds, without having to say how good each of them is: we merely identify all the ones that tie for best, and then determine which way of acting has the best chance of leading to one of those worlds. This, however, is certainly wrong.[2] Suppose that in a certain emergency, ten men are at risk, and you have only two options. If you ϕ, you have a 1 per cent chance of rescuing all ten, and a 99 per cent chance of saving none. If you π, you have an 80 per cent chance of rescuing eight, and no chance of rescuing all ten. Only ϕing has any chance of leading to the best upshot, but nobody would think it the right thing to do. Rather, we should calculate the expectable utility of each way of behaving. To ascertain the expectable utility of my now ϕing, I associate a Number with each world that could result if I ϕ; the Number is a function of two numbers, one for how probable the world is, the other for how good it is. The expectable utility of my ϕing is a function of all the Numbers associated with worlds that could ensue if I ϕ. I shall not explore the problems of devising a suitable value metric, or of getting from probability and value numbers to Numbers, and from those to expectable utility.[3] From now on, indeed, I shall write in terms of actual consequences; everything I say could, routinely though laboriously, be translated into terms of expectable utilities.

Utilitarianism keeps us on a rein that is tight, but it may allow some slack by permitting non-moral choices between courses of action that would result in equally good worlds. Still, that may not be much. There

---

[1] I ignore the fine-tuning: distributive fairness, the measurement of well-being, and so on. None of these affects the issues to be discussed in this chapter.

[2] For a brief, helpful discussion, see J. J. C. Smart, 'An Outline of a System of Utilitarian Ethics', 37 ff.

[3] For good help with some of the complexities, see John Broome, *Weighing Goods*, sect. 6.1.

might always be a unique best accessible world, so that between what is required and what is prohibited there is no room to wriggle. Also, any space that is left, whether large or small, is uncomfortable. Each gap between what is required and what is forbidden is kept open by opposing moral pressures rather than by an absence of any—the tense calm at the centre of a hurricane rather than the relaxed peace of a halcyon day.

Some ways of attributing significance to making/allowing still leave the reins just as tight. Consider the following moral system:

> At time T, many worlds are accessible to Agent: he could make any one actual by how he acts. At each world, evaluate each state of affairs that would—if that world were actual—be a consequence of how Agent behaved at T, and give it a positive or negative score according to how good or bad it is. Then modify each score as follows. If it is the case that *If S had obtained, Agent would have (positively, actively) made it do so*, then multiply S's score by 2. If it is the case that *If S had obtained, Agent would have (negatively, passively) allowed it to do so*, then divide S's score by 2. Add up the *modified* scores for each world. Agent acts rightly at T just in case he actualizes the world with the highest total.

Replace multiplying and dividing by 2 by any algorithm you like; the details do not matter here. Nor do the problems of individuating states of affairs and evaluating them separately. We have here a schema for a coherent morality which gives basic moral significance to the difference between making and allowing, but not in such a way as to loosen the moral reins.

For that to happen, we need a bigger and less threatened area of sheer permission. Most common moralities achieve this by treating making/allowing as *categorial* or *structural*: they more or less sternly forbid making bad things happen, but treat allowing them to happen in a quite different way—usually speaking about it quietly or intermittently or with an uncertain voice. Such a morality's judgements about makings come from a completely different part of it from its judgements about allowings. Most of these moralities, for example, merely require us to help people in need sufficiently often and generously; so that they judge our dual-hurtings—our failures to help—not one at a time but rather according to how large they loom in our behaviour as a whole. This is categorially unlike their approach to our hurtings, which they forbid severally. As long as their idea of 'sufficiently often' is mild enough or

characterized vaguely enough, a morality of this sort leaves many practical questions unanswered, loosening the reins and leaving elbow-room
for the soul. We can challenge such a morality by arguing that mak-
ing/allowing is morally neutral; but our case for this rests on taking an
analytic view of the distinction, and adherents of the common moralities I have been discussing may be unmoved by this, regarding the
moral significance of the difference between hurting and not-helping as
so secure that no analytic scrutiny should be allowed to dislodge it (see
Section 3 above). Indeed, they had better take that view of the relevance
of analysis to moral judgement; if they do not, their moral position is
unsustainable.

It is sometimes said that the reins must be loosened if there is to be
room for acts that are supererogatory (meaning: better than merely
right). This is seen as a problem for utilitarians, who judge the mere
rightness of behaviour in terms of its leading to the best accessible
world, leaving no space for supererogation. The latter is not listed in
the index of Sidgwick's utilitarian classic, but he does address its cus-
tomary companion, praise: 'From a Utilitarian point of view . . . we
must mean by calling a quality "deserving of praise" that it is expedi-
ent to praise it, with a view to its future production: accordingly, in dis-
tributing our praise of human qualities, on utilitarian principles, we
have to consider primarily not the usefulness of the quality, but the usefulness of the praise.'[4] As a statement of how praise looks from 'a
Utilitarian point of view', this is perfectly correct, but it warns us that
most of the reality of praise lies outside the purview of utilitarianism.
Sidgwick's correct, chilly account of utilitarian praise gives no hint that
when we praise we celebrate, expressing surprised joy over someone's
performance. We can readmit that element without tying praise to
supererogation; the time-honoured link between those two seems to me
wrong. (I am trying here to get straight about praise, not to rescue
Sidgwick.) If you think in a broad and realistic way about how praise
figures in our lives, I predict that you will see clearly that praise—even
moral praise—goes far beyond 'better than merely right' judgements.
Praise in general is a way of expressing pleasure at the goodness of a
physique, a high jump, a proof, a generous and self-sacrificing action.
Only the last of those will elicit *moral* praise, but it can do so without
one's judging that the action was supererogatory. If doing the right
thing were always easy, we would never get a shock of pleasure from

[4] Henry Sidgwick, *The Methods of Ethics*, 428.

someone's achieving it; and then moral praise would indeed be confined to behaviour judged to be supererogatory. All of us, however, utilitarians and others, realize that it would often be astonishing if Agent acted as he ought, or even came close; and in such cases we shall praise his acting nearly as he ought, not conditioning him but doing what we always do in genuine praise—celebrating.

47. Morality as too Demanding: The Thwarting of Desires

The 'tight reins' kind of morality that I looked at first, namely a making/allowing symmetrical form of utilitarianism, is also for many of us demanding in the second of the two ways that I identified. To state the point in terms of probabilities: The expected utility of my selling most of my belongings, living in a studio apartment on a subsistence diet, giving up travelling, and sending all the money I can to Oxfam is greater than that of my continuing on my present path. Symmetrical utilitarianism condemns me for not taking this course of action, which savagely conflicts with my non-moral desires.

This 'thwarting' kind of exigency is not necessarily a feature of that kind of morality. It arises only because of some facts about human life on our planet. They certainly *are* facts, however, so the demands are made. The early utilitarians thought otherwise, but they had no good reason for this. Only a minor philosophical mistake, it seems, shielded their eyes from the demanding glare of their own morality. Here is Mill:

> The multiplication of happiness is, according to the utilitarian ethics, the object of virtue: the occasions on which any person (except one in a thousand) has it in his power to do this on an extended scale—in other words to be a public benefactor—are but exceptional; and on these occasions alone is he called on to consider public utility; in every other case, private utility, the interest or happiness of some few persons, is all he has to attend to.[5]

This passage does not rely on the making/allowing distinction. On the contrary, it clearly implies that in the rare case where Agent can bring happiness to many people, he behaves wrongly if he does not do so, which is to say that he will be behaving wrongly in allowing a utility level which he could have made higher. No moral significance is being accorded to making/allowing.

Rather, Mill is making a mistake. Rightly saying that I can help

---

[5] John Stuart Mill, *Utilitarianism*, 19 (two-thirds of the way through ch. 2).

relatively few of the people now alive, he wrongly takes this to lighten my moral burden. Apparently he does not see that even if I can help only a few, utilitarianism demands that while there are people worse off than myself I should give up things for myself in order to benefit them, if this can be done without a net loss of utility; and in today's world, as in Mill's, I could do this only by giving up almost everything I have. Even if I do so, I cannot help many people; that is Mill's point, and now we see that it does not save me.

Mill thinks it does, and I have a suggestion about why. His phrase 'the interest or happiness of some few persons' suggests that we all know which 'few' are in question: if I cannot be a large-scale public benefactor, I should be a small-scale private one, which means that my beneficiaries should be myself, my immediate family, and my friends. This defends me against the threat of exigency, because of a contingent fact that holds for me and almost anyone who reads this book, namely that nobody in our inner circles is in such penury as are most people in sub-Saharan Africa. That is one reason why doing good to my near and dear may not seriously interfere with the activities that keep me cheerful and prosperous. Also, less contingently: the closer people are to me in the indicated ways, the more likely it is that my welfare matters to them, so that in guarding my own interests I am to some extent looking after theirs. Conversely, also, to the extent that I naturally, pre-morally care about the welfare of my near and dear, doing things for them is not burdensome to me.

Alas, Mill's line of thought is mistaken. Even if I cannot significantly help more than five people, say, there may be millions of people any five of whom I could help, and utilitarianism requires me to 'attend to' the millions in order to know which I could help the most. The mere fact that I cannot be a public benefactor on the large scale does not imply, through any utilitarian argument, that my proper moral arena should be what is small-scale and close to home rather than small-scale and remote.

Bentham seems to have made the same mistake: 'The greatest happiness of all those whose interest is in question [is the] only right and proper and universally desirable end of human action.'[6] The phrase 'those whose interest is in question' suggests a narrowing of focus to which Bentham is not entitled. Something similar happens when Sidgwick writes: 'Each person is for the most part . . . not in a position

---

[6] Jeremy Bentham, *An Introduction to the Principles of Morals and Legislation*, 1 (footnote added in 1822 edn.).

to do much good to more than a very small number of persons; it therefore seems, on this ground alone, desirable that his chief benevolent
impulses should be correspondingly limited.'[7] Sidgwick openly makes
this a reason for attending primarily to the welfare of one's family and
friends. He has reasons for such a narrowing of focus, as we shall see
later; but when he says of his purely numerical premiss that 'on this
ground alone' we should attend primarily to our near and dear, he is
wrong.

So the threat of undue exigency still stands. I have derived it from a
form of utilitarianism in which making/allowing is taken to be neutral.
Even if it were not, morality's demands might still be overwhelming. In
a forthcoming book Peter Unger writes that he neither knows nor cares
very much whether the making/allowing distinction has any moral significance. He argues, through intuitive attention to examples, that any
moral significance it has is small enough to be easily drowned by other
factors; on which basis he argues for drastic conclusions about how we
ought to live. Unger's examples are unusually detailed, and his handling
of the details is alert, thorough, and fair; altogether he sets a new standard for this kind of work. It is the wrong kind of work for my project,
which is to *understand* our best moral thinking—not merely to show
what it implies about how we should behave but to grasp how it does
so, what the elements are, and how they interact. Arguments from
examples, however delicately handled, cannot answer these questions,
which require that we analyse our potentially important moral concepts.
Only an analysis can show us whether and why the making/allowing
distinction makes a basic moral difference, and how big a difference it
is. Still, Unger and I have something in common in this area: we both
raise the question of the moral significance of the difference between
making bad things happen and allowing them to happen; we see that
distinction as one ingredient in certain concepts that we use in moral
thinking, and are willing to pick the latter apart sufficiently to consider
this element on its own, asking for its moral credentials. This contrasts
with what I believe to be the real position of many moral theorists, for
whom making/allowing is too deep and structural to be open to this
kind of challenge.

Someone who is not willing to protect making/allowing from analytic
scrutiny can try to reduce the threat of an intolerably exigent morality
in another way, namely by backing off from the 'optimizing' idea that

---

[7] Sidgwick, *The Methods of Ethics*, 434.

is the heart of utilitarianism. Let us look into the most promising way of making that attempt.

48. Morality of Self-interest

We can leave utilitarianism with its making/allowing symmetry while weakening it so as to lessen its demands, as follows. Adopt a morality according to which the moral status of Agent's conduct depends purely upon the value$_{Agent}$ of its overall consequences, where the value$_{Agent}$ of a total state of affairs depends upon two independent variables: how good or bad its various components are for Agent, and how good or bad they are for everyone else.[8]

Many different functions might be found attractive. (1) Some systematically weight Agent's good, allowing it to count as though he were two people, or ten, or a thousand. At one end of that scale the extra weight is zero, and we are back with utilitarianism; at the other, it is infinite, and we have purely egoistic morality. The intermediate territory is more interesting. (2) Then there are functions according to which, if the value for Agent is low enough, the state of affairs has the lowest possible value$_{Agent}$. Such a function would set a limit to the degree of morally permitted self-sacrifice—perhaps implying that nobody should submit himself to being slowly burned to death, no matter what horrors this would spare others. (3) There are functions that combine aspects of the first two kinds—but their details do not matter here. I shall use the phrase 'morality of self-interest' to embrace every morality according to which the value$_{Agent}$ of a state of affairs is sometimes higher than its impersonal value because of how good it is for Agent, that is, how well it satisfies his non-moral desires. That will cover the kinds of function I have mentioned, and many others.

I have sketched moralities of self-interest as saying that Agent *ought* to give special weight to what is good for him; but some of them say only that Agent *may* do this. According to these systems, slanting things towards himself is an option that he is morally permitted but not required to take. It would be easy to rewrite my paragraph about kinds of function so that it addressed permissive rather than mandating moral systems; for example, replacing 'a limit to the degree of morally

---

[8] This idea is sketched in my 'Morality and Consequences', 78 f. It became a major theme in Samuel Scheffler, *The Rejection of Consequentialism*.

permitted self-sacrifice' by 'a limit to the degree of morally required self-sacrifice'. The choice of functions is independent of the difference between mandating and permissive forms of self-interest morality.

Most of us are inclined to think that we ought to have a special concern for the welfare of our near and dear, and these 'special obligations' are perhaps a special case of a mandating morality of self-interest. I want, however, to discuss the general idea that one ought to have a special concern for one's own welfare, whether or not that involves anyone else.

The permissive form of self-interest morality is easier to defend than the mandating one. For one thing, a permissive morality not only helps with the exigency complaint but also loosens the reins. A mandating morality of self-interest says 'required' or 'forbidden' as often as utilitarianism does, differing only in how it distributes them across the options. Also, most of us think that conduct can be supererogatory—beyond the call of duty, or better than merely right—and room is made for this by a permissive but not by a mandating morality of self-interest (assuming that it is at least sometimes better not to avail oneself of such a moral permission). So it is not surprising that recent moral philosophy has tended to ignore mandating self-interest moralities, attending to the self-interest idea only in its permissive form.[9] The neglect of mandating moralities of self-interest has shown up in the use of the phrase 'agent-centred *permissions*' as though it defined the whole idea of self-interest moralities; and malpractice with that phrase has had a seriously distorting effect on recent work in moral theory. But this is not the place to go into all that. I began with the mandating version of self-interest morality to protest the current tendency to define it out of existence, and also because it is of interest in itself. I shall stay with it, parenthetically, until the end of this section.

Something like it occurs in work of Bernard Williams. When he protests against the utilitarian idea that value should always be maximized, he does it through a stress on Agent's *projects*, i.e. the long-term endeavours that he cares about most and that give structure to his life. Agent may have a choice between positively pursuing his projects and thereby behaving in a manner that is negatively relevant to the loss of some good, and neglecting or turning away from his projects in order positively to produce some good. This choice raises two issues: one's own projects versus the good of others, and making versus allowing. I

---

[9] An honourable exception: Rolf Sartorius, 'Utilitarianism, Rights, and Duties to Self'.

shall filter out the latter, and focus on the former, which is Williams's real concern.[10]

A person's long-term projects (especially the deeply espoused ones that Williams calls 'commitments') are constitutive of her identity, making her the person that she is; so Williams maintains. If that is somewhere near right, then to relinquish one's projects and commitments is not heroism or quixotry or imprudence but rather the destruction of one's own wholeness and unity along the time line. This involves a loss of *integrity*, Williams says, using the word in its old sense of integralness, undivided wholeness. For the billions who can afford only one project, survival, that is an understatement. Considered as agents, though, those folk lie outside the scope of our topic, which is utilitarianism's demand that projects be relinquished in the interests of others. No sane morality would demand this of someone who must struggle to stay alive.

Williams's emphasis on my right to pursue my projects combines two ideas: I am entitled to tilt the scales somewhat in my own favour, and my good depends largely on how my projects fare. The latter is not about my projects, but about projects: when I think about how my behaviour affects others, I ought—according to the second idea—to give special weight to my effect on *their* projects.

Granted that I am entitled to give more weight to my projects than to anyone else's, is this *just* because of that general slope towards myself that also entitles my pleasures, pains, etc. to count with me more than theirs do? Williams seems to answer No, taking the slope of legitimate self-favouring to be steeper with projects than with other values—as though the moral force of 'my own projects' were not reached merely by summing the forces of 'my own' and of 'projects'. I am not sure how he would defend this, though his paper 'Persons, Character and Morality' gives some help.

Some moralists, though probably not Williams, have been absolutists about this, holding that nothing could make it right or reasonable to give up one's deepest and most enduring projects on behalf of others. That was Nietzsche's view:

I only need to expose myself to the sight of some genuine distress and I am lost . . . The sight of a small mountain tribe fighting for its liberty would persuade

[10] Bernard Williams, 'A Critique of Utilitarianism', 108–18. For evidence about the focus of Williams's concern, and for other helpful discussion, see Nancy Davis, 'Utilitarianism and Responsibility'.

me to offer it my hand and my life . . . All such arousing of pity and calling for help is secretly seductive, for our 'own way' is too hard and demanding and too remote from the love and gratitude of others, and we do not really mind escaping from it.[11]

That has a certain hardness and grandeur about it, as has Thoreau's boast: 'Probably I should not consciously and deliberately forsake my particular calling to do the good which society demands of me, to save the universe from annihilation.'[12] These passages express disdain for self-sacrifice, suggesting that there is something contemptibly yielding about it; their moral equivalent would be a severe mandating form of morality of self-interest.

49. Affections

An outright morality of self-interest—whether permissive or mandating—provides one defence against undue exigency. There is another, having to do with the interests of the people one naturally cares about—one's near and dear. These connect with self-interest in three ways, as I noted in Section 47 above: because I love certain people, their flourishing counts as a good for me; because they love me, my flourishing is a good for them; and because they are relatively well-off, I could without drastic loss to myself bring my well-being onto a level with theirs. Of these points, two are necessary and the third contingent.

There is also an independent basis, not invoking self-interest, on which a utilitarian might allow or even require an emphasis upon one's near and dear. Just as a given morality, conjoined with some psychological facts, might imply that we should usually look for guidance to some *other* morality (see Section 7), so a morality might imply that it would be best if we were sometimes guided not by moral concerns but by our affections for other people. This would be empty if it applied only when the issue is trivial, or morally balanced between pro and con; but I am talking about a morality which invites us sometimes not to ask it what we should do, even though it has an answer and the stakes are large.

This is different from the place that affectionate feelings can be given within a utilitarian morality, as remarked by Smart: 'There are very good utilitarian reasons why we should by all means cultivate in

---

[11] Friedrich Nietzsche, *The Gay Science*, sect. 338.
[12] Henry Thoreau, *Walden*, 73.

ourselves the tendency to certain types of warm and spontaneous feeling.'[13] Sidgwick puts it more coolly when he says that it is 'conducive to the general happiness that each individual should distribute his beneficence in the channels marked out by commonly recognized ties and claims'.[14] His reasons for this rely on contingent facts about the role of affections in producing human well-being. The most interesting is a deep point about motivation. There is self-love, there are the special affections, and there is benevolence towards all. Utilitarianism makes calls on the third of these, but we are grounded in the first. The best route from there to the third is through the second, so the special affections are instrumentally valuable: 'Such specialized affections as the present organization of society normally produces afford the best means of developing in most persons a more extended benevolence, to the degree to which they are capable of feeling it.'[15] This provides a utilitarian reason for cultivating such affectionate feelings, quite apart from the fact that having and acting on them is pleasurable, and thus valuable, in itself.

Sidgwick also holds that some important goods are unlikely to be produced unless people love and favour their children. Although utilitarianism requires us to do the best we can for everyone, he says, in trying to help strangers we tend to harm them: 'The happiness of all is on the whole most promoted by maintaining in adults generally (except married women), the expectation that each will be thrown on his own resources for the supply of his own wants.'[16] On the other hand, where natural affections already exist, 'the practical objections to spontaneous beneficence . . . are much diminished in force' because in this special context 'kindnesses . . . have less tendency to weaken the springs of activity in the person benefited; and may even strengthen them by exciting other sources of energy than the egoistic'.[17] I shall not comment on how true this is today.

What if my affections impel me to behave in a way which—even with the above points taken into account—is not for the best overall? Here is Sidgwick's laconic reply: 'All special affections tend occasionally to come into conflict with the principle of promoting the general happiness: and Utilitarianism must therefore prescribe such a culture of the feelings as will, so far as possible, counteract this tendency.'[18] The saving phrase is 'so far as possible'. To the extent that it is not possible,

[13] Smart, 'An Outline of a System of Utilitarian Ethics', 45.
[14] Sidgwick, *The Methods of Ethics*, 433.   [15] Ibid. 434.   [16] Ibid. 436.
[17] Ibid. 433.   [18] Ibid. 434.

utilitarianism has a choice between suppressing personal affections entirely and encouraging them in the knowledge that sometimes they will lead us to act wrongly. The latter option is the one I mentioned before taking a detour through Sidgwick. The point is that a properly informed utilitarianism might imply that we should sometimes act on our feelings—giving no thought to morality, or being emotionally driven to defy it—even though that will lead us to do what utilitarianism says is the wrong thing to do in the particular case.

That is Peter Railton's position in an important paper on how feelings relate to what he calls 'consequentialism'. That is not a term that I have used in this book, because it is more trouble than it is worth; but in this section I shall adopt it, so as to stay with Railton's terminology. That will do no harm. The topic is Railton's distinction between two kinds of 'consequentialism', which could as well be two kinds of utilitarianism—the difference between them being just the same. When I speak of 'consequentialism' here I shall have in mind the broad kind of utilitarianism that I have been considering.

While rooting himself in consequentialism, Railton values the affections for more than what they promote or produce. He quotes Rawls as saying 'purity of heart' would involve seeing and acting from a strictly impartial point of view, and comments:

This may or may not be purity of heart, but it could not be the standpoint of actual life without radically detaching the individual from a range of personal concerns and commitments. . . . The fact that so purely abstracted a perspective is portrayed as a kind of moral ideal should at least start us wondering. If to be more perfectly moral is to ascend ever higher toward [complete impartiality], perhaps we made a mistake in boarding the moral escalator in the first place. Some of the very 'weaknesses' that prevent us from achieving this moral ideal—strong attachments to persons or projects—seem to be part of a considerably more compelling human ideal.[19]

This implies that affectionate feelings are valuable in themselves. It is hard not to agree. Try to imagine the human condition deprived of all behaviour based on such feelings. If the picture repels you, that gives you a utilitarian reason for not trying to squelch your affections or their influence on your behaviour. That is where Railton stands: he accepts a morality whose central aim is the production of what has value; he

[19] Peter Railton, 'Alienation, Consequentialism, and the Demands of Morality', 139 f. For a rich presentation of this theme in a non-consequentialist framework, and for much more, see Lynne McFall, 'Integrity'.

thinks there is intrinsic value in our having and acting upon affection-ate feelings; and he sees that acting on those feelings sometimes involves acting against one's morality. He distinguishes 'objective consequential-ism', which may be a true theory about what makes conduct right or wrong, from 'subjective consequentialism', which says that practical choices should always be guided by the thought of what would yield the best consequences. The former could be right while the latter is wrong, Railton says; and he stands up for an objective form of consequential-ism which implies nothing about where one should look for guidance.[20]

This is a hard saying. What can be going on when someone accepts a morality in its 'objective' form but does not in general consult it as a guide? One might answer like this: 'His acceptance of it consists merely in his believing it to be true. That implies nothing about the practical role that he gives it.' That would confine Railton's position to moral realists, who think that moral judgements have truth-values. It has indeed been said that for a non-realist for whom 'the truth of moral claims consists in their acceptability . . . moral truth and acceptance value could not be distinguished so as to justify the claim that utilitar-ianism can be a standard of rightness without being a decision proce-dure'.[21] In fact, the difference between realism and non-realism has nothing to do with the issue about moral decision procedures, and the phrase 'acceptance value' is off the mark. Railton's consequentialist *does* accept consequentialism, either by taking a practical attitude or by believing a moral proposition. What is special about his position is that this acceptance does not manifest itself in his always seeking conse-quentialism's guidance on how he is to behave.

Then how is it manifested? William Wilcox has asked how a man can relate to consequentialism at a time when he helps his wife in perfect awareness that he could do more for a stranger. He offers four options—hypocrisy, moral weakness, apriorism, and this:

Finally, he could be a self-deceived consequentialist with a moral blind spot where his wife's welfare is concerned. He would convince himself, probably by muttering something about having the sort of character of which a consequen-tialist could approve, that he does have an overriding commitment to

---

[20] Railton's principal distinction and his reason for it were both anticipated by Sidgwick, *The Methods of Ethics*, 413. For an attack on it, see Bernard Williams, 'A Critique of Utilitarianism', 128; for a response to that, see Robert M. Adams, 'Motive Utilitarianism', 475–7.

[21] David O. Brink, 'Utilitarianism and the Personal Point of View', 428 n.

impersonal value and that even though such a commitment would seem to require him to sacrifice his wife's welfare, the sacrifice is not really required.[22]

This 'moral blind spot' diagnosis—stripped of the stuff about self-deceptive muttering—points in the right direction, though it is not right as it stands. Our man may have moral thoughts at the time of action; they simply do not dominate how he acts.

Wilcox implies that when a Railton person helps a friend instead of helping someone else more, there is something wrong with either his consequentialism or his friendship. On the contrary, he is a genuine consequentialist at that time because he accepts this: it is all right to give rein to the feelings that now drive him, only because it is better, overall, that he should have and sometimes act on such feelings. He is also a genuine friend. He is moved by feelings that come from the bottom of his heart. If he raises any moral issues, he does not let them dictate his behaviour on this occasion. That is the sort of person he is: one who often acts on his affectionate feelings. He accepts, Sidgwick fashion, that he ought to change himself in this respect if that would be overall better, so that for him this aspect of his nature stands under a certain condition; but individual expressions of it do not. When he reaches out in love to his friend, it is not with the thought 'I wouldn't be doing this if . . .'. His friendship is as unconditioned and absolute as any friendship can rationally be. If he is not a moral idiot, there are presumably some consequentialist conditions on this particular act: it had better not be the case that he would bring his friend this help even if it brought ruin and death to an entire city. So his consequentialism might be involved in that way, as setting limits in individual cases. What Railton puts under the spotlight, however, is not that involvement but rather the consequentialist basis for allowing oneself to be a person of a certain kind instead of trying to change. What could be more consequentialist than that?

Why should I accept the role that my natural affections have in causing my conduct? If it is *only* because I think the world would be worse if I did not, then this is where I stand:

> I contemplate the possibility of cleansing myself of those affectionate feelings, or of breaking their link with action; I see that the only ways I might do that would lead to overall states of affairs

[22] William H. Wilcox, 'Egoists, Consequentialists, and their Friends', 83. For another unconvinced discussion of this matter, including many references to the literature, see William L. Langenfus, 'Consequentialism in Search of a Conscience'.

that are worse than if I left myself alone; and for this reason I reject the proposal that I try to change in this respect.

Where I actually stand, however, is here:

> I contemplate the possibility of cleansing myself of those affectionate feelings, or of breaking their link with action, and I reject it.

Just that. I am not willing to cut that deeply into that part of myself, and that is not because of what that change would lead to in the rest of the world. This is not to disagree with Railton about how people ought to behave, or to deny that those judgements can be justified on consequentialist grounds. It is to question whether that justification is required, because I would regard myself as morally permitted to be like that even if my being so did not tend to maximize value. This is to say that I accept an emphasis on affectionate feelings as part of the morality of self-interest—that is, as *a departure from* utilitarianism rather than as *implied by* it in the manner explored by Sidgwick and Railton. Let me be a spontaneously loving person *ut ruat coelum*? Of course not. If enough turned on it, I would see myself as morally required to try to lose all my affections and all my spontaneity.

50. The Collapse of the Self-interest Defence

I have invoked the idea of a morality of self-interest as a way of justifying at least some of my conduct in not preventing harms that I could prevent. The idea was that I might be protected against the demands of an intolerably exigent morality if I could claim a basic moral entitlement to give more weight to my own wants than to those of other people. Two vast difficulties in that project were anticipated in my second Tanner Lecture: 'The conclusion I have so far come to is uncomfortable. Even if I may tilt the moral scales in my own behalf, does this entitlement go as far as the premature deaths of other people? And do murderers have it too? Am I saying that we are as bad as murderers, but that they are better than they are made out to be?'[23] The first difficulty is that few of us could in good conscience accept a morality of self-interest that would justify all, or even most, of our unhelpful conduct. The second is sharper: it is that when a morality of self-interest

---

[23] Bennett, 'Morality and Consequences', 81.

is combined with the thesis that making/allowing is neutral, one gets shocking results. If I am morally entitled to keep my house warm in winter rather than spending that money on saving the life of someone in Ethiopia, then the neutrality of making/allowing would entitle me to kill someone in Ethiopia if that was needed to keep my house warm. Indeed, even if making/allowing has some basic moral significance but makes only a limited difference of degree, the trouble will remain. If we defend our life-style through a morality of self-interest, while holding that making/allowing carries a less than mountainous moral weight, we shall still be committed to approving some possible behaviours that would in fact disgust and horrify us.

My Ethiopian example is a little extravagant, because the penal code—which is heavily asymmetric along the making/allowing line (see Section 25 above)—does not require me to help Ethiopians but does forbid me to kill them; and there are utilitarian reasons why legal requirements nearly always create moral ones. Still, if the law furnishes the only moral barrier to such killings, something seems to have gone wrong.

That was the point of my question about the permission to favour oneself—'Do murderers have it too?' I went on to argue that things are less simple than the question might suggest; I adduced a pair of examples which were as alike as possible given that one was the making/allowing dual of the other, and invited the reader to agree that those two cases did intuitively seem to be morally on a par. This was not an argument for the neutrality of making/allowing—merely evidence that the latter does not collide with common opinion as directly as is sometimes thought. This did not, as I acknowledged, lead me back to the question about ourselves and murderers. The case of 'making suffer' that I there presented was devised as the making/allowing dual of a fairly typical case of not helping such a village (see Suit and No-help in Section 33 above); the two were unalike in the making/allowing respect but did not differ in any of the other ways that tend to accompany that one. The result was that the 'making' member of the pair was not a typical case of hurting, making suffer, behaving in a way that is positively or actively relevant to someone's suffering harm; so it did not typify the range of trouble that I had uncovered by contending that making/allowing is morally neutral.

In a nutshell: If we adopt a morality of self-interest as our only defence against an unduly exigent morality, we thereby permit or require ourselves to further our interests by hurting people, killing them, and so on. Scrupulous attention to 'other differences that tend to accompany making/allowing' cannot much lessen the impact of this point.

One pair of 'other differences', however, is such a potent distraction that it had better be discussed. If I kill someone, e.g. by poisoning her, a finger points from her to me as the person who kills her, and one points from me to her as the person whom I have killed. On the other hand, when I do not send help to Chad, nobody dies in Chad of whom it is true that if I had sent help she would have lived; and when someone dies in Chad, no finger points straight at me as the person because of whose inaction she died. Either of these might seem to make a moral difference.

In fact, neither does, as is shown by the following pair of examples (due to Jonathan Glover). (1) A gang of thirty bandits overpowers a village with thirty inhabitants; each bandit deprives one villager of all his or her food, and the villagers die. (2) The same bandits take over the same village, and each bandit takes from each villager one-thirtieth of all his or her food, and the villagers die. In (1) a finger points in each direction: killers and victims are paired. In (2) no bandit has a unique victim, and no villager a unique killer. It would be absurd, though, to discriminate morally between the behaviour in (1) and that in (2)— unless in (2) some bandit does not think that the others will do what he is doing, and therefore does not expect his behaviour to be part of a lethal pattern.

Still, let us consider the two pointing fingers separately. The fact that when someone dies in Chad there are many of us who might have saved her, though it can be expressed disjunctively—She would have survived if I had helped her *or* you had helped her—can also be put conjunctively: She died because I did not help her *and* you did not help her. The conjunction is better: it brings out that we were in this together, each doing his negative bit;[24] so there is after all a finger pointing straight at me. One also points straight at you, but that does not make me less responsible; compare a case where one terrorist plants a bomb and a second detonates it. Morally speaking, there is no safety in numbers.

Conversely, what are we to make of the fact that if I do not send help to Chad, nobody dies of whom it is true that if I had sent help she would have lived? Well, an agency with a monopoly on charity in some

---

[24] Or his passive bit. My present point goes through equally well on the active/passive understanding of the making/allowing distinction.

distressed region could arrange to pair potential victims with potential donors. Imagine receiving a letter giving you details, including a photograph, of the 10-year-old girl whose chance of living for another year depends upon you alone. This would strike you as oppressive, bullying, unfair—but why? You knew already that you could send money which would result in one fewer deaths in the coming year; this agency has merely made it the case that there is one identified person whose survival depends in this way on your charity. Why has that so much power? It is probably because, for many of us, the conscience is an imaginative faculty; our victims can visit us in the night, so to speak, filing past with promises to meet us at Philippi. The parade may be long; but it cannot be disjunctive, with each fist being shaken on the condition that the others are not; and so if the deaths of my victims are all disjunctive consequences of my neglect, there is no parade; and this may help me to sleep soundly. You may find this disgraceful; or you may think—as I am inclined to—that it reflects something so deep in our natures that we had best accept it, align ourselves with it, build it into our moralities. It has some relevance to our neglect of needy people in the Third World, but nowhere near enough to abolish the exigency problem—to which I now return.

That problem looked soluble through an appeal to a morality of self-interest, but that turned out to permit behaviour that we are sure must be wrong—unless we give to making/allowing a structural or categorial status that has the effect of treating it as almost infinitely weighty. We meet essentially the same difficulty if, instead of invoking self-interest directly, we espouse a morality which allows us to be influenced by affectionate feelings. Whatever its basis, the permission to favour those one loves combines with making/allowing symmetry to yield results that none of us will accept. It permits me, for instance, to ruin one person's career in order to further my son's.

So we are left swinging, on the pivot of the neutrality of making/allowing, between a morality that permits us to further our own interests by behaving in ways that appal us and one that requires us to repent of and change much of what we cherish in our own behaviour.

51. Arguing for Making/Allowing Asymmetry

Some philosophers have adduced this situation as itself constituting evidence that making/allowing is not neutral. Mostly they have looked at it without the aid of a morality of self-interest; so they have seen it not in the pivotal role which I have just described, but simply as threatening us with a morality that is unbearably demanding. Their argument is simple. We start with the premiss that a correct morality will not demand more than so much of us; if making/allowing is neutral the demands will go further than that; so making/allowing is not neutral.[25] We do not have to anatomize it, asking *why* it has moral significance; it is enough *that* it does, and of this the exigency threat assures us.

How is the moral realist to entitle himself to the premiss about morality's demands? Parfit has presented this challenge: '[If] a moral theory is something that we *invent* . . . it is plausible to claim that an acceptable theory cannot be unrealistically demanding. But, on several other views about the nature of morality, this claim is not plausible. We may *hope* that the best theory is not unrealistically demanding. But, on these views, this can only be a hope. We cannot assume that this must be true.'[26] Any realist who does argue in the challenged manner is presumably relying on his 'intuition' that true morality does not make such demands as that. In theorizing about morals, most of us rely on intuitions at various points, and I make no issue of that. However, if ever there was a moral intuition whose credentials should be suspected, especially by moral realists, it is this one.

From the non-realist standpoint, the force of the exigency threat is different. To accept a moral principle, in my non-realist view, is not to recognize a truth but rather to take a stand or adopt a policy—to be or become willing to hold oneself to certain standards of behaviour. For me, then, the proposed morality is too demanding (not to be *plausible*, but) to be *acceptable*: I am unwilling to hold myself to such a standard.

This awkward position is reached by combining moral constraints against positively harming people with the view that allowing is morally on a par with making, a combination which pretty much leads to utilitarianism. So I have a powerful reason for not letting those two moral doctrines run free in my moral scheme of things, but how to constrain them is a problem calling for further moral theorizing. It might be objected: 'You call it theorizing, but really it's just you trying to *decide* what to accept, like trying to decide which apple to pick from the tree'. I have explained in Section 5 why that is not right. Although it is ultimately a matter for decision, it is not isolated like the choice of an apple; it is more like deciding on a move in chess, or where to put the stair-

---

[25] e.g. Heidi Malm, 'Directions of Justification in the Negative–Positive Duty Debate'.
[26] Derek Parfit, *Reasons and Persons*, 29.

case in a new house, or what textbook to use in a philosophy course. What I decide about the troublesome pair will not satisfy me unless I can lock it firmly into a coherent moral system whose fundamental principles are highly general. Furthermore, this has to be a system that I really do accept; any factual matter which it says makes a moral difference must be one which I am willing, when fully conscious of what I am doing, to let make that difference in my life. This is no trivial requirement; and trying to satisfy it while fending off the exigency threat is hard.

I have failed to do it. There seems to be no way out of the difficulty adumbrated in my second Tanner Lecture except either to accord fundamental moral weight to the making/allowing distinction or to accept the tremendously exigent morality's condemnation of our conduct, as some have done and I will not.[27]

[27] For instance Shelly Kagan, *The Limits of Morality*, and a forthcoming book by Peter Unger.

10

ATROCITIES

52. Crises

The thesis that making/allowing is neutral bustles disturbingly through two areas of moral theory, with two threats. In the area I have been discussing, it threatens us with unendurably severe moral demands; in the one to which we now come, it threatens to be unduly lax in what it permits. The former topic is not a mere matter of theory: it sits at the centre of our lives. The latter—the permissiveness—is less immediately and urgently practical.

Here is a reason for doubting that. 'If not saving a life is as bad—*ceteris paribus*—as taking one, it seems to follow that we are morally entitled to steal from some people in order to save the lives of others, for example robbing a bank and sending the takings to Oxfam. This conclusion will be widely resisted, and the resistance will rely on giving moral weight to the making/allowing distinction. So the latter's status threatens a moral permissiveness that concerns us in a close and immediate way.' There is something in that, but I wish to set such matters aside and to look elsewhere. Moral objections to Robin Hoodery are largely based on views about property and the criminal law. Where either of those institutions is in play, it is difficult to discern how much (if any) further work is being done by a moral discrimination between making and allowing.

If we look for cases where law and property are not involved, and where an unwanted moral permissiveness clearly comes from the neutrality of making/allowing, we find them in a kind of set-up that seldom if ever occurs in the lives of most of us; which is what I said two paragraphs back. Unusual as this kind of situation is, though, we ought not to neglect it: if we do not think about our reactions to it, we shall to that extent lack an understanding of ourselves.

I refer to what I call *crises*—contexts where Agent knows that only by doing some atrocious, revolting, horrible thing can he avert a calamity that is still worse. Although such crises are mostly

philosophers' inventions, they merit attention because they challenge us
to clarify some of our moral thinking, becoming conscious of what concepts we are using and how. In the philosophical literature on them, the
atrocious behaviour that is in question usually involves physical harm,
up to killing, and I shall follow suit; but such atrocities are only a sample. An atrocity might consist in ruining someone financially, causing
her to be incurably contemptuous of herself, depriving her of friends,
blackening her name, undermining her trust in someone she loves.

Absolutism about φing is the thesis that it could never be right to φ;
opposed to it is what I call *relativism* about φing, according to which it
would be right to φ in some possible circumstances.[1] The term 'relativism' is commonly used to name one or other of a certain range of
views about the nature of morality as such, but this common use of the
term should be dropped. It does not give 'relativism' a single precise
meaning, there is not even a clear understanding of exactly what range
of meanings it tolerates, and none of the range does justice—as my proposed use does—to the fundamental, time-hallowed idea that 'relative'
is the antonym of 'absolute'.

The terms 'could' and 'possible' have different strengths, so absolutism can be more or less strong, and relativism less or more so. On
this continuum of readings, one terminus is set by causal possibility: the
strongest absolutism about φing that we need to consider holds that
φing could not be right in any causally possible state of affairs. Then
there is a range of weaker forms, according to which φing could never
be known to be right, could never be right in any sociologically possible situation, could never be right in any state of affairs that is likely
enough to be worth thinking about in a practical way, and so on. I start
with the strongest kind of absolutism.

Some of the kinds of behaviour that absolutists fix upon involve consequences in a limited way: killing an innocent person, for example,
entails moving in a manner that has an innocent person's prematurely
dying as a causal consequence. None of these kinds, however, is defined
in terms of overall consequences. There is no absolutist/relativist dispute about the wrongness of φing where 'φ' stands for 'kill an innocent
person when there is no good to be achieved, or bad to be lessened, by
so doing'. I shall also exclude from my discussion kinds of behaviour
that are defined in terms of motives; so I shall not consider, for example, absolutism about killing innocent people purely for fun. (That

---

[1] In this usage, 'absolutism' *simpliciter* names the view that for some value of φ, absolutism about φing is correct; and 'relativism' *simpliciter* is the contradictory of that.

raises the general question whether behaviour which would otherwise be right can be made downright wrong by being done for a discreditable reason—an issue in substantive first-order morality, about which I have nothing to say, except for one small corner of it that will be my topic in Chapter 11.) My concern here is with absolutism about φing versus relativism about φing for values of φ that are defined in terms of what is done, not in terms of why. The values of φ are definable in non-moral terms, of course: 'impermissibly killing someone' is not one of them. In this context, an 'innocent' person is one who has not broken any law and is not trying to do any harm.

For some values of φ for which absolutism is plausible, there could be cases in which Agent had to choose between φing and dual-φing. He might be so placed that if he did not kill someone several people would die prematurely, this being something he has allowed to happen. If their deaths come about through the intervention of someone else, Agent will not have dual-killed them, because his conduct will have related to their dying in a mediated way, which means that it will not have differed from killing *only* as allowing differs from making. In the meantime, however, let us keep other agents out of the picture, taking cases where the alternative to φing really is dual-φing. Of course there could be a crisis where Agent had to choose between φing and allowing to happen something even more appalling though of a different kind from anything involved in φing; but the choice is easier to think about clearly if the options differ only in the making/allowing way and also in some matter of degree—e.g. how many innocent people are killed.

In every such case, the neutrality of making/allowing implies that in theory the choice should depend purely on which upshot is worse—for example that it could be right to kill one innocent person if the alternative is that two such people die prematurely, or to kill ninety-nine to save a hundred. When the value difference between the atrocity and the alternative calamity is small enough, however, and especially when it is a small proportion of the (dis)value of either, this should amplify any doubts about whether those really are the only options. Even by the standards of 'neutrality', therefore, the chances of being right in practice are much smaller for a one-for-two atrocity than for a one-for-five one. That is one reason why crises are usually illustrated with cases where the imbalance is greater—killing one to save five, say. Increasing the imbalance also has the effect of widening the range of moralists who are challenged by crises, making trouble for those who hold that the moral status of (say) torturing a person differs, but only in degree, from that of allowing a person to suffer extreme pain. As long as making and allowing are, so to speak, in the pans of a single balance, there is the prospect of its being right to act atrociously.

Someone who accepts a strict absolutist moral principle must, I think, hold to something like the following. 'That it could never be right to ϕ is deeply axiomatic, and there can be no question of demanding its credentials. Analytically inclined moralists invite me to compare ϕing with other ways of behaving that differ from it in certain respects and are not absolutely forbidden, and to consider whether the differences should make that moral difference; but this is a misunderstanding of my moral position. The absolute wrongness of ϕing is not something that has to prove itself by withstanding that kind of scrutiny. If the latter leads people to think that it might sometimes be right to ϕ, that shows that analysis provides bad discovery conditions for moral truth [see Section 3 above].' Someone who takes this view for ϕ = torture, for instance, might resist analytic scrutiny at either of two points. He or she might hold that it is morally misleading to think of torturing as behaving in a manner that has, in a 'making' way,[2] the consequence that someone continuously or repeatedly suffers extreme pain, or that it's morally misleading to think analytically about the making/allowing distinction. The resistance, that is, could be to the intellectual moves that expose making/allowing as an ingredient in the notion of torture, or to the further moves that display what making/allowing ultimately amounts to. I am not sympathetic to this attitude in either of its versions, but, as I said in Section 3 where I first mentioned it, I have no arguments to bring against it.

53. Forms of Absolutism

Elizabeth Anscombe holds, for some values of ϕ, the strongest kind of absolutism—for instance that it could never be right to kill an innocent person. We might try to break her hold on that conviction by describing a possible context in which the Church of which she is a member is at risk for its very existence unless some innocent person is killed. However, she is defended in advance against that. For her, moral absolutism is a matter of obedience—'We have to fear God and keep his commandments, and calculate what is for the best only within the

---

[2] And a way that is direct rather than mediated (see Section 2 above); in this paragraph I allow making/allowing to stand in for direct/mediated as well.

limits of that obedience'—and that is made bearable by 'a definite faith in the divine promises, that makes us believe that the Church cannot fail'.[3] So if we ask 'How should we behave if the Church's failure were avoidable only through an atrocity?', she can answer that the question is improper because the Church cannot fail. That puts a stop to that line of argument, but there remain all the other kinds of calamity which seemingly could loom on one side of a crisis.

Those could be covered by a view in moral theology that went Anscombe's way and then on beyond her, as follows. For various values of ϕ God forbids us to ϕ, and we can rely upon him not to let obedience be too burdensome. For each forbidden value of ϕ he will set a limit to how bad things will become if we refuse to ϕ. If we believed in that limit (for whatever reason), that could help to make absolutism about ϕing reasonable *for us*, independently of God's commanding it. There would remain a question, though, about what could make absolutism reasonable *for God*. This is a non-issue for theologians who hold that all moral thinking must start from God's commands, which cannot themselves be evaluated. Others, however, think that God issues his prohibitions because they are right or reasonable in some manner that we could dimly understand; these are the theologians who think it worth while to support their moral positions with reasoning. Their view allows us to ask what reasons God could have for these absolute prohibitions; and it is hard to see how they can answer.

From now on, I shall take it that crises (always in my sense of the term) can occur. Even in a crisis, where a calamity could be averted only by doing something atrocious, Anscombe would say that the atrocity is wrong. According to a variant kind of absolutism, the atrocity might not be wrong but would not be right either. Charles Fried allows that there could be crises which challenged some seemingly absolute moral principle:

We can imagine extreme cases where killing an innocent person may save a whole nation. In such cases it seems fanatical to maintain the absoluteness of the judgment, to do right even if the heavens will in fact fall. And so the catastrophic may cause the absoluteness of right and wrong to yield, but even then it would be a non sequitur to argue (as consequentialists are fond of doing) that this proves that judgments of right and wrong are always a matter of degree, depending on the relative goods to be attained and harms to be avoided. I believe, on the contrary, that the concept of the catastrophic is a distinct concept just because it identifies the extreme situations in which the usual cate-

[3] G. E. M. Anscombe, 'War and Murder', 61.

gories of judgment (including the category of right and wrong) no longer apply.[4]

Fried is wrestling with a usually neglected problem. For a strict absolutist about φing, the wrongness of φing is basic and axiomatic; it stands immovably, with no risk of being eroded by thoughts of situations in which the only alternative to φing is dual-φing. For a near absolutist like Fried, on the other hand, the usual wrongness of φing may have to 'yield' in certain extreme circumstances, and this poses a threat. It starts to sound like this: 'Making/allowing makes only a moral difference of degree; because the difference is so large, an enormous imbalance the other way is needed to make φing permissible; but still, all of this is a matter of weighing one thing against another, and is nothing like absolutism'. That is what Fried is trying to head off in this passage, where he wants to show how the prohibition might have to 'yield' without being *outweighed*.

His solution to the difficulty is ingenious: Although *in extremis* the prohibition of φing may have to 'yield', it is not outweighed—does not enter into calculations involving 'a matter of degree'—because the 'yielding' is of a special kind. If the prohibition were merely outweighed, that would mean that φing is right or permissible in an extremity; but Fried holds not that φing is all right in such contexts but rather that in them 'the usual categories of judgment (including the category of right and wrong) no longer apply'. He writes later:

> I do not know . . . whether I would be willing to kill an innocent person to save the whole of humanity from excruciating suffering and death. There are boundaries to each of these concepts [of right and wrong], and the concepts themselves often become blurred, indeterminate, subject to judgments of prudence at those boundaries. We can accept this without at all concluding that therefore the concepts . . . are subject throughout to judgments of degree.[5]

Ingenious as this is, it is hard to accept. Granted, most of us are not armed to cope with crises: life has not required us to think about how we should act in them. If they make the concepts of right and wrong break down, however, such thinking is impossible for us: we cannot consider how we ought to behave in a crisis. Fried gives us no reason to believe this.

Bernard Williams describes a similar position, without quite adopting it. He merely reports that some people are 'prepared to take

---

[4] Charles Fried, *Right and Wrong*, 10.
[5] Ibid. 31. I have Fried's warrant for inserting '[of right and wrong]'.

seriously' someone whose position it is, which puts him at three removes from it; but in inviting us to think about the position he seems to take it seriously himself. It includes the idea that some states of affairs cannot be thought about morally, so that it is 'insane, if not merely frivolous' to try to think about how one should act in them. Setting aside the startling charge of insanity, which seems to come from word-play,[6] we are left with the sober claim that one cannot think morally about certain extreme states of affairs.

I want to say to Fried and to the person Williams describes: 'You agree that you could find yourself in a crisis. Once there, you would have to act somehow. How can there not be a question as to how you should act?' Williams's man replies that the contexts in question 'so transcend in enormity the human business of moral deliberation that from a moral point of view it cannot matter any more what happens'.[7] That, taken literally, is such an ugly answer to my question that I must suppose Williams means it some other way; but I do not know what that is. I do understand the thought: 'If things become as bad as that, I want out; I would kill myself rather than try to cope morally with such a choice'; but killing oneself is not dodging the question 'What am I to do?', but rather answering it decisively. Furthermore, it would take a strenuous moral solipsism to carry one from 'I shall kill myself' to 'It doesn't matter what else happens', as though what will not affect oneself does not matter.

Alan Donagan defends what he calls 'traditional morality', and carefully makes it stop short of the strongest absolutism (Anscombe) or the next strongest (Fried, Williams): 'In laying down that its precepts are to be observed no matter what the consequences, traditional morality does not imply that they are to be observed, let us say, if the consequences should be the death of everybody on earth.'[8] If the price of obedience to one of those 'precepts' should be a 'tragedy' such as the death of a whole community, we must pay, Donagan says; but if it would be a 'calamity' such as the death of all mankind, the precept no

---

[6] 'Rationality he sees as a demand not merely on him, but on the situations in, and about, which he has to think; unless the environment reveals minimum sanity, it is insanity to carry the decorum of sanity into it' (Bernard Williams, 'A Critique of Utilitarianism', 93).

[7] Ibid. 92.

[8] Alan Donagan, *Theory of Morality*, 206. Donagan distinguishes 'tragedy' from 'calamity' on the same page. I adopt his special sense of 'calamity' in this paragraph; but hereafter I shall revert to using it to stand for any terrible state of affairs that could be averted, in a crisis, by atrocious behaviour.

longer binds. Yet he usually sounds like an absolutist, and does not offer his concession about what he calls 'calamities' as really weakening the moral principles in question. He twice speaks of calamities as 'unforeseeable',[9] which suggests this: Traditional moral bans on atrocious behaviour, though obedience to them could lead to calamity, should be treated as absolute because we *could* never be rightly confident that the alternative is calamitous. Moore went even further in this same direction, but Donagan's view (if that *is* his view) is strong enough to be implausible. It is, I submit, clearly possible that we should rightly be sure that if we did not perform a certain atrocity a doomsday machine would be triggered, obliterating the human race—this being Donagan's one example of a calamity.

Anscombe has implied that crises of the sort I have been envisaging are unlikely to occur or to be known to have occurred.[10] That is of interest, though it has no bearing on any of the kinds of absolutism I have discussed. If it is true, that must bring comfort to both sides in the absolutism/relativism dispute, just because a crisis must distress each side: it would be dreadful to kill an innocent person, and dreadful to allow many to die. As a relativist on these matters (that is, someone who thinks that any kind of action could be right in some possible circumstances), I should like to believe that crises are virtually unthinkable—that they could not occur at any 'possible world of the sort with which common morality has to do',[11] and that examples of them are all 'fantastic'.[12] Unfortunately, it is not so. There is nothing fantastic about the range of examples, which I first learned from Anscombe in 1965, in which a man is stuck in a pot-hole and only by lethal means can be removed in time to save the people below him from drowning. Other dismayingly credible examples will be given later.

54. *Atrocity and Policy*

Stuart Hampshire has eloquently defended a position which sounds much more like absolutism than like anything that might be reached through attending to the nature and conceptual roles of the making/allowing distinction. Still, he stops short of the strongest kind

[9] Ibid. 201, 209; see also 207.
[10] G. E. M. Anscombe, 'Modern Moral Philosophy', 40 n.
[11] Donagan, *Theory of Morality*, 148; see also ibid. 35 f.
[12] G. E. M. Anscombe, 'Does Oxford Moral Philosophy Corrupt Youth?', 267.

of absolutism, and therefore needs to address the case where a near-absolutist prohibition yields to something stronger. What Hampshire says about this is different from the offerings of Fried and Donagan. It is also complex, elusive, and interesting.

Hampshire's cherishing of the language of absolutism might make one think that he would allow of no exceptions. He writes of 'things that cannot be done, or that must be done, and that are ruled out as impossible by the nature of the case', says that this modal language 'marks the unqualified, unweakened, barrier to action', and helpfully shows how 'must' contrasts with the weaker 'ought' in morality and elsewhere.[13] Despite the phrase 'unqualified barrier', though, Hampshire is careful to qualify. He speaks of 'moral prohibitions . . . which a man acknowledges and which he thinks of as more or less insurmountable, except in abnormal, painful, and improbable circumstances';[14] and he associates outrage with 'a sense that a barrier, assumed to be firm and almost insurmountable, has been knocked over'.[15] Repeatedly, he uses and stresses forceful absolutist language while stopping short of outright absolutism. Given that he concedes that an atrocity could be right, and implies that it could be known to be so, what sort of absolutist is Hampshire? *When a near-absolute prohibition rightly yields, according to him, is that because one value is outweighed by another?* If so, then for him making/allowing figures in mere moral balancing, and he is even further from absolutism than he seems to be. Here is Hampshire's answer to my question:

In the circumstances of conflict he has to make a choice, and to bring himself to do one of the normally forbidden things, in order to avoid doing the other. He may finally recognize one overriding necessity, even though he would not be ready to generalize it to other circumstances. The necessity that is associated with types of action—for example, not to betray one's friends—is absolute and unconditional, in the sense that it is not relative to, or conditional upon, some desirable external end; but it is exposed exceptionally to conflict with other necessities.[16]

So the prohibition on betraying one's friends can be made to yield not by its conflicting with 'some desirable external end' but by its conflicting with 'other necessities'; and this is evidently meant to imply that what is going on in these cases is not a matter of outweighing. But does it imply this? Since the 'other necessities' can be made to yield, they

---

[13] Stuart Hampshire, 'Morality and Pessimism', 88.   [14] Ibid. 87.
[15] Ibid. 89.   [16] Ibid. 93.

are not strictly necessities; so Hampshire really ought to say that when a nearly absolute prohibition is made to yield, that happens through a conflict with another nearly absolute prohibition. Any relativist might accept that much, I suggest. Relativists will agree that for an atrocity to be right the alternative must be a calamity of a sort that we are in general strenuously required to avoid—this being the sort of requirement that Hampshire might call a necessity.

Hampshire could disagree, however. Although he describes how bad life is for a community with no shared system of nearly absolute prohibitions, Hampshire denies that he is 'arguing for the truth of a doctrine by pointing to the evil consequences of its being disbelieved'.[17] The prohibitions are justified ultimately by their role in a chosen ideal 'way of life', he says, and such an ideal may be chosen for many different reasons, a prominent one being that 'a particular way of life . . . has in history appeared natural, and on the whole still feels natural, both to oneself and to others'.[18] That implies that even when one 'necessity' clashes with another, the deliberation that is called for does not involve balancing and weighing as these are ordinarily understood. This should not convince us, I suggest, until something is said about what such deliberation *does* involve.

A large part of Hampshire's position is something we might all accept. He wants to encourage the psychological attitudes of the absolutist; it is dangerous, he thinks, for us to be aware that behaviour which is ordinarily base and disgusting could sometimes be right. He associates 'morally impossible action' with 'a feeling that, if this horrible, or outrageous, or squalid, or brutal, action is possible, then anything is possible and nothing is forbidden, and all restraints are threatened'.[19] This can be understood in terms of Sidgwick's or Hare's two-level view of morality (see Section 7 above): in theory, atrocities would sometimes be right, but it will be better if in our everyday lives we think, feel, and behave as though they were absolutely barred. Once we allow for excusing circumstances, we risk looking for them too often and 'finding' them when they do not exist.

This is probably true in general. We have sad evidence of its truth when governments do not subject themselves to quasi-absolutist constraints: at that level, arguments about ends justifying means seem often to be profoundly corrupt. It does not follow, however, that ends cannot justify atrocious means—merely that it is dangerous to think, in a practical way, that they can. That, however, does not mean that it is dangerous to hold this opinion as a matter of moral theory. The view that it *is* is implicit in a famous remark of Anscombe's: 'If someone really thinks, *in advance*, that it is open to question whether such an action as procuring the judicial execution of the innocent should be quite excluded from consideration—I do not want to argue with him; he shows a corrupt mind.'[20] This infers corruption purely from the person's having a certain moral opinion, irrespective of his reasons for it or its effects on the rest of his life. The accompanying refusal to 'argue', which includes a refusal to listen to opposing reasons, is disconcerting when it comes from a philosopher.

It would be comforting to agree with Hampshire about the dangers of thinking and feeling like a relativist in everyday life; but this comfort should not be gained on the cheap. There are atrocious kinds of behaviour which we could safely entertain under some circumstances. Consider the following crisis: Several people are dying for want of suitable organs to be transplanted into them, all the needed organs could be provided by a single healthy person who has nothing to do with them except that he is tissue-compatible, and there is no other source for the organs. In such a case, all that is needed to save several lives is that one innocent person be murdered and organs transplanted. Given our society and law as at present organized, such a murder would be profoundly wrong; but on relativist principles it might be justified as a matter of moral theory, if the social surroundings were appropriate. John Harris has persuasively described a society in which such murders are accepted policy.[21] It would be a kind of lottery, in which reasonable people would accept a small chance of being sacrificed, in return for a larger one of being saved through the sacrifice of someone else. Victims would not be suddenly pounced on; rather, the computer program that selected them would send advance warnings of increasing probability of selection, so that the deaths of organ providers would be heralded about as gradually and uncertainly as are, now, the deaths of people whose organs fail.

This 'survival lottery' would have to exclude people who have damaged their bodies through tobacco or other drugs, obesity, lack of exercise, and so on. If they were included, they would for obvious reasons have too much chance of gain and too little of loss; and excluding them, Harris acknowledges, would raise hard criterial problems. Peter Singer

[20] Anscombe, 'Modern Moral Philosophy', 40.
[21] John Harris, 'The Survival Lottery'.

holds these to be insoluble, and says that there would never be a good relativist case for instituting the survival lottery.[22] Well, maybe, but let us suppose a society all of whose members eat properly, exercise regularly, and do not take harmful drugs: might the survival lottery be a good idea in that society? Relativists ought to say Yes—unless their view of the making/allowing distinction leads them to reject the survival lottery on the grounds that no one sacrifice would save *enough* lives.

I have found that some people object to the survival lottery—and to relativism in general—on prudential grounds. In a world that is dangerous enough anyway, they feel, relativist policies would expose us to the further threat of being harmed by do-gooders trying to avert something worse. The fear that the do-gooders might make mistakes is reasonable; but that is a practical matter, which leaves the theoretical issue untouched, as can be seen from its irrelevance to a well-run survival lottery. A five-for-one version of the latter would give you an *n* per cent chance of being killed as a donor, and a 5*n* per cent chance of having your life saved as a recipient. People who see the lottery as risky, in face of the plain facts about the odds, are probably manifesting what T. M. Scanlon, in an illuminating phrase, has called 'the bias of the lucky against the unlucky'.[23] Many of us do tend to count ourselves among the lucky so far as life-threatening illnesses are concerned, and therefore to view the survival lottery and its like as a threat to 'us' in the interests of 'them'. This is obviously irrational; in the relevant sense there are no lucky or unlucky people.

The survival lottery is a good example of what emerges from thinking of such crises in terms of two kinds of relevance of conduct to upshot. 'Just so!' an objector may say. 'If on one side of a crisis Agent murders someone, while on the other he does not, it is obvious which way he ought to go. Your use of technical, abstract, humanly empty terms such as "kind of relevance of conduct to upshot" is a distraction, leading our thoughts away from the reality of one person's killing another. Your comparisons of the values of consequential states of affairs is a smoke-screen that blocks us from seeing what really counts, the act itself.' That is a paradigm of what I am opposing in this book. Where this objector says that I am *disguising* the reality, I claim to be *clarifying* it. The objector may reply that in clarifying it I am distorting our moral vision. I do not accept this, but I have no arguments against it.

---

[22] Peter Singer, 'Utility and the Survival Lottery'.
[23] T. M. Scanlon, 'Rights, Goals and Fairness', 109.

55. *Absolutism and Moral Character*

Absolutists sometimes connect this opinion of theirs with moral character. Laurence Thomas argues convincingly that people of good moral character have held sharply opposing views in moral theory, but he adds something that absolutists might exploit: 'A moral theory has to yield terrible consequences in a quite systematic way before we are inclined to think that only those of bad moral character could subscribe to it.'[24] Some absolutists would hold that anyone who cleared his mind and remained a relativist would be assenting to 'terrible consequences' and would thereby stand convicted of being a bad person.[25] When I apply this to myself as a relativist, I do not agree, but I see what they mean.

I would love to take an absolutist view of certain kinds of behaviour— e.g. of killing innocent people, and of torture. The thought of torturing someone appals me, and it would be comforting to think: 'That is ruled out absolutely, always, in all possible circumstances'. It would be naïve to deny that I could become so corrupted that I could calmly torture someone; but I tame that frightening thought by disowning the corrupted *me* in question. That defence is not available against the idea that for myself as I am, with the character and values that I now have, the role of torturer is a possibility. Absolutism about torture would shield me against that, and I wish I could call upon it to do so. When I think clearly about crises, however, I cannot bring myself to wear that shield; I cannot accept absolutism about any kind of behaviour, such as torture or killing the innocent, that is defined in non-moral terms and without mention of overall consequences of the behaviour and of alternatives to it. I hate this relativist position of mine, and would rid myself of it if I could honestly do so.

Whether that clears my character of opprobrium, at least as far as this topic is concerned, may depend on whether in a crisis I could live up to my relativist convictions. I am not sure that I could. Some philosophers say that no really good person could do so, and that is credible. In judging someone to be a good person, we go partly by what moral principles he accepts, more by whether he abides by those principles in

---

[24] Laurence Thomas, *Living Morally*, 8.

[25] I distinguish this from the random libels that have, perhaps without much thought, been aimed at relativists and 'consequentialists': they do not attach fundamental value to truth (Fried, *Right and Wrong*, 62), they value survival above honour (Donagan, *Theory of Morality*, 183), they regard the sincere moral scruples of others as mere squeamishness (Williams, 'A Critique of Utilitarianism', 102–4).

his everyday life, and perhaps more still by facts about things he does, without thought of morality, because they present themselves to him as natural, inevitable, unquestionably to-be-done; and it may be that the only people who would strike us as being thoroughly good are ones who would be quite unable to behave atrociously in a crisis. But what has that to do with the issue in moral theory? One's answer to this will depend on where personal goodness fits into one's moral scheme of things, and on that there is a spectrum of opinion. Near one extreme: The thought of how a good person would act is the basis for all moral thinking. Near the middle: The 'good person' thought deserves an equal billing with anything else that might be brought to bear in theorizing about morality; as in James Cargile's view that it is 'confusing' to consider whether it would be right to do something that no good person could do.[26] The truth, I believe, is out near the other extreme: The concept of a morally good person belongs to the superstructure of our moral thought, not to its foundations. That does not mean that it is unimportant. We have reason to be glad that there are good people, and to fear bad ones; but good people have no authority on the morality of hard cases, and moral principles are not be fixed or defined in terms of them.

The concept of moral character is buried away in something else that is sometimes urged in defence of absolutism, namely that it is required by a certain kind of attitude to other people. Donagan, for instance, holds that 'unconditional prohibitions of certain kinds of action' are a necessary feature of 'any member of the class of deontological systems in which the sole fundamental principle ordains respect for beings of a certain kind'.[27] He adds, mildly, that he does not think his opponents (he names me) 'would maintain that members of that class are as such irrational'. Well, 'irrational' is too abrasive, but it is not entirely wrong. Donagan has to understand 'respect' asymmetrically along the making/allowing axis; the demand for respect has to forbid killing not just more strenuously than it forbids letting die but in a quite different way. If we cannot see how making/allowing can have so much power, we should conclude that a morality founded on a demand for such respect cannot withstand scrutiny. All that remains is the rejoinder that *scrutiny* as I understand it is irrelevant (or worse) as an aid to moral inquiry.

A related line of thought has been offered by Nagel. He aims it at

---

[26] James T. Cargile, 'On Consequentialism'. For a criticism, see R. G. Frey, 'What a Good Man can Bring himself to Do'.
[27] Donagan, *Theory of Morality*, 158.

crises of a kind I shall discuss in Section 57 below—ones where Agent must choose between atrocious behaviour and allowing someone else to bring about a calamity—but his general point goes beyond those confines:

> Faced with the question whether to murder one to save five from murder, one may be convinced that fewer people will be murdered if one does it; but one would thereby be accepting the principle that anyone is legitimately murderable, given the right circumstances. This is a subtle but definite alteration for the worse in *everyone's* moral status. Whereas if one refuses, one is saying that all murders are illegitimate, including of course the five that one will have refused to prevent.[28]

That is one way of putting it. Here is another:

> If one does it, one is saying that people are legitimately rescuable by murder from murder; if one refuses, one is accepting the principle that nobody is legitimately rescuable by murder from murder, which makes a subtle but definite difference for the worse in everyone's moral status.

What could justify Nagel's claim over that mirror image of it? He does not say; but he acknowledges Frances Kamm as the source of his 'status' idea, and she has subsequently developed it on her own account.[29] She writes about how the 'constraints' that she defends make us morally 'inviolable' in a certain way, show us to be 'important', defend us against 'disrespect', and testify to our 'significance', 'dignity', and 'status'. Eventually she asks: 'Why is one not a less significant creature because one is not the sort for whose sake one may permissibly violate others?' That was my question. Declaring it to be 'difficult', Kamm addresses it as follows (the wording is mostly mine). The moral status of all human beings is the same. Any rise in status that we might all get from being creatures who are helpable by violating others has to be matched against the lowering of our status that comes from our being violable in the interests of others; and *the lowering would be greater than the rise*, or, as Kamm says, the latter kind of status is 'more important' than the former. That is all Kamm offers us. It is what the 'why?'-question was concerned with; it raises the question; it does not answer it.

---

[28] Thomas Nagel, *Equality and Partiality*, 148.

[29] Frances Myrna Kamm, 'Non-consequentialism, the Person as an End-in-Itself, and the Significance of Status', esp. 386–9.

56. Comparative Value of Upshots

In discussing this issue in terms of cases where the only alternative to Agent's killing one innocent person is the premature deaths of several, philosophers have assumed that when it comes to the avoidable death of innocent people, one is not as bad as several. This has been denied, sometimes on the grounds that the disvalues of One and Several are equal because each is infinite. Grisez and Shaw write that if absolutism is rejected, 'it would then make no sense to speak of the "infinite value" of the human person. Far from being infinite, the value of a person would be quite specific and quantifiable, something to be weighed calculatingly in the balance against other values.'[30] The analogy is with transfinite arithmetic: if set S_1 contains infinitely many members, then set S_2, which contains all those plus one more, has exactly the same number of members as S_1 does. Once you have infinity you cannot get a higher number by adding or multiplying. This enables those philosophers to say that since One is infinitely bad, Several is not worse; and since it is not better either, the disvalues are equal. The protest 'They cannot be equal if one includes all the bad of the other and some more' is not valid. It is like 'There cannot be as many even positive numbers as there are positive numbers'—a natural thing to say, but known to be wrong.

Could anybody really abide by this position? It implies that the first time something as bad as One occurred, the universe thereby became infinitely bad—and thus as bad as it could be—so that no later events could make it worse. The equality theorist has to say that as the serial murderer dispatches his successive victims things are not worsening. The analogy with transfinite arithmetic, I suggest, has got out of hand. Without it, however, it seems quite absurd to say that One and Several are equally bad.

It might be held that Several is not worse than One because their values are not comparable: neither is worse than the other, and they are not equally bad either. Grisez and Shaw offer this too:

Human life [should be] regarded not as a concrete, specific, essentially quantifiable object but as a good in which each person participates but which none exhausts or sums up in himself. In such a view of reality it is simply not possible to make the sort of calculation which weighs lives against each other . . .

[30] Germain Grisez and Russell Shaw, *Beyond the New Morality*, 131.

and thus determines whose life shall be respected and whose sacrificed. The value of life, each human life, is incalculable, not in any merely poetic sense but simply because it is something not susceptible to calculation, measurement, weighing, and balancing.[31]

We are told that 'the value of each human life is not susceptible to balancing', which must mean that two lives are not together more valuable than one. This would hold not only in crises but also in triage problems. If a medical resource could save this one person or those two who are equally threatened but more easily savable, most of us would think it right to give it to the two, other things being equal. Opponents of 'balancing' cannot agree with this, or anyway not for our reason, namely that the survival of two is better than the survival of only one. I am not alone in being puzzled that anyone should adopt such a view.

If the one is not one of the two—if, that is, it is a question of saving either James or both John and Andrew—there might be a problem about comparability. To know that the premature death of both John and Andrew would be worse than that of James one must know some details. For example, we need to know that this is not the case: James is 15 years old, healthy, talented, decent, and full of promise, while John and Andrew are terminally ill nonagenarians. The possibility of cases like that, however, does not secure the position that I have been discussing, according to which comparisons based on numbers of lives never make a moral difference.

Faced with a crisis, anyone might naturally feel that in being asked to compare those upshots she is being overloaded, required to make a decision that is too big, asked to play God; and this feeling might be expressed by saying that the comparison cannot be made. Still, the person on the spot *will* choose one option or the other: she will perform the atrocity or she will allow the calamity to occur; a crisis (in my sense) is so structured that the protagonist cannot avoid doing one or the other. The requirement to play God comes from the objective set-up, not from any moral opinion about it. That anyone should have to face such a choice is terribly unfair; this is an unfair world; but that has no bearing on moral theory.

Philippa Foot has attacked relativism's value comparisons more radically, by challenging the values that are supposed to be compared. She means this to undermine the broad kind of utilitarianism that is often

---

[31] Germain Grisez and Russell Shaw, *Beyond the New Morality*, 132. For something similar, see John Taurek, 'Should the Numbers Count?'

called 'consequentialism', including its welfare demands on us; but most of her paper is concerned with the other flank on which it seems vulnerable, namely relativism about atrocious behaviour in crises, according to which any kind of atrocity could be right in some possible circumstances. She announces herself as struck, as anyone must be, by how one is drawn towards the basic utilitarian idea yet repelled by what it seems to imply about atrocious behaviour in crises. She claims to release this tension by exposing as spurious the supposed notion of 'better state of affairs' upon which utilitarianism, and thus relativism, depends:

Must it not be irrational to prefer the worse to the better state of affairs? This thought does indeed seem compelling. And yet it leads to an apparently unacceptable conclusion about what it is right to do. So we ought . . . to wonder whether we have not gone wrong somewhere. . . . We go wrong in accepting the idea that there *are* better and worse states of affairs in the sense that consequentialism [= relativism] requires.[32]

If the concept of an interpersonally good state of affairs were all right, Foot seems to hold, relativism would carry the day. We are saved by the fact that there is no such concept.

She allows two basic uses of value terms. The propriety of 'good hiking-boot' or 'bad radio' obviously does not help with 'good state of affairs'. The other use that she recognizes is speaker-relative: Rain starts falling and I say 'That's good' while you think 'That's bad', because I want my vegetables to grow and you want a picnic. Our attitudes conflict, but we are not attributing different values to the rain. I mean that rain's falling is good from my point of view, you that it is bad from yours, and we are both right. States of affairs may be called good or bad in this way, but those evaluations, being subjective, are not what relativism needs.

That is all, Foot says. We have no legitimate uses of value terms that are neither subjective nor relative to purposes. She acknowledges that it is sometimes plausible to say that a state of affairs is dead good or dead bad,[33] as distinct from good for me or bad for you:

---

[32] Philippa Foot, 'Utilitarianism and the Virtues', 198 f.

[33] 'For the human system whiskey is truly more intoxicating than coffee . . . but what a strange way of vindicating this real, though relative distinction, to insist that whiskey is more intoxicating in itself, without reference to any animal; that it is pervaded, as it were, by an inherent intoxication, and stands dead drunk in its bottle! Yet just in this way Mr Russell and Mr Moore conceive things to be dead good and dead bad' (George Santayana, 'The Philosophy of Bertrand Russell', 146).

[It] seems preposterous . . . to deny that there are some things that a moral person must want and aim at in so far as he is a moral person and that he will count it 'a good thing' when these things happen and 'a good state of affairs' either when they are happening or when things are disposed in their favour. For surely he must want others to be happy. To deny this would be to deny that benevolence is a virtue—and who wants to deny that?[34]

The last sentence is crucial. According to Foot, our sense of 'good state of affairs' comes from our sense of what it is to be benevolent, of what kinds of states of affairs that virtue will lead us to promote. This is not an independently grounded concept of 'good state of affairs': when it is properly reined in, it extends only as far as benevolence goes.

That enables Foot to explain the pull of utilitarianism, and to allow it to draw her a certain distance, stopping short of crises. She goes with it just so far as benevolence speaks for it; but that is only one virtue; there are others, including justice; and there is no question of someone's being led *by benevolence* to behave unjustly—that is not how the virtues are related. Is it better that few innocent people die prematurely than that many do so? Foot writes: 'If it were a question of riding out to rescue a small number or a large number then benevolence would, we may suppose, urge that the larger number be saved. But if it is a matter of preventing the killing *by* killing (or conniving at a killing) the case will be quite different.'[35] One might object: 'In such a case benevolence *does* prima facie urge the behaviour that Foot condemns; it is just not true that benevolence is silent here.' Foot could accept this, and reply that killing an innocent person would be unjust, and that justice outranks benevolence. Her overall position, I think, could be based on limits to what the various virtues demand *or* on a ranking among them. Either way, the position is ingenious; but there are two points at which it seems weak.

(1) It relies on the thesis that evaluations of states of affairs are parasitic on thoughts about benevolence. What is Foot's basis for this? It seems to be the claim that the concept *good state of affairs* cannot be swallowed whole; it needs to be explained somehow; and hers is the only or the best explanation. That last clause is doubtful. Even granting that the concept must be explained in terms of propositions about kinds of people, Foot's is not the only way to do this. Instead of equating '*x* is a better state of affairs than *y*' with 'A benevolent person would seek to produce *x* rather than *y*', we might, in words that Foot herself

[34] Foot, 'Utilitarianism and the Virtues', 204.   [35] Ibid. 206.

uses, equate it with 'A moral person would want x rather than y to be the case'. Many of the resistance cell would be arrested, tortured, and killed unless a captured Gestapo agent was made to talk, which would require torture. Pierre was not there at the time, but he knew what was at stake. Without any thoughts about benevolence, he hoped that the man was tortured into revealing what he knew, welcomed the news that this is what happened, preferred this to the torture of the resistance fighters. Foot may say 'He ought not to have welcomed it, because torturing the man would be wicked', but she needs a fresh reason for saying so. The shape of benevolence will not help. Or she may say that the explanation in terms of benevolence is better than mine. That too needs support. Foot uses both explanations, as though they were equivalent; given that they are not, we need reasons for preferring one to the other.

(2) Foot proposes a morality which guides our conduct by reference to the virtues, which she takes to be asymmetric along the making/allowing axis. This asymmetry comes mainly from *justice*, which prohibits ϕing but does not prohibit dual-ϕing for some values of ϕ. (See Section 27 for a reminder of what dual-ϕing is.) This morality, then, gives a fundamental structural role to the difference between making and allowing, and we are entitled to ask why. This is not to ask why justice is making/allowing asymmetrical; that might be a feature of the concept of justice about which nothing much can be said. Rather, it is to ask: Given that justice is asymmetrical, why should first-order morality be dictated by it rather than its symmetrical analogue, that is, something that equally condemns killing an innocent person and not saving an innocent person from being killed?[36]

57. *Other Agents*

Much of the 'atrocities' debate is focused on crises in which Agent must choose between atrocity and calamity because of the behaviour or dispositions of someone else, whom I shall refer to as 'the Other'. Some philosophers think that this feature makes a moral difference, but it is not clear why.

To consider the issue, we need a taxonomy of kinds of case. One division is into (1) cases where the Other is a link between Agent's not ϕing

[36] For a different kind of agent-relativity, which is also supposed to bear on the problem of atrocities in crises, see Amartya Sen, 'Rights and Agency', and 'Evaluator Relativity and Consequential Evaluation'.

and the calamity and (2) cases where the Other is merely a scene-setter. In (1), if Agent does not (atrociously) φ, that will lead to the Other's producing a calamity. For example, if Agent does not turn on the warning light (thereby electrocuting his assistant, who is mending it) the Other will continue driving his train along the main line to a place where it will hit a stalled bus full of children. If the train hits the bus, Agent's behaviour is relevant in a mediated way to the Other's conduct (see Section 2 above). In (2), the Other has so organized things that if Agent does not φ, that will—unaided—lead to a calamity. For example, the Other sets the train running down the hill, so that the only way it can be diverted from hitting the bus is by Agent's throwing a switch, thereby crushing the fingers of his assistant, who is trying to mend it. If the train hits the bus this time, the behaviour of the Other and of Agent are both relevant, but the latter's relevance does not run through the former's. (On the left of the making/allowing line, the difference between links and scene-setters affects whether Agent φs or not—where 'φ' stands for 'wreck the bus', 'kill the children', or whatever; see Section 2 above. Just now, though, we are on the right of that line, so that there is in any case no question of Agent's φing.)

There are many frames of mind in which the Other, whether scene-setter or link, might make the crisis exist; but let us attend to one line through them. On one side of it, the Other is *coercive*. In creating the crisis, the Other is motivated by some interest in Agent's φing: he wants Agent to φ, or wants to test whether he will φ, or wants to make him agonize over whether to φ, or the like. In *non-coercive* frames of mind the Other is not motivated in any such way. That leaves room for great variety. The Other may be trying to bring about the calamity, not knowing that an atrocity could head it off, or knowing that it could and hoping it won't. Or he may not realize that he is making a calamity likely—for instance the train driver heading towards the bus. All the varieties of malevolence and innocence can be combined with either role—that of the link and that of the scene-setter. Devising examples of each pairing is left as an exercise for the reader.

Now, some people think that how Agent should behave in a crisis depends on whether the critical conditionals—*If no atrocity, calamity* and *If atrocity, no calamity*—are made true by another person. I can think of three reasons they might give for this.

(1) The first applies only to links, whether malevolent or not. The crisis exists for Agent only if he is morally sure of the critical condi-

tionals; and he might think that he is not entitled to be so sure. It is not safe to perform an atrocity on the strength of a prediction about something as uncertain and variable as human behaviour.[37] There is something in this, but not much, because people are in fact all too predictable across much of their behavioural range. A coercive crisis-maker might often have uttered such threats and always kept his word; and we might have a psychiatric understanding of why. An innocent one might be going about his business in an utterly predictable way. The claim that one should not be morally confident about the behaviour of others is too weakly supported to imply anything for moral theory.

(2) The second reason applies to coercive crises, whether with scene-setters or links. A case can be made against the atrocity, in most such cases, on the grounds that compliance with threats is bad policy. The readier we are to forestall calamity by performing an atrocity, the more likely it is that we shall be threatened again. If we all handle problems like this by performing the less bad atrocity so that the Other won't bring about the still worse calamity, we increase the chance of receiving more such threats in the future.[38] This is a sound point, which relativists should accept—as a truth about policy, however, not moral theory.

(3) The third reason pertains to crisis-makers who are malevolent even if not coercive, whether scene-setters or links. If Agent refuses to perform the atrocity, and the Other brings the calamity about, it will be the Other who is primarily and centrally to blame; and this result in second-order morality points to the first-order conclusion that it was morally all right for Agent to behave as he did. This is wrong, however. Even if the Other is as thoroughly to blame as anyone could be, it does not follow that Agent is not to blame also. A man has been executed for making a bomb that a second used to blow up an aeroplane; we would condemn a third who sold explosives to the bomb-maker for that purpose; and so on back down the line. My point is not legal but moral: we do not automatically blame someone less severely for an outcome just because we also blame someone else for it. Moral discredit is neither an indivisible atom nor an exhaustible quantum.

---

[37] See e.g. Donagan, *Theory of Morality*, 181, 207.
[38] For an extravagant version of this point see Donagan, *Theory of Morality*, 181. Bernard Williams, *Morality*, 104 f., *seems* to point the same way, but the passage is obscure. Its likening of coercive crises to the so-called Prisoners' Dilemma is especially puzzling.

Our attitude to the two villainous bombers makes the general point that blame can increase by being divided; but Agent is not a villain, and that may make a difference. Suppose that Agent refuses to φ, profoundly regretting that this will lead to the Other's doing something vile—in *this* situation cannot our blame for the Other serve to clear Agent from discredit? To make this plausible, we have to think of Agent, the Other, and the rest of us as morally competent members of one community. In our group what do we want to say, and to whom? Shall we round on Agent, criticizing him for not φing when he knew that only this would prevent the calamity? This seems inappropriate, because it treats the Other as machinery, a feature of the landscape, something to be reckoned with, steered around, predicted, and not as a real person who is there in front of us, vastly more in the wrong and a fit target of our moral wrath.

When Agent confronts the practical problem, however, he is on his own: he must act here and now, in the light of how things—including the Other—are hooked up in the world outside him. Agent's feelings about the Other, and his thoughts about how their shared community will feel about each of them, have no bearing on this practical problem. What matters is that the critical conditionals are true; something may later be made of the reasons for their truth, their roots in the Other's past behaviour or present dispositions; but here, on the spot, what counts is the biconditional itself: Calamity if and only if no atrocity.

58. Their Projects

The philosopher who has most emphatically claimed moral importance for the role of the Other is Bernard Williams. The emphasis seems irresistible when it is said to come from 'the idea . . . that each of us is specially responsible for what *he* does, rather than for what other people do'.[39] This is too easy, though. No moral theory denies that I am especially responsible for what I do, and Williams cannot mean to imply otherwise. He means, I suppose, to contrast my doing things with my not preventing you from doing things. Within a concern for what I allow to happen, or could but do not prevent, he wants us to attend to cases where what I do not prevent is voluntary behaviour by someone else. There is a discussable idea here, but when stated accurately it seems less glaringly obvious.

[39] Williams, 'A Critique of Utilitarianism', 99.

Williams emphasizes the Other when he discusses his famous story about a captain of gendarmes who convincingly threatens to have twenty innocent people killed unless Agent kills one. Some moralists think it is 'obviously' right for Agent to kill the one, Williams says, because they have not 'taken seriously' some aspects of the scene that count the other way—not decisively, perhaps, but strongly enough to make the decision hard.

(One of these can be parenthetically got out of the way. If Agent sincerely believes that he ought not to kill the one, his 'integrity' is at issue, Williams says, and utilitarianism is wrong to brush this conviction aside as mere squeamishness.[40] Williams is here unfair to his opponents; but anyway the point is irrelevant to our problem. Agent is a stand-in for us; we are asking what we ought to do in a crisis; and it is irrelevant to bring in a different Agent who already has his answer. Still, there is a relevant point about squeamishness that Williams could be making. Whatever Agent concludes about how he *ought* to behave, if he is decent he would find it horrible to shoot an innocent person, going clean contrary to the life he has tried to lead and the person he has tried to be. Thus to violate his deeply held working morality, at the bidding of a judgement from the critical level, would cost him more than a mere transitory unpleasant feeling. His sense of his own limits would be changed for ever, and his long-term memory would have an ugly intruder squatting immovably in the middle of it. If that is how things stand, then morality is demanding a vast sacrifice from Agent, and any weighing of profit against loss should fully take it into account.)

Williams subordinates the making/allowing distinction to the fact that if Agent does not kill the one, the twenty will die through the agency of someone else:

The distinction between action and inaction, between intervening and letting things take their course . . . is certainly of great moral significance, and indeed it is not easy to think of any moral outlook which could get along without making some use of it. . . . But I doubt whether the sort of dilemma we are considering is going to be resolved by a simple use of this distinction. . . . The distinction between my killing someone, and its coming about because of what I do that someone else kills them [is] based, not so much on the distinction between action and inaction, as on the distinction between my projects and someone else's projects.[41]

[40] Ibid. 102–4. Joel Kupperman, *Character*, 11 f., notes that 'integrity' in this sense raises quite different issues from wholeness along the time line, which Williams also calls 'integrity' (see Section 48 above).

[41] Williams, 'A Critique of Utilitarianism', 109, 117.

This brings in not only the Other but also his 'projects', which are also stressed here:

While the deaths, and the killing, may be an outcome of Agent's refusal, it is misleading to think, in such a case, of Agent having an *effect* on the world through the medium (as it happens) of the Other's acts; for this is to leave the Other out of the picture in his essential role of one who has intentions and projects, projects for realizing which Agent's refusal would leave an opportunity. Instead of thinking in terms of supposed effects of Agent's projects on the Other, it is more revealing to think in terms of the effects of the Other's projects on Agent's decision. This is the direction from which I want to criticize the notion of negative responsibility.[42]

What are the effects of the Other's projects on Agent's decision? Well, the Other's dispositions create Agent's crisis, by making true the conditionals *If no atrocity, calamity* and *If atrocity, no calamity*. Williams invites us to 'think in terms of' this fact, but he does not guide us in doing so. We will find it 'revealing' to approach the case in that way, he says, but he does not say or show how.

It is not clear how much weight Williams gives to the malevolence of the Other in his story, or how much it matters that the Other is a link rather than a scene-setter. When he writes of the Other's projects as having 'so structured the causal scene that' etc., and of the utility network 'which the projects of others have in part determined', he covers scene-setters generally. Usually, though, he seems to have links in mind: he writes of the significance of 'whether the causation of a given state of affairs lies through another [person] or not', and stresses that sometimes 'a vital link in the production of the eventual outcome is provided by someone else's doing something'.[43] If we knew whether to focus on the malevolence of the Other, and/or on his linking role, that might help us to know what Williams's view is. His emphasis on the Other's projects throws no light on either question. Such projects might be furthered as much by scene-setting as by linking; and they could be malevolent or innocent.

Anyway, what is the point about the Other's projects? We have seen how Williams connects projects with utilitarianism's demands (see Section 48 above); but that concerned Agent's projects, not an Other's, and it concerned help for the needy etc., not crises. The two areas have little in common, and the role that projects play in one does not help

---

[42] Williams, 'A Critique of Utilitarianism', 109. I substitute 'Agent' for 'Jim' and 'the Other' for 'Pedro' throughout.

[43] Ibid. 94.

us to give them work to do in the other.[44] If they matter to Williams's moral diagnosis of the crisis, he should care whether the offer 'Shoot this one or I'll have all twenty shot' comes from a mere passing whim, albeit an immovable one, or rather from an enduring project; but how would that difference affect the morality of what Agent does? If we are to understand that even a whim is a transitory project, then we can remove 'projects' from this discussion and take Williams to be emphasizing merely that the crisis results from the will of another person. That is where we started, however. The hope had been that by attending to projects we could get some understanding of *why* this makes such a moral difference.

In Williams's story, in short, Agent is faced with a choice between ϕing and not ϕing, in a context where if he does not ϕ his conduct (1) will be negatively or passively relevant to a calamity, because (2) another person makes the critical conditionals true, doing this (3) as a link between Agent and the calamity, (4) with malice aforethought, and (5) in the furtherance of a project. We need to be told which of these elements carries weight in Williams's moral estimate of how Agent should behave, and why.

One naturally has a sense of rebellious fury at the thought of being in a coercive crisis. Some foul person is trying to force me to act as though I were as wicked as he is: how can I not defy him? This understandable reaction does not tell Agent what to do. In this man-made crisis, he is hemmed in by a bad person, as good people sometimes are: if he ϕs he has been manipulated into terrible behaviour, but if he does not ϕ he has been manipulated into allowing results that are even worse. His inescapable status as victim comes not from his behaviour but from the world in which he finds himself. It may be replied: 'If he refuses to perform the atrocity, at least he has not been manipulated into *doing* anything bad, and that makes all the difference'. That takes us straight back to the making/allowing distinction, about which I have no more to say.

59. Deontology

The emphasis on other agents (never mind their projects) runs through a certain debate in current moral theory—a debate which is said to have

[44] As is pointed out by John Harris, 'Williams on Negative Responsibility and Integrity', 272 f.

'deontologists' on one side of it and 'consequentialists' on the other. The exact nature and location of the battle line between the two kinds of moral theory is a matter of debate, to which I have tried to contribute,[45] but I have had enough of that. The question of just what marks off moral theories properly called 'consequentialist' now strikes me as uninteresting. However, I have a little to say about deontology, the essence of which can be related to themes of this book, and especially of this chapter. I shall sketch the relations here, hoping thereby to illuminate the ways of moral thinking that are commonly called deontological.

Consider a state of affairs in which Agent is morally certain of the following:

> Victim, who is extremely conscientious in his work, is about to submit a report to his superiors which will lead them to instigate a course of events in which several people will be tortured. The only way to block this is to get Victim to turn in a false report: that would not do any great harm, and it would forestall the dreadful causal chain that a true report would start up; but there is no chance of convincing Victim of all this, and indeed the only way to get him to submit a false report is to coerce him through torture. Merely locking him up so that he submits no report will not suffice.

I want to contrast two fundamentally different approaches to this case. One is that of a morality M_c which is profoundly opposed to torture, enjoins us *so to act that there is as little torture as possible*, and therefore commands Agent to torture Victim. The other is that of a morality M_d which enjoins us *not to torture people*, and therefore commands Agent not to torture Victim. M_d is so-called because it exhibits the characteristic feature of moralities that are commonly called 'deontological'. I am not confining this to versions of it which are absolutist or nearly so; I want to take in any first-order morality which forbids torturing people in a different way, on a different basis, on the strength of different basic principles, from anything it says about trying to avoid situations in which people are tortured.

The contrast between M_d and M_c is often described in terms of the difference between the act itself and the consequences of the act, and this is reasonable when applied to the torture example. M_d says 'Do not

---

[45] Jonathan Bennett, 'Two Departures from Consequentialism'.

torture him' while M_c says 'Do not behave in a way that fails to mini-
mize torture', where that failure is a consequence of how Agent
behaves. What we cannot do, however, is to generalize from this example, characterizing M_d as a morality which in general focuses on the act
itself rather than the consequences of the act. The reason why that
won't do has been stated several times in this book: the only clear-cut
absolute use we have for 'the act itself' is to pick out movements people make, considering only their geometrical properties, because all
their other properties are relational. (Well, perhaps things are not quite
as bad as that. In the context of a contrast between 'the act itself' and
'the consequences of the act' we might allow the former phrase to bring
in not only the movement's intrinsic properties but also relational properties that do not involve causal consequences. That sounds promising
until we notice that it draws the line in some peculiar places—between
lying in the American Sign Language and lying in English, for instance.
In the ASL, the movements themselves bring falsity because of what
they mean, whereas in English what bears a meaning is the sound or
inscription which the movements cause.)

This trouble that 'the act itself' gets into disappears if the phrase is
understood in terms of specific kinds of acts that might be identified
through verb phrases such as 'torture someone', 'help a stranger',
'betray', 'lie', 'break a promise', and so on. When someone's conduct
falls under language like this, an act is performed; we can consider that
act, in itself, independently of what flows from it; and this does not confine us to how fingers move or larynxes vibrate. That is precisely what
happened when 'the act itself' was applied to the difference between M_d
and M_c in so far as it concerned the torture example. But now we are
back with the problem of whether, and how, we can make a general
statement about how moralities like M_d differ from ones like M_c.

We cannot do it like this: 'M_d is characteristically concerned with
kinds of act, while M_c is concerned with the bringing about of kinds of
states of affairs'. The trouble is that those two characterizations have a
vast area of overlap. An individual behavioural episode can be brought
under the 'act' language in many different ways; seldom is there one
line between what he did and what resulted from what he did; rather,
any line we draw is a creature of some choice of descriptive language.
What he did was to *close a gate*, with the result that traffic was stopped,
a collision was prevented, and a life was saved. This puts the fact that
the gate came to be closed on the act rather than the consequence
side of the line. On the other hand, what he did was to *extend his arm*

northwards, forcefully, parallel to the ground, with the result that the gate came to be closed, the traffic was stopped, etc.; and now the gate's closing is a consequence. Or we can go the other way: What he did was to *stop the traffic*, with the result that a collision was prevented etc.; and now the traffic's stopping is incorporated in the act. This distinction between act and consequence, though it slides, is real; and it has its uses. It lets us cleanly distinguish *Agent's φing* from *the consequences of his φing*, for particular values of φ. But it does not offer much promise that we can usefully characterize a whole moral approach by saying that it focuses on kinds of act rather than on consequential states of affairs. The real, robust behaviour/consequence distinction is always drawn relative to some verb phrase; we draw it on the basis of some prior way of conceptualizing the facts.

The best way to see deontological morality, I contend, is as presenting a list of kinds of behaviour, and saying something about the morality of behaving in one of those ways. Just as strict absolutism holds that for certain values of φ it could never be right to φ, so deontological morality holds that for certain values of φ there is something specially wrong about φing. Though less strong than absolutism, it shares a structural feature with it: each makes sense only as a moral doctrine about specified kinds of behaviour such as lying, killing the innocent, and so on; neither can be fully characterized in terms more abstract than that.

Deontological morality is something essentially conservative, inherited, tied to some received ways of looking at behaviour, rather than a product of high-level moral theory.[46] Attempts to defend it theoretically—usually worded as attacks on 'consequentialism'—focus on certain elements in the meanings of the verb phrases which are deontology's real core. The thread that runs through the meanings of most of those verb phrases are the ones I identified in Section 2 above: each phrase speaks of someone's moving in a manner that (1) has a certain consequence, (2) in a making rather than an allowing way, (3) directly rather than in a mediated way, and (4) not by an unstable causal chain. Of these, (1) and (4) are not relevant to the issue between consequentialism and deontological morality; our focus must be on (2) and (3)—making/allowing and direct/mediated.

The nearest thing we have, then, to a clean theoretic account of the nature of deontological morality is this: It is the doctrine that if Agent's

---

[46] One of the many merits of Hampshire's 'Morality and Pessimism', discussed in Section 54 above, is its openness about this.

ɸing has a bad consequence U, the relevance of that fact to the morality of U's ɸing—whether it counts at all, if so how much, and in what way—depends on whether Agent by ɸing would *make* U obtain, and on whether Agent's ɸing would bring about U *directly*, that is, not by a causal chain running through the will of someone else. Deontological moralists do not arrive at their position by reflecting on these two points, I think; rather, these are the theoretical points that they fall back on when their position is challenged.

11

INTENTIONS

60. *Intentions and First-Order Morality*

Some philosophers have thought that morality forbids some conduct for reasons having to do with the concept of intention. In many possible crises, performing the atrocity will involve not merely bringing about something terrible but *intending* to bring it about as a means to averting a calamity; and this 'intending as a means' is thought to make a big moral difference. There are sharp differences of opinion on this issue; properly to grapple with it, we need a good understanding of what it means to say 'Agent intends to bring it about that P'. I mean what he intends *in* or *by* φing; what he now intends (plans, purposes) to do later are irrelevant here.[1] So are problems about what intentions are: there may be no such items as intentions; and all my uses of that noun 'intention' could be replaced by uses of the verb 'intend'.

Statements about what Agent intends in φing can be explained in either of two ways. (1) When someone acts, she has beliefs about what states of affairs she is bringing about (causally or otherwise), and some of these will constitute her reason for acting. She thought that by wiping his brow she would make him feel better, and that she would make the handkerchief wet, but only the former belief helps to explain why she wiped his brow. That means that in wiping his brow she intended to make him feel better. (2) When someone acts, she has desires regarding what will result from her conduct, and some of these will help to explain her acting as she does. She wanted her wiping his brow to make him feel better, and she wanted it to make him grateful to her, but only the former desire helps to explain her wiping his brow. That means, again, that in wiping his brow she intended to make him feel better.

What a person intends in φing is defined, therefore, by which of her consequential beliefs explain her φing and by which of her desires do so. This is really a single story told in two ways: explaining behaviour

---

[1] On the difference, see John R. Searle, *Intentionality*, ch. 3.

in terms of cause–effect beliefs essentially involves explaining it also in terms of desires. Her belief that wiping his brow would make him feel better could not—except in a pathological way—explain her conduct unless his feeling better was something she wanted; and conversely.

How does the concept of intention figure in first-order morality? (1) Well, it might be thought to mark the latter's boundary, since first-order morality attends only to behaviour that is intentional or voluntary, not what happens under hypnosis, sleep-walking, epileptic fits, and the like. That is wrong, however, for there can be voluntary behaviour in which the person does not intend anything—as when you cross your legs without giving it a thought.[2] Voluntariness certainly is the frame for first-order morality, and need play no part within it, as Elizabeth Anscombe has pointed out: 'A rule as you consider it in deciding to obey or disobey it does not run: do not *voluntarily* do such-and-such, for you cannot consider whether to do such-and-such voluntarily or not. ... The voluntariness is presupposed in [the person's] *considering whether* to do [such-and-such]. Thus it does not come into his considerations of what to do.'[3] Now back to intentions, properly so-called. (2) First-order morality can take account of any facts about how the world is—including ones about what people did, do, will, or would intend. What I intended in turning in that report on your work may affect how I ought to behave towards you now. It may be wrong for me to φ because that would lead me, or lead you, to form certain intentions. This is plain sailing.

A question remains: Does first-order morality address the immediately future intentions of its adherents, telling them what they may or must intend, as it does how they may or must behave? I used confidently to answer No, but Michael Stocker and others have shown me that Yes could be right. My error was based on two truths: (1) What I intend in φing is defined by which of my beliefs and desires I am motivated by; and (2) I cannot turn beliefs or desires on and off at will. From these I inferred that (3) I cannot turn intentions on and off at will, which implies that (4) intentions are not under the command of first-order morality.[4] The wrong step is from (1) and (2) to (3). Although it does not make sense to forbid me to believe P and want Q, it does make sense to forbid me to act on this belief and desire.

² I was alerted to this point by Carl Ginet, *Action*, 3.

³ G. E. M. Anscombe, 'Two Kinds of Error in Action', 8.

⁴ Essentially this argument can be found in W. D. Ross, *The Right and the Good*, 4 f. For detailed discussion of it, see Michael Stocker, 'Intentions and Act Evaluations'.

If I cannot φ without intending Q, I am still free to obey 'Do not act intending Q!'—I obey this by not φing. What if my morality forbids me to intend Q and commands me to φ, and I cannot φ without that intention? Here is an example:

> In wartime a ship is torpedoed, there are survivors in the water, and there is a friendly cruiser nearby. Its captain knows where the opposing submarine is, and is sure that if it escapes it will kill thousands more sailors. To destroy it he must speed straight at it, thereby killing some of the survivors in the water. He could not bring himself to do that if it were not for the fact that he recognizes one of them as a personal enemy.

The captain might be morally required to go after the submarine, morally forbidden to do it in order to kill his enemy, and unable to do it except with that intention. Philosophy does not help with this problem. If a given morality requires from a person behaviour which he cannot produce except with a forbidden intention, the final judgement on what he ought to do can only come from the morality that creates the problem. This is like a case where your morality tells you to be truthful and to keep your promises, and you are in a fix where you cannot do both.

I conclude that a first-order morality could intelligibly use the concept of intention, though only in a manner that is limited in scope and indirect in effect. When that concept is placed at the centre of first-order morality, that is because the latter is not being properly distinguished from second-order.

61. The Principle of Double Effect

The moral view about intentions that I want to consider has come to the fore as part of a doctrine that was first explicitly formulated by Roman Catholic moral theorists in the nineteenth century—the principle of double effect. I shall say a little about this as a whole before turning to the part of it that is my chief concern. The principle is permissive. It permits certain conduct that predictably leads to bad results, if it also leads to good ones and the following are all true:

(1) The behaviour is not bad in itself.
(2) The agent's intentions are good.
(3) The good does not flow from the bad and/or the agent does not intend the bad as a means to the good.

(4) The good is good enough, compared with the bad, and there is no better route to the former.

The third condition is my main topic in this chapter.

The first condition is that the behaviour must not be bad in itself. My doubts about what this means have not been removed by fairly extensive reading of the literature. No behaviour is 'bad in itself' if that means 'bad for reasons that do not involve any of its relational properties'; for that would rule out only behaviour that involved bad trajectories of limbs or the like. (See Section 14.) So the first condition must rule out the behaviour's being bad or wrong because of its relational properties. That, however, is ambiguous. It could be ruling out behaviour that

(*a*) has some feature that counts towards its being wrong;
(*b*) is actually wrong in these particular circumstances;
(*c*) is of a kind that is always wrong.

(*a*) cannot be what is meant, because all the conduct to which the principle of double effect is relevant has the feature *causes something bad*, which counts towards its being wrong. Nor is (*b*) a possible reading. According to the principle of double effect it is wrong for me to φ in these circumstances if my φing would not satisfy all four conditions; if one of the four is that it is not wrong for me to φ, I am caught in an absurd circle. There remains only (*c*), which makes the first condition say: 'Nothing is permitted by this principle that conflicts with the absolute prohibitions laid down elsewhere in the moral system'. This is vacuous for anyone who is not a moral absolutist about some ways of behaving; for others, including many Roman Catholic moralists, it is a mere reminder of which part has primacy.[5] The second condition requires that the agent must not be seeking the bad for itself. Some quick visitors to these regions have taken it to concern what the agent intends as a means to the good, but that is wrong. It is about ends only, with intended means being a topic of the third condition. The second, then, merely rules out malevolence. The fourth condition has the effect—roughly speaking—of ensuring that the principle of double effect does not permit conduct that even relativism (so-called 'consequentialism') would condemn.

---

[5] Elizabeth Anscombe sees the principle of double effect as more intimately connected with absolutism than this, and not through its first condition. Puzzlingly, she depicts a person who accepts a moral injunction never to φ, and then begins to waver in his obedience to it, as being comforted and strengthened by the principle of double effect. G. E. M. Anscombe, 'War and Murder', 58.

I have stated the third condition as saying that the good state of affairs G must not flow from the bad one B *and/or* that the agent must not intend B as a means to G. First we must tighten up the indeterminacy of 'and/or'. I shall discuss it in terms of this example: *There is a terror raid, in which civilians are killed, which leads to a lowering of enemy morale, which increases the probability of the enemy's being defeated. The civilian deaths are on the causal path to the enemy defeat.* It is stipulated that the defeat of this enemy would be an enormously good thing, and of course that it is bad for civilians to die in war. Let us suppose that the leader of this raid expects it to kill civilians, and expects this to shorten the war, which is why he conducts the raid. We have, then, the objective fact: *The enemy's increased willingness to capitulate is a consequence of the deaths of civilians in the raid*, and the subjective fact: *The leader of the raid seeks the deaths of the civilians as a means to making the enemy more likely to capitulate*. The objective fact concerns a causal structure, the subjective one a frame of mind, specifically a fact about what someone intends as a means to something else.[6] The third condition of the principle of double effect is usually stated as prohibiting both of these: G must not be caused by B, and the agent must not intend B as a means to G. How are they supposed to be morally related to one another? There are three possible answers:

(*a*) The intention and the causal structure are both, independently, forbidden. Charles Curran takes the third condition in that way, alluding to a bad thing that must be 'neither directly intended nor directly done', and asking when one may 'directly kill the attacker both in the intentional and in the physical orders'.[7]

(*b*) The causal structure alone is forbidden. I do not know of any double effect theorist who has taken this view, though Frances Kamm has said something even stronger: 'It is permissible to cause harm to some in the course of achieving the greater good of saving a greater number of others from comparable harm, if . . . events which produce the greater good are at least as intimately causally related to the production of the greater good as they are to the production of the lesser harm.'[8] This, strangely, forbids acting in a manner that will lead to G through a long causal chain an early part of which launches a short side-

---

[6] Strictly speaking, it does not have to be causal: one might set out to kill all the villagers as a means to killing the guerrillas among them. See Thomas Nagel, 'War and Massacre', 61. In what follows I shall ignore this wrinkle.

[7] Charles E. Curran, *Ongoing Revision in Moral Theology*, 176 and 189.

[8] Frances Myrna Kamm, 'Harming Some to Save Others', 232.

chain leading to B.[9] My interest is in its less surprising prohibition of producing harm as a means to good, and its silence about intentions. Although it says nothing about intentions, the principle does constrain them. If you *obey* the injunction never to produce G out of B, you will think you are conforming to it; so you will not act believing that you are producing the sequence G through B or, therefore, intending to produce G through B. On this objective reading of it, therefore, the third condition says nothing about intentions yet has the effect of forbidding one to intend bad as a means to good.

On either of the readings (*a*) and (*b*) the third condition is quite implausible: there is no evident reason why a morality should forbid the G-from-B causal structure except for what it implies about intentions that may lie behind its production.[10]

(*c*) What is basically forbidden is the intention. To obey this is to avoid *acting in a way that one thinks will lead to the G-out-of-B causal structure, and being motivated to act by that belief*. This does not, even implicitly, forbid one to produce that structure. I could φ expecting this to lead through B to G but not being motivated to φ by that expectation. In that case, I would be knowingly producing the G-out-of-B structure but would not be infringing the third condition on our present reading of it. Here is a light-weight example which illustrates the structure that is involved here: I promote x (who is brilliant), intending by this means to make him happier and thus more likely to stay in the department; I expect this action also to have the effect of making y (who is competent) so despondent and angry that he will probably leave the profession altogether; that will take him out of the department, thereby contributing in a different way to x's contentment. The version of the third condition that we are now examining says that it may be morally all right for me to promote x knowing that this will contribute to his happiness through y's departure, but only if what motivates me is not that connection but something else.

I believe that double effect moralists have usually meant to focus on the subjective condition (*c*), and have not been clear in their minds about how if at all the objective condition (*b*) fits in. All the standard defences of the third condition address its subjective component, and statements of it put the emphasis there, sometimes omitting the objective side altogether. Here, for example: 'In waging a just war a nation

[9] For criticism, see Eric Rakowski, 'Taking and Saving Lives', 1084–90.
[10] For a good discussion, see R. G. Frey, 'Some Aspects of the Doctrine of Double Effect', 279–83.

may launch an air attack on an important military objective of the enemy even though a comparatively small number of noncombatants are killed . . . If the direct purpose of the attack were to kill a large number of noncombatants so that the morale of the enemy would be broken down . . . the attack would be sinful because the third condition would be broken.'[11] Jean-Pierre Gury's statement of the principle of double effect, which has been vastly influential in Roman Catholic moral theology, also focuses on its subjective part, saying that the reason for the third condition is that if it is infringed 'then good is being sought through bad' (*tunc bonum ex malo quaeritur*), which, he says with a reference to Romans 3: 8, is condemned by St Paul's injunction that we are not to do evil that good might arise.[12] The phrase 'sought through', like the Latin that it translates, involves the concept of intending something as a means. From now on, I shall be concerned only with the subjective clause in the third condition, assuming that it stands on its own feet; and I shall usually call it *the means principle*.

A word about history. Double effect moralists often refer to Romans 3: 8 and Romans 6; but these biblical passages, taken in context, do not condemn every intention to produce bad as a means to good. In 3: 8 Paul merely says that we ought not systematically to lie about God so as to get him to make our lies work to his greater glory. The second passage, read as the comment on chapter 5 which it explicitly is, has an equally limited scope. It is also wrong to bring Thomas Aquinas into the story. The expression 'double effect' comes from his discussion of ways in which you might kill an aggressor while defending your own life; but what he says about this is nothing like the third condition, and sounds more like the fourth.[13] Catholic scholars tend to agree these days that Thomas did not commit himself to the means principle.[14] The history of the principle of double effect, indeed, is clear only back into the nineteenth century.

---

[11] F. J. Connell, 'Double Effect, Principle of'. The contrast between small and large numbers of civilian deaths is a smoke-screen.

[12] Jean-Pierre Gury, *Compendium Theologiae Moralis*, 14.

[13] Thomas Aquinas, *Summa Theologiae*, II–II. 64. 7.

[14] For references and discussion, see Curran, *Ongoing Revision in Moral Theology*, 174–82; Daniel F. Montaldi, 'A Defense of St Thomas and the Principle of Double Effect'.

62. *Intentions as Explanatory*

In the terror bombing raid described above, the protagonist does something which he rightly expects to cause civilian deaths, and he is willing to do this as a price for shortening the war. Those two facts do not entail that he intends the deaths as a means to victory, however, for they also hold here:

> There is a tactical raid, in which a munitions factory is destroyed; this reduces the enemy's military capacity and thus increases the chance of his defeat, and it also inevitably leads to the deaths of civilians who live close to the factory. Here the civilian deaths are not on the path to the enemy defeat, but are a by-product of something on that path.

I stipulate that the protagonist in this raid believes the above account of what the raid will accomplish, and how, and is motivated to go through with it by that belief. So the terror bomber intends that civilians shall die while the tactical bomber does not: the latter expects them to die, but does not intend this to happen.

In saying that the tactical bomber does not intend the deaths, I am taking seriously the now common view that one's intentions in acting are defined by which of one's beliefs about consequences explain one's acting in that way. I have relied on this already in this chapter, but now it comes under the spotlight. It underlies this passage from a pioneer work:

If he is asked 'Why did you replenish the house water-supply with poisoned water?', his reply is, not 'To polish them off', but 'I didn't care about that, I wanted my pay and just did my usual job'. In that case, although he knows concerning an intentional act of his . . . that it is also an act of replenishing the house water-supply with poisoned water, it would be incorrect, by our criteria, to say that his act of replenishing the house water-supply with poisoned water was intentional.[15]

I prefer the idiom of 'he intended to bring it about that P' to that of 'his act of bringing it about that P was intentional' (see Section 9 above). With the main thrust, however, I agree: what someone intends to achieve by φing depends upon which of his beliefs about his φing's consequences explain his behaviour.

[15] G. E. M. Anscombe, *Intention*, 41 f. For development of this idea, see my *Linguistic Behaviour*, chs. 2 and 3.

If that is right, then the disclaimer 'When I φed I did not intend to make her angry' means 'It is not the case that my φing is explained by my expecting it to make her angry', which is equivalent to *Either (1) I did not expect her to become angry, or (2) I expected her to become angry but that does not explain my φing.* Yet people would often hear the disclaimer as tantamount to an assertion of (1) rather than of the weaker disjunction of (1) and (2). Is this evidence against the now standard view about what the disclaimer means? Yes, but the evidence is weak, and can easily be explained away, using the kind of pragmatics that I sketched in Section 42 above, which showed how a speaker can imply more than his sentence means. Alastair Norcross showed me how to explain it, as follows.

The disclaimer will be apt to occur in making excuses, which are ways to fend off anticipated criticisms. The usual criticism will be that the person behaved wrongly because he made her angry; the objection that he behaved wrongly because he was motivated by a desire to make her angry is a rather subtle and specialized affair that will not occur often. To meet the most likely criticism, therefore, the speaker needs (1) rather than the weaker disjunction of (1) with (2); so we 'hear' his sentence in that way, even though the disjunction is what it actually means. (That does not explain why someone who wants to communicate (1) should say something that means the disjunction of (1) with (2). If his aim is to disavow a certain expectation, why does he say 'I did not *intend* . . .'? I cannot explain this. It may be a mere verbal habit that has grown up accidentally, with no semantic principles behind it.)

Notice that the extra implication can be cancelled. It all happened long ago, and the speaker cannot remember whether he anticipated her anger; but he is quite sure that if he did, that is not what motivated him to act as he did. He, then, might say: 'I can't remember whether I expected her to become angry, but when I confronted her I did not *intend* to anger her'. That sounds like the disjunction of (1) with (2), and is evidence that that is what the original sentence conventionally means.

The linguistic fact that I have been explaining helped to make Sidgwick willing 'to include under the term "intention" all the consequences of an act that are foreseen as certain or probable'.[16] It may also underlie the refusal of English law to distinguish what an agent intends from what he confidently foresees.[17] But Sidgwick's position, and per-

---

[16] Henry Sidgwick, *Methods of Ethics*, 202.
[17] See Anthony Kenny, 'Intention and Purpose'.

haps the law's too, also reflects a moral view, as does Hector-Neri Castañeda's treatment: 'An action that one ponders and places as a side action in a plan leading to a goal action, is an action that one . . . *accepts* in spite of how painful it is, in order to attain that goal. This deliberate toleration is of the same family as the acceptance we call intending. It is harsh [*sic*] to cast a tolerated action aside and declare it nonintentional, just because it is not in the path of the goal.'[18] Castañeda seems to be expressing the view that there is no moral difference between intending and merely foreseeing a bad upshot. Of something that is foreseen but supposedly not intended, he says severely that 'The side action is considered by the agent, and his putting it in the [plan], with deliberation, does signify that it is not undesirable enough to lead him to the cancellation of the [plan].' That remark belongs to morality rather than meaning analysis. I urge that the two be kept apart. In taking the concept of intention to be essentially explanatory, and thus maintaining the intended/foreseen distinction, we do not give moral significance to the latter. We merely ensure that those who do give it significance will get their day in court and will be allowed to speak clearly.

63. Delimiting the Means: Acts and Events

Two matters of terminology should be cleared away before the discussion goes further. From now on, whenever I contrast 'intend' etc. with 'foresee' etc. I am contrasting what is intended as a means with what is foreseen as a by-product of one's means. This is mere shorthand. The second matter is more substantive. I have quoted both Curran and Connell using the terms 'direct' and 'indirect' in ways that are sadly typical of this literature. I shall explain now what is wrong with them, and choke back further comment when they are echoed by Warren Quinn in some important work of his that I shall discuss. In the double effect literature it is sometimes implied that the tactical bomber whom I described 'indirectly intends' the civilians to die. I reply that, given that he does not intend their deaths as an end or as a means, he does not intend them at all; and to say that he 'indirectly' (or 'obliquely') intends them is just to muddy the waters. Much worse than that, however, is the frequent assertion that the tactical bomber does

---

[18] Hector-Neri Castañeda, 'Intensionality and Identity in Human Action and Philosophical Method', 255.

not 'directly kill' the civilians. In any reasonable sense of the words, it would be hard to kill a person much more directly than by dropping a bomb on him! The idea that he does not directly kill the civilians sometimes leads on to the thought that he does not kill them at all, and this takes two equally absurd forms. In one, intended/foreseen is equated with making/allowing: the tactical bomber does not kill the civilians, but only allows them to die. In the other, intended/foreseen is aligned with action/consequence: he does not kill them, but only acts in a way that results in their dying. In the following excerpt from a published discussion of intended/foreseen (never mind what or whose), both of these absurdities occur and are treated as equivalent: 'I do not have a foolproof criterion for identifying the results we intend and distinguishing them from those we merely allow to happen, for distinguishing . . . between what one does to people and what happens to them as a result of what one does.' Now back to philosophy.

Means principle theorists sometimes judge cases differently because they do not draw the intended/foreseen line in the same place.[19] The latter disagreement reflects an underlying conceptual difficulty that can be seen in the following example. A nearly born child is blocked; its mother is near to death, and her heart cannot stand a Caesarian delivery; to extract the child, the surgeon crushes its head, thereby killing it. Did the child's dying lie within the scope of what the surgeon intended, or did he intend only to change the shape of its head, its death being a foreseen but unintended by-product? If the former, this operation is forbidden by the means principle; but if the death was not intended, the principle gets no grip. Means principle moralists are divided on this: most would condemn what this surgeon does, but a few would not. On the other hand, none would condemn the removal of a cancerous womb, even if the woman is pregnant and the hysterectomy would certainly be fatal to the foetus.

The root of the trouble is unclarity about how to distinguish what is a part of one's means from what results from one's means. Philippa Foot has suggested that those who condemn the head-crushing might say that the child's dying is 'much too close' to its head's being crushed to count as a mere result, and thus 'too close' for an intention to include one and exclude the other.[20] She remarks that they may 'have considerable difficulty in saying where the line is to be drawn' around what is

---

[19] For evidence see Albert Di Ianni, 'The Direct/Indirect Distinction in Morals'.

[20] Philippa Foot, 'The Problem of Abortion and the Doctrine of Double Effect', 268 f.

too close. As well as knowing where the line is, I would add, we need to know *what* it is. The metaphorical use of the word 'close' does not explain that. Fried uses a similar metaphor: 'One may always be able to designate some aspect of the result as the chosen means and another aspect as an undesired side-effect. And the gambit can be blocked only if we find some way of saying that certain consequences come in such tightly bound units that they may not be disaggregated.'[21] Indeed, we need a principled basis for distinguishing units that are invincibly 'tightly bound' together, or pairs of items that are 'too close' for the expect/intend line to fall between them.

We might look to the act concept for help. It is in general a clumsy device for saying what people intend (see Section 9 above); but two ways in which it might be thought to solve the 'too close' problem should be considered.

The first involves *identity of caused events*. The argument runs as follows. The collapse of the child's head is its death; these are two descriptions of a single event; so the surgeon cannot intend to bring about 'one' without intending to bring about 'the other'. In contrast with that, the surgeon who does the hysterectomy does not intend the death of the foetus, but only the removal of the uterus; that these really are two events is shown by their occurring at different times. Similarly with the tactical bombing raid: the destruction of the factory is a distinct event from the deaths of the civilians because they occur to different things and in slightly different places.

This approach had better not be based on the idea that intentions are directed towards particular events. My intention to make her angry did not consist in my relating in a certain way to her fit of anger; I could have had that intention and failed, in which case there would be no fit for me to relate to. Intending, believing, expecting, and the rest are *propositional* attitudes: each is reported in statements that relate a person to fully propositional items, states of affairs. The object of an intention can be expressed by an infinitive or noun-infinitive construction:

I intended *to win*, I intended *Mary to win*,

but it can always be expressed with a whole nested sentence:

I intended it to be the case that *I won*, I intended it to be the case that *Mary won*.

---

[21] Charles Fried, *Right and Wrong*, 24.

What one intends is always to bring it about *that P*, where 'P' stands for a complete sentence.

Still, we could haul events into the propositional story by saying that a person intends to bring it about that *an* event of such-and-such a *kind* occurs: in intending to make her angry he intended that *a fit of anger* should occur; in intending that they should lose all their money, he intended that *a loss* should occur; and so on. Let us see whether this can help with the 'tight binding' problem. The story would have to be that if these three all hold:

(1) The surgeon intends to cause a collapse of the child's head,
(2) He expects thereby also to cause a death of the child,
(3) He thinks that if there is a collapse and a death, the collapse will be the death,

then in intending to cause a collapse he also intends to cause a death. This brings in *a belief about* event-identity, rather than the thing itself. That is because what the surgeon intends must depend on what his beliefs are and not on whether they are true; as with his intending the collapse as a means to the mother's survival, which depends not on its doing so but on his thinking that it will. Let us simplify things, though, by attending only to informed, sensible people who accept all and only the event-identities that cannot reasonably be rejected.

What event-identities *can* be reasonably rejected? All the clear cases fall into two classes, both of which I have already appealed to. Sometimes the question 'Where and when did it occur?' has one determinate answer for e_1 and a different one for e_2, and that is enough to establish that e_1 is not e_2. Sometimes, also, two events can be distinguished by their having different subjects: the ruin happens to the factory, the deaths to the civilians; so those are different events. Those event non-identities, however, provide a rather liberal solution to the 'tight binding' problem. For example, the collapse of the head and the death of the child have different subjects, and occur a second apart; so these are two events, not one. Similarly with a dropped rock's displacement of water and its fall to the bottom of the pond, a bullet's puncturing the victim's skin and its reaching his heart. This 'event-identity' approach sets no limits to how finely we can cut into space and time in marking out possible trajectories for the intended/foreseen line.

Whether location and subject are the whole truth about event-identity is controversial; if they are not, then the present approach may leave unbound yet further items that we want to bind together. I shall not lead us into that morass, however. What the approach says while standing on firm ground is bad enough, especially with respect to time. Almost without limit, temporal parts of events are themselves events; so one that takes time has a first half and a second half, which are distinct; so, according to the 'event-identity' approach, a person could intend to cause the first half while only expecting to cause the second. This will not meet all the 'tight binding' needs of any serious means principle theorist.

It is, anyway, artificial and peculiar to describe the surgeon as intending or expecting to cause collapses and deaths, rather than as intending or expecting the head to collapse and the child to die. Dragging events into this in the first place is a philosophers' dodge, which from the outset looked unlikely to clarify our thoughts about what people intend.

The second attempt involves *act-identity*. When the surgeon crushes the child's head, he performs an act—it is his crushing of the child's head. At the same time, he kills the child, which means that he performs an act: his killing of the child. Furthermore, some events theorists hold that this is not a pair of acts but a single act described twice. Perhaps that helps with the 'tight binding' problem: if the crushing of the child's head was the killing of it then the surgeon cannot intend 'one' without intending 'the other'. Fried may be expressing this line of thought when he writes: 'It is inadmissible to say that one intends to put a bullet through a man, stab him, crush him, or blow him to atoms but does not intend to harm him. All of these things just *are* harming him.'[22] Identity does indeed firmly bind act to act: to separate the crushing from the killing or the harming, on this view, would take a pull strong enough to separate Cicero from Tully. (Strictly, what will block 'He intended to crush the child's head but didn't intend to kill it' is not that the crushing was the killing but that the surgeon believed that it was. Let us continue to steer around that wrinkle.)

Most of those who hold that the crushing was the killing base this on a particular thesis about act-identity, originated by Anscombe. According to this, if you win by jumping, the jump is the victory; if you betray someone by reporting him, the betrayal is the report; and so on. The Anscombe thesis is controversial,[23] and anyway it delivers far too many act-identities to solve our 'tight binding' problem; it ties

[22] Charles Fried, *Right and Wrong*, 44. Fried uses the language of facts ('harming him'), but I think events are meant. Construed as asserting fact-identities what he says is too obviously false.
[23] The controversy is evaluated in my *Events and their Names*, ch. 12.

together hosts of items which *nobody* would think are too close—too tightly bound—for one to be intended without the other. For example, it implies that the tactical bomber's destruction of the factory is his killing of the civilians, because each is identical with certain movements that he makes up in his aeroplane.

Perhaps we could go part of the way with the Anscombe thesis. If there are non-equivalent pairs of act descriptions which pick out the very same act, but not as many as the Anscombe thesis says there are, perhaps we can after all solve the 'tight binding' problem with help from act-identity. Such a semi-Anscombian theory might identify the crushing of the child's head with the killing of it while not identifying the destruction of the factory with the killing of the civilians. This is mere whistling in the dark, because nobody has developed such a theory; and there is no chance that one will be found that accounts for our common intuitions about the scope of intentions. That is because of a fundamental fact about the latter: *If you do not believe that in ϕing you will be πing, then it is not the case that in ϕing you intend to π.* Because of this, you can intend to falsify the date on the document without intending to break the law; you can intend to move the log without intending to raise it; you can intend to answer the question without intending to insult the questioner; you can intend to kill the old man at the crossroad without intending to kill your father. If each of these corresponds to a pair of acts, then your lie about the date is one act and your breach of the law another, your moving of the log is one act and your raising of it another, your answer is one act and your insult another, your geronticide is one act and your patricide another—even if only one movement of muscles or larynx is involved. (In the last case, indeed, there is one muscular movement, one effect, and one victim.) This is hopeless. As I have argued elsewhere, a theory according to which 'acts' are as plentiful as this must really be talking about *facts* and giving them the wrong label.[24] Facts—and more generally states of affairs—are what we should be talking about.

64. Delimiting the Means: Facts

Our problem, then, is to find a clear sense in which one state of affairs is so 'close' to another that one could not intend only one while expect-

---

[24] The controversy is evaluated in my *Events and their Names*, ch. 5.

ing both. We are trying to understand and explain not the thesis that the crushing of the child's head (an event) is too close to the child's death (another event), but rather the thesis that the *child's head's being crushed* or *the proposition that the child's head is crushed* is too close to *the child's dying* or *the proposition that the child dies*. Our best understanding of the logical form of intention statements demands that we pose the question in this way.

What determines whether Agent can intend that P without intending that Q will not be how P is related to Q but rather how Agent thinks they are related. As before, I shall attend to the relations themselves, confining myself to agents who are well informed about them. Now, the two best-known relations between states of affairs will not serve as the 'tight binding' or 'too close' tie that we are looking for. One is too weak, logically speaking: it binds pairs that we do not want to bind. The other is so strong that it does not apply to many that we do want to bind.

The weak candidate is causal necessitation: this holds between S_1 and S_2 if the obtaining of S_1 makes S_2 inevitable. This holds between *The child's head is crushed* and *The child dies*, and between any pair that the means principle theorists would want to bind; but it also holds between many that they do not want to bind. When a hysterectomy is performed early in pregnancy, for instance, it is causally inevitable that the foetus will die; in the tactical raid that I described, it is inevitable that if the bombs are dropped the civilians will die. In general, the means principle aims to contrast bad effects that are intended means to one's end with bad effects that are *inevitable* by-products of one's means. It is common ground throughout all this literature that one may intend M and only foresee B without intending it, even if it is (known to be) causally impossible to have M without B.

The strong candidate is entailment: this holds between S_1 and S_2 if it is absolutely, logically impossible that S_1 should obtain unless S_2 does too. We may grant that if someone intends to make S_1 obtain, and that entails S_2, he intends to make S_2 obtain—unless he is so thick that he does not see the entailment. This implies that if the bomber intends the bombs to fall he intends them to move, and that if the surgeon intends the child's head to be crushed he intends its shape to change; but it will not help with any of the claims that have troubled the friends, and indeed the enemies, of the means principle. For example, it does stop us from thinking that the surgeon intends the child's head to be crushed but does not intend it to die, for the crushing does not absolutely, conceptually entail the dying: there are worlds where God steps in and restores the ruined head to its former condition, and others where crushing a head is the first step in a helpful curative procedure. If entailment is our only 'binding', countless pairs will be left loose that most means principle moralists want to be bound.

One might suspect that that is their fault: if they properly grasped their own concept of 'intended as a means', and applied it accurately, they would permit much of what they now condemn. Indeed, a few means principle moralists do hold that when the surgeon crushes the child's head he does not intend it to die, from which they infer that it is morally permissible for him to do what he does. Let us follow through on this, interpreting the means principle in terms of what I'll call the entailment proposal: *If B is not itself needed for G, and is necessitated only causally and not logically by the means M to G, then Agent's intending to produce M as a means to G does not imply his intending to produce B.* This puts on the 'foreseen' side of the line some states of affairs that *nearly* all means principle moralists put on the 'intended' side. Rather than concluding that this refutes the entailment proposal, should we accept the proposal and on that basis claim victory for the minority party? I am afraid not. The entailment proposal yields results that seem outright crazy to all the friends and all the enemies of the means principle.

Consider first this tale: A political leader takes action against a trade union, intending to bring about a month-long state of disintegration in which the locals split off from the parent body and severally fall into further disunity. This is his intended means to the union's being unable to call a strike at Christmas. He knows that if the union falls apart for that long it will never be reconstituted, but he has no interest in that: he would be equally motivated to move against it even if he were sure that it would recover in January. By the entailment proposal, this politician intends the at-least-temporary inaction of the union, and does not intend its permanent destruction, its death: the former is all he needs for his end, and it does not entail the latter. This upshot of the proposal seems intuitively all right.

So much for the killing of a union. Now try the killing of people—for instance of civilians in the terror raid. I said that the raid leader intended to kill the civilians so as to lower enemy morale, but the truth is finer-grained than that. Really, he intended only that the people's bodies should be in a state that would cause a general belief that they were dead, this lasting long enough to shorten the war: nothing in that scheme requires that the dismaying condition of the bodies be permanent; so nothing in it requires that the people become downright dead rather than merely seemingly dead for a year or two. It would not enter the bomber's head that he could achieve the lesser thing without achieving the greater; but the greater thing is complex, and only one constituent is intended as a means.

Instances of this difficulty abound—for example, the arsonist who does not intend the building to be permanently destroyed, just that it be reduced to ashes for long enough for the insurance company to pay up. These mad results all concern some reversal of change that is causally but not logically impossible, so the difficulty does not infect some uses of the concept of 'intended as a means'. For example, it makes no trouble for the idea that if we torture the captured Gestapo man to get him to speak, his suffering is our intended means to our end. What is bad about his suffering lies in the horrible process itself, not in any irreversible change of state. Still, although many uses are not threatened, far too many are. Since they all concern the logical possibility of reversing causally irreversible changes, we might try to draw their sting by ruling that the intended/foreseen line cannot separate states of affairs that are related as *x is F up to time T* relates to *x is F from T onwards*. That, however, would disqualify not only the absurd results concerning the terror bomber and the arsonist and his like but also the wholly reasonable one about the political leader's moves against the trade union.

What basically matters, as I noted earlier, is not what relations obtain but what ones the agent thinks obtain. So my statement of the entailment proposal was a simplified stand-in for this more accurate one: *If Agent thinks that B is not itself needed for G, and thinks that it is necessitated only causally and not logically by his means M to G, then his intending to produce M as a means to G does not imply his intending to produce B.* If we interpret 'He thinks that P' to mean that he explicitly, consciously has this thought, this would dispose of many of the absurd results, because the relevant thought is unlikely to occur much. The theoretical problem would remain, however, for we would still be left with countless possible absurdities—for instance an arsonist who plays with the idea of the world's continuing to the point where the insurance company pays off and then the events in the building itself running in reverse, like a film played backwards, so that the building comes to be intact again. He might even note with amusement that if he did expect this it would not affect his plans, as would his expecting that the building would not catch fire or that the insurance company would not pay up. The new proposal counts this arsonist as not intending the building's permanent destruction. The absurdity has not been reduced much.

Since I first presented the entailment difficulty, the one philosopher who has stared at it without blinking is Warren Quinn in a paper which I greatly admire without much agreeing with it.[25] Offering no criterion except the entailment one, he said that maybe the terror bomber *doesn't* intend the civilians to die (as distinct from being dismantled for some months), and he thought this was my view. In fact, I had said it was absurd, but that I could not see how to escape from it. Quinn, in contrast, was willing to go along with this fantastically narrow understanding of what an agent intends: and he thought he could find something special marking off the terror raid from the tactical one, without having to claim that the terror bomber intends that civilians shall die. The crucial difference, he said, is that the terror bomber does—even by the narrow entailment standard—intend to 'involve' the civilians; he does intend to have *some* effect on them; whereas the tactical bomber does not. Reluctantly adopting Quinn's indefensible terminology, I shall express this by saying that the terror bomber's harm to the civilians is an instance of *direct agency*, the tactical bomber's *indirect agency*. Similarly, the surgeon who crushes the head of the unborn child intends to have an effect on it, so this is direct harmful agency; the surgeon who performs a hysterectomy through which the foetus dies does not intend to affect it in any way, so this is indirect harmful agency.

Although this openly abandons the notion of 'intending bad as a means to good', which is the heart of the clause in the principle of double effect which I call 'the means principle', Quinn says he is discussing 'the doctrine of double effect'. He must think that his category of 'direct harm' captures the very same cases that means principle moralists have sought to mark off through the 'intended as a means' idea. In fact, however, his direct/indirect line does not coincide with the one ordinarily drawn between intended means and foreseen by-products. His category of direct harmful agency includes everything that would ordinarily have been counted as 'bad which is intended as a means', but it also includes cases which *everyone* would classify as 'bad which is only a foreseen by-product of the means'. Here is one:

Some people have a highly infectious and dangerous disease; there are treatments that may succeed, but for the next week we will not have

[25] Warren S. Quinn, 'Actions, Intentions, and Consequences: The Doctrine of Double Effect'.

any of the special masks that are needed to protect the health workers from being infected. So we put the patients in quarantine for a week, although it is almost certain that a week from now their disease will have gone too far for successful treatment and they will die from it.

Nobody would say that we intend their dying as a means to anything, and no friend of the means principle would say that *it* condemns this act of quarantining. Yet in it we clearly intend to 'involve' the infected people; our purpose essentially requires us to affect them by keeping them away from everyone else. If we left them alone and moved ourselves, even this would involve an 'intention to involve' them by altering their distance from us; but the means principle as ordinarily understood would not condemn it. Presumably Quinn overlooked such possibilities, being led astray by considering too narrow a range of cases.[26]

He found a way to steer around the 'tight binding' problem; but his detour, we now see, led to a real change of subject—replacing the contrast that the means principle addresses by one that is extensionally different from it. Let us get back to where we were. There must be some sense in which the terror bomber intends the civilians to die; if the entailment criterion does not yield it, then we should find something that does.

The best I can find is rather loose, but it may be the whole truth about our intended/foreseen distinction. Not only is there no chance of turning the ashes back into a building, or the smithereens back into people, or of crushing the baby's head without killing it—these things are what the plain man would call *inconceivable*. We can fairly easily imagine getting technology that would allow bombs to be aimed much more precisely, or would allow a foetus to be brought to term outside the mother's body; whereas the idea of destroying the head but not the baby, or of restoring a person who has been burnt to a cinder, is sheer fantasy. Without denying that it is conceptually possible, something God could do, we have not the faintest idea of what it might be like to have the means to bring it about. That, I suggest, is the 'tight binding' that we have been looking for.

[26] Rakowski, 'Taking and Saving Lives', n. 23, says that Quinn's response to the difficulty I raised 'seems promising', but he does not discuss it. Its departure from the principle of double effect is pointed out by John Martin Fischer, Mark Ravizza, and David Copp, 'Quinn on Double Effect: The Problem of Closeness', *passim*, and by Frances Myrna Kamm, 'Non-consequentialism, the Person as an End-in-Itself, and the Significance of Status', 378.

65. *The Morality of the Means Principle: 'Intend'*

From now on, I shall assume that the terror bomber intends that civilians shall die as a result of his raid while the tactical bomber does not. The friends of the means principle hold that *ceteris paribus* the terror bomber acts worse than the tactical bomber, or that the former acts wrongly while the latter does not. Or perhaps that the former is more blameworthy than the latter: I shall not strain to confine the discussion to first-order morality. If the means principle is defensible anywhere in morality, that is worth knowing.

The moral view expressed in the means principle can sometimes be appealed to instead of the making/allowing distinction. In the crisis where if I do not torture the Gestapo man several better men than he is will be tortured, my torturing him might be opposed on either of two grounds. (1) Making pain occur is worse than allowing it to occur, and if you don't torture him you will only be allowing pain to come to the others. (2) It is worse to intend pain as a means to your end than to foresee it as a side-effect of your means. Torturing the Gestapo man would involve intending pain as a means; not torturing him would not, because the suffering of your friends would not be your intended means to the comfort of the Gestapo man. Moralists who are near the absolutist end of the 'atrocities' continuum differ among themselves in what they emphasize—making or intention.

Although making/allowing sometimes falls across a situation in the same place as intended/foreseen, the two are orthogonal. A means principle theorist could, and some do, hold that it is wrong to allow something bad to happen as your intended means to some good end; and on the other hand many bad by-products which the means principle permits fall squarely on the 'making' side of that line. In the rest of this chapter, I shall keep making/allowing out of sight, in order to focus on the means principle. What sort of case can be made for it? I shall give a section each to three attempts.

Some means principle theorists write as though 'He intended the civilian deaths' were all we need to secure the moral point. 'It is nonsense to pretend that you do not intend to do what is the means you take to your chosen end,' writes Elizabeth Anscombe, as though that settled the moral matter.[27] It is true that in general a person's inten-

---

[27] Anscombe, 'War and Murder', 59.

tions have much to do with how we morally judge him; but two of the reasons for that seem irrelevant to the means principle. (1) What someone intends to bring about is something he is willing to bring about: the terror bomber voluntarily produces the civilian deaths, knowing what he is doing, and that says something about what sort of man he is. This, though, is equally true of the tactical bomber: he too would rather produce civilian deaths than call off his raid. I have quoted Castañeda to that effect, and here is Thomas Aquinas: 'If a man wills some cause from which he knows a particular effect results, it follows that he wills that effect. Although perhaps he does not intend that effect in itself, nevertheless he rather wishes that the effect exist than that the cause not exist.'[28] (2) There is great moral significance in what a person intends as his end, what he pursues for its own sake; but that is irrelevant to our topic. Neither the terror nor the tactical bomber seeks or values civilian deaths for their own sake; each may regard them as deplorable—something he would not bring about if it were detachable from his hastening of victory in this just war. (That will itself be a means to yet further ends; but here we can treat it as ultimate.) In short, each man does what he knows will kill civilians, and neither man values civilian deaths for themselves. We are still looking for a moral difference.

Granted that intending something bad as a means is different from intending it as an end or wanting it for itself, perhaps the two are alike in some morally significant way. Let us dig for it. We now have to consider *three* men: the malevolently punitive bomber who wants to kill enemy civilians out of hatred for what their country has done to his, the terror bomber seeking to shorten the war by killing enemy civilians and thus lowering morale in the enemy country, and the tactical bomber seeking to destroy a munitions factory while knowing that he will thereby kill civilians. We want a clear similarity between the first two that does not carry over to the third.

Well, our hand-hold on intentions is the idea that a person's intentions in acting are settled by which of his beliefs explain his behaviour; so let us ask our men about that. If we were trying to analyse 'intending as a means', the question we should have to put to the terror bomber is: 'If you had thought that your raid would not cause civilian deaths which would hasten victory, would you have called it off?' That, however, is no use to me. I want to interrelate our three bombers by

---

[28] Thomas Aquinas, *Commentary on the Nicomachean Ethics*, vol. i, ch. 512.

comparing and contrasting their answers to some one question about their beliefs and behaviour. The above question means nothing to two of the three, and therefore does not serve. The question 'If your raid hadn't caused civilian deaths, would it have been worth doing?' is not apt either, because it does not ask about the motivating frame of mind in which the raid was conducted.

For comparative purposes, the question we need is this: 'If you had thought that your raid would not cause civilian deaths, would you have called it off?'[29] On the face of it, we might expect these answers from the three bombers:

> Punitive: Yes.
> Terror: Yes.
> Tactical: No.

There, one might think, is the whole story. The admittedly bad man is *moved by a desire for something bad*, and he shares this with the terror and not the tactical bomber. What more could we want? Well, we could want more precision. Each man is being asked: Would you have behaved differently if . . . ? If what? What is the possible state of himself that he is asked to entertain? It is to include his thinking that his raid will not lead to civilians dying, and whatever other differences from his actual state may follow logically from that, and . . . what else? There are three ways we might go on.

(1) . . . *and in no other way from his actual state.* In that case, we are leaving the tactical man with his belief that his raid will destroy the factory, and the terror man with his belief that his raid will lower morale. While the punitive bomber will answer 'Yes, I would call the raid off' to this version of our question, each of the others will answer No. This question, then, does not yield the grouping that the means principle moralist wants.

(2) . . . *and by including whatever follows from that by virtue of his causal beliefs.* The punitive bomber will still answer Yes, and now the terror bomber will say Yes too: He is being asked whether he would call the raid off if he thought that it would not kill civilians and therefore would not shorten the war. However, the tactical bomber will also answer Yes, he too would have called off his raid; he is saying how he

---

[29] When I first used this in my 'Morality and Consequences', 100 f., I was not clear in my mind that I was not—and did not need to be—analysing 'intending as a means'. Kwong-loi Shun, 'Intending as a Means', easily shows that the question would be wrong for such an analysis.

would behave if he thought that no civilians would die and thought that the munitions factory would not be destroyed. The first change of belief brings the second with it, because he thinks that he cannot destroy the factory without killing civilians, which is to say that the civilians cannot survive his raid unless the factory does too.

Of those readings of our question, the first supposes too little change in the antecedent state, the second too much. We need something in between.

(3) . . . *and by including whatever follows from that by a causally down-stream inference.* This version of our question calls for pretended belief adjustments concerning upshots, not prerequisites. So the terror bomber is asked to envisage thinking that no civilians will die and that enemy morale will not be lowered; while the tactical bomber is asked to envisage thinking that no civilians will die without also thinking that the factory will survive—since the factory's fate is not causally downstream from what happens to the civilians, it is protected from the scope of our counterfactual question. To this version of our question the terror bomber will answer Yes (as will of course the punitive bomber), while the tactical bomber will answer No.

At last we have the terror bomber sounding like the punitive bomber in a context where the tactical one sounds different. Is there a moral conclusion to be drawn from this? It seems unlikely. We achieved this result with help from the distinction between consequences of one's means and presuppositions of them, and this has nothing to do with the punitive bomber. It is true that we have managed to get the punitive and terror bombers answering Yes to a question to which the tactical bomber answers No; but the terror bomber's Yes essentially depends on a complex clause in the question to which the punitive bomber is not even listening.

Looking past this formal point into the content of the discussion, there still seems to be no moral conclusion to be drawn. Neither the terror nor the tactical bomber would call off his raid if his beliefs changed only in not including the belief that it would kill civilians. Each would call it off if his beliefs changed in that way and in every way that causally follows from it. To get them apart we had to specify what causally follows downstream as distinct from what causally follows upstream. Why should that difference matter morally? It obviously matters when it is a question of being upstream or downstream from the agent's conduct; but the civilian deaths are downstream from

the bomber's bodily movements in each of the raids we are considering.

66. *The Morality of the Means Principle: 'Means'*

Having civilian deaths as your means involves using people as a means
to your end. The terror bomber does this, while the tactical bomber
does not; and some moralists hold that to be the crucial difference,
because (they say) we are morally required never to treat people as
means.

In what sense is it wrong to treat someone as a means? Not, presumably, in the literal sense that would imply that I ought not to hire
someone to build bookshelves for me. If there is a morally binding 'end,
not means' principle, it presumably forbids us to treat a person *just* as
a means, affecting her interests without care for what they are. That is
a good principle, but it applies equally where the effect on the person's
interests is one's means and where it is a by-product of them, and thus
yields no moral difference between those two. I can find no reading of
the 'end, not means' principle which makes it both plausible and relevant to our present question. If there is one, it must not only clear the
tactical bomber of using the civilians as a means, but must imply that
he is treating them as ends. Tell that to the civilians! What the tactical
bomber does to the civilians, indeed, is in a way worse than treating
them as means. He is treating them as nothing; they play no part in his
plan; he is not *even* treating them as means. Objection: 'They might figure in his plan in this way: if he expected more than 5,000 of them to
die, he would call off his raid'. That is true, and could also be true of
the terror and even of the punitive bomber, neither of whom has to
think that the sky is the limit. Morally speaking, I would add, the sky
had better not be the limit. I have been arguing that what the terror
bomber does may be morally all right, but I do not accept that it could
be all right for him to behave in this manner without compunction,
without considering the cost to the civilians, without looking for less
lethal alternatives. All of this holds equally, of course, for the tactical
bomber.

Warren Quinn counts it against the terror bomber that he is 'treating people as means' yet openly admits that the tactical bomber is not
treating them as ends.[30] As I reported two sections back, Quinn con-

---

[30] Quinn, 'Actions, Intentions, and Consequences: The Doctrine of Double Effect'.

trasts the cases not in terms of (1) harm which is a means to a good end versus (2) harm that is a by-product of a means to good end, but rather in terms of (3) harm brought about in furtherance of a plan which essentially involves the people who are harmed versus (4) harm which is not brought about in that way. So he is not defending the means principle's discrimination between (1) and (2), because he thinks it has been put out of business by my extreme version of the 'binding' problem. He defends instead what I'll call (adapting Quinn's own terminology) the direct agency principle: other things being equal, it is worse to harm people in the furtherance of a plan which essentially involves them than in one which does not. His defence of this overlaps things that might be said in support of the means principle; so in tracking Quinn I am not entirely losing my way.

Quinn divides direct harmful agency into two species. In *opportunistic* agency, the agent sees the victim as an advantage, an opportunity to be exploited. In the terror bombing case, for example, the fact that civilians are present and can be involved is a help to the agent's project of shortening the war. In the *eliminative* cases the agent sees the victim as a difficulty, an obstacle. When the unborn child's head is crushed, for instance, the fact that the foetus is present is a threat to the agent's project of saving the mother's life, the threat being removable only by involving the foetus. This is a sound distinction, with many examples on each side of it.

What we have to look at are Quinn's reasons for attaching moral significance to the opportunistic kind of direct harmful agency. He admits that his position is less plausible when applied to the eliminative species; I contend that in that application it is entirely implausible, and that Quinn has nothing significant to say in its defence. Almost everything he says about the moral status of direct harmful agency is really addressed to the opportunistic species: he borrows phrases from that and applies them across the whole genus, but he does not even try to defend doing so. The little he says that really is about the entire genus—including its eliminative species—is weak and unpersuasive.

Our topic, then, is Quinn's defence of the opportunistic agency principle, which says that it is prima facie more wrong to harm people through opportunistic agency than to harm them in other ways.

This picks out some of the cases that means principle moralists have talked about, though not all; and it includes some that they would put on the other side of the line as not involving bad that is intended as a means. Here is an example from fiction. The storm has swept the ship on to the rocks just outside the harbour mouth, and the sailors have little chance of surviving unless a line is got to them. The only chance of that is for Otho to tie one end of the line to himself, swim out to the entrance to the harbour, and then let the current carry him to the ship. It is virtually certain that in the final stages he will be hammered to death on the rocks, but the line's reaching the ship does not depend on that either way. The plan goes through and the sailors are rescued; Otho is dead by the time the current bears his body to the ship. This is not a case where, by ordinary standards, Otho's dying—or indeed his risk of dying—is intended by us as a means to our end. What is intended is his swimming to one place and being carried by the current to another; his dying is pure by-product. Yet the agency is clearly opportunistic in Quinn's sense: in this emergency, Otho represents an opportunity, not an obstacle.

Yet there is a special reason for attending to opportunistic agency, namely that it is precisely the class of cases in which a person is used as a means to someone else's ends. I am talking not only about the opportunistic cases where harm is intended but also ones, like my shipwreck example, where the harm is a by-product. If the concern is with using *people* as means, not merely making *some fact about them* obtain as a means, then opportunistic agency is what we should be talking about. To think of the victims of direct eliminative agency as 'used' is 'less plausible', Quinn writes; I say that it is downright wrong. If our concern is with using people as means, opportunistic agency should be our focus, which is why I have fought through Quinn's underbrush so as to reach this point. Now that we have reached the point, what shall we do with it? Quinn's rationale for giving a special moral status to opportunistic harmful agency must be gleaned from two remarks—each ostensibly about all direct harmful agency, but really appropriate only for the opportunistic species.

(1) 'Someone who harms by direct agency must take up a distinctive attitude towards his victims. He must treat them as if they were then and there *for* his purposes.'[31] If taking up a distinctive attitude to one's victims is having a certain belief about them, then that is wrong. An opportunistic harmful agent, acting in what he takes to be a good cause, can believe anything that Quinn believes about what the victims 'exist for' or are 'there for'. One might say: 'Whatever he believes, he is treat-

[31] Quinn, 'Actions, Intentions, and Consequences: The Doctrine of Double Effect' 348.

ing his victims as though they exist for his purposes'. But what does that mean? The eighteenth-century philosopher William Wollaston defined wrong action as action which implies something false: not going to church implies that God does not exist, but he does; stealing someone's property implies that it is yours, but it is not; and so on. It is obvious why this purported moral algorithm is useless: What connects (A) my taking this book from your shelves with (P) the proposition that it is mine is that A is wrong unless P is true; and similarly with the other examples. So Wollaston's notion of 'implying a falsehood' rests on prior moral judgements, and therefore cannot serve—as he thought it could—as a criterion to tell us which acts are wrong. The same mistake seems to occur when we are told that opportunistic harmful agency is wrong because in it the agent behaves as though the victims were there for him or existed for his purposes: all I can make of this is that he behaves in a way that is wrong unless they exist for him. This presupposes that the behaviour is wrong; so it cannot give a reason why it is wrong.

(2) 'In discriminating to some extent against both forms of direct agency, the doctrine reflects a Kantian ideal of human community and interaction. Each person is to be treated, so far as possible, as existing only for purposes that he can share.'[32] Properly called 'Kantian', the ideal concerns treating people as ends; and has nothing to do with any distinction Quinn is drawing, as he acknowledges. With that removed, it is not clear that there is more to the ideal than that each person is, so far as possible, to be treated in ways that he can agree to; but that again applies all across our 'harmful agency' domain, and is not confined to the kind that Quinn calls 'direct'.

67. The Morality of the Means Principle: Character

Moral character is sometimes introduced into defences of the means principle. An issue about character might be lurking behind this suggestion: *The terror and tactical bombers differ in what they hope for, or what they would welcome. One wants civilian deaths, though not for themselves, whereas the other does not want them at all.* There is truth in that, but let us be careful. The terror bomber will be glad when he hears that civilians have died, because he needs this for his end; but the tac-

---

[32] Ibid. 350.

tical bomber will also be glad when he hears that civilians have died, because that is evidence that something has happened that he needs for his ultimate aim. Because the raid on the factory will inevitably kill many civilians if it succeeds in its purpose, it would be bad news for the tactical bomber if he heard that few civilians had died, for that would show that something had gone wrong—his bombs had not exploded, or had fallen in open countryside. What contradicts that bad news is good news.

The two welcomes of the news of civilian deaths do admittedly differ: one man is glad because of what will flow from the deaths, the other because of what will flow from what must have preceded them; one is downstream glad, so to speak, while the other is upstream and then downstream glad. They do not differ, however, in how greatly glad they will be, or, therefore how greatly they will hope for and want civilian deaths.

The tactical bomber's wish for the civilian deaths is a reluctant one: if he could, he would destroy the factory without killing civilians. But the terror bomber too, if he could, would drop his bombs in such a way as to lower enemy morale without killing civilians.

'That is not fair', you may think. 'There is some chance of bombing the factory without killing civilians, whereas there is none that the terror raid will lower enemy morale unless civilians are killed by it. The tactical man's regret about killing civilians could generate a sane, practical desire for more precise bombing or for a coincidence in which all the civilians happen to be out of town; whereas the terror man's so-called "regret" about killing civilians could only lead to a sigh for a miracle.' That is true, but only because of a difference in probability, which is an unwanted accident of this example. The means principle is ordinarily understood to distinguish behaviours which have equal probabilities of causing harm, including probability $= 1$; so it contrasts bad intended means with bad that is foreseen as an *inevitable* by-product of one's means. This inevitability has been crucial at several points in my discussion. I shall return to it in the next section.

Here is a related matter which has been adduced as showing that one man should be judged differently from the other. Suppose that each bomber expects only one civilian death—yours. The tactical bomber is sure his raid will kill you; but if that turns out to be wrong and he sees you staggering to your feet amidst the rubble of the factory, he has no reason not to rejoice. On the other hand, if the terror bomber sees that you have survived his raid, he has reason to drop another bomb on you, since his purpose will be defeated if you survive. The two bombers differ in how intensely or thoroughly hostile they are: if something goes awry with the terror bomber's expectations, he will adapt, ducking and weaving his way right up to your death. That is not so with the tactical bomber.

That is because the line from what the terror bomber does through to your death is part of the line from what he does through to his goal; whereas the line from what the tactical bomber does through to your death includes a segment that is not on the route to his goal, so that if that bit were broken he could still pursue his goal. From the point of view of the potential victim, you, the two cases feel different; but what does the difference consist in? It does not concern the probability that you will be killed: we are investigating the means principle, which is never made to say that in the permitted case there is some chance of getting the good effect without the bad. Indeed, it seems usually to be assumed that all the probabilities are inevitabilities. (But see the next section.)

Anyway, I cannot see that the difference in how it feels to you generates a moral difference between the two men. Each is prepared to manœuvre towards your death: the tactical bomber may work to overcome political resistance to his raid, evade the defences that try to keep him away from you, solve the mechanical problem with the bomb-bay doors, and so on, using all his skill, ingenuity, courage, and plasticity to keep on a path that has your death on it. It is true that eventually the path to your death forks away from the path to his goal, and his ingenuity goes with the latter. Still, he has in common with the terror bomber that he relentlessly and ingeniously pursues, *for as long as he has any reason to*, a path that inevitably leads to your death. The moral difference eludes me.

The line of thought just criticized shows up briefly in a discussion of Thomas Nagel's, whose main thrust is diffferent. Having pointed out that 'action intentionally aimed at a goal is *guided* by that goal', Nagel draws this conclusion:

To aim at evil, *even as a means*, is to have one's action *guided* by evil. One must be prepared to adjust it to insure the production of evil: a falling off in the level of the desired evil must be grounds for altering what one does so that the evil is restored and maintained. But the *essence* of evil is that it should *repel* us. If something is evil, our actions should be guided, if they are guided by it at all, towards its elimination rather than towards its maintenance. That is what evil *means*. So when we aim at evil we are swimming head-on against the normative current. Our action is guided by the goal at every point in the direction dia-metrically opposite to that in which the value of that goal points.[33]

The undeniable prima-facie power of this is due, I think on reflection, to our taking the phrase 'guided by evil' in a manner to which Nagel is not entitled. The terror bomber is guided by the thought of killing civil-ians, which he knows to be in itself evil; that is common ground, agreed on all sides. The force of Nagel's treatment comes from our thinking of being 'guided by evil' as being guided in a way which essentially involves the thought of evil; that really would be swimming against the normative current; but it is not what the terror bomber is doing.

68. A Limited Success

In my last two points, as elsewhere in this unremittingly negative dis-cussion, I have relied on the idea that the bad by-product of the means is inevitable and believed to be so. I have stipulated that the tactical bomber knows that he *cannot* destroy the factory without killing civil-ians. When that is so, I submit, the means principle is indefensible. The picture changes, however, when we turn to pairs of cases where the probability of harm is lower. I have recently been made aware of this by Judith Lichtenberg.[34]

Suppose that the tactical bomber's destruction of the factory is only likely to kill civilians, and that his conduct of the raid can increase the chance that it will not do so. In that case, he can at least try, consis-tently with his ultimate end, to act in a way that does not cause any-thing bad. And even if he cannot *try*, he can unfancifully *hope* that few civilians will be killed. This is not true of the terror bomber. For him, anything that lowers the probability of civilian deaths *ipso facto* lowers the probability of ultimate success.

I am not contrasting the bombers by assigning different probabilities of harm to them. If the probability of civilians dying is higher in the terror raid than in the other, that makes a moral difference, but not one that arises from intend/foresee. I am still supposing the probabilities to be the same for both, but am considering cases where it is less than 1 = certainty. That leaves room for one bomber but not the other to

[33] Thomas Nagel, 'The Limits of Objectivity', 132 f.
[34] Personal communication. Lichtenberg detects seeds of the idea in Philippa Foot, 'The Problem of Abortion and the Doctrine of Double Effect', 270 f., and Michael Walzer, *Just and Unjust Wars*, 174.

manœuvre away from the civilian deaths, or—more realistically—to try to cause as few of them as possible; and, failing that, it leaves room for him to hope that through sheer good luck few will be killed.

This does not establish the means principle, or imply that the terror bomber acts more wrongly than the tactical bomber. All I conclude is that the former lacks a certain moral advantage which is possessed by *many* of those who foresee bad as a by-product of their means. These are the agents who can reasonably try to make the bad by-product less probable, or probably less bad, or can reasonably hope that the world will do it for them. Such a 'by-product' agent has a window of moral opportunity through which he can act consistently with his plan, and the 'bad means' agent lacks this.

We can tie this to my discussion in Section 64 of what to include in Agent's means and what to regard as only a by-product of them. Here are two ways in which states of affairs can be related:

> *Conceive*: We have some idea of what it might be like to have the technical means to make S_1 obtain without its leading to S_2.

> *Try*: Someone who plans to make S_1 obtain could reasonably try or hope to do this without its leading to S_2.

It looks as though Conceive is needed for S_2 to be a by-product rather than a part of S_1, while Try is needed for S_2's by-product status to have moral significance. Since Conceive is a major ingredient in Try, the two results have a satisfactory fit.

What I have offered with Try, however, falls doubly short of justifying the means principle. For one thing, it makes a point about *some* 'foreseen by-product' cases, which it contrasts with all 'intended means' cases and the remaining 'foreseen by-product' ones, namely those where the agent cannot reasonably try or hope to avert the bad by-product. Also, what I have been saying about the agent who can try is that he has a certain moral advantage or benefit, not that he acts less wrongly or more creditably.

BIBLIOGRAPHY

ADAMS, ROBERT M., 'Motive Utilitarianism', *Journal of Philosophy*, 73 (1976), 467–81.

ALSTON, WILLIAM P., 'Expressing', in Max Black (ed.), *Philosophy in America* (Ithaca, NY: Cornell University Press, 1964).

AMES, JAMES BARR, 'Law and Morals' (1908), in Ratcliffe, *The Good Samaritan and the Law*.

ANSCOMBE, G. E. M., *Intention* (Oxford: Blackwell, 1957).

—— 'Does Oxford Moral Philosophy Corrupt Youth?', *The Listener*, 57 (1957), 266 f. and 271.

—— 'Modern Moral Philosophy' (1958), repr. in her *Ethics, Religion and Politics, Collected Philosophical Papers*, iii (Minneapolis: University of Minnesota Press, 1981).

—— 'War and Murder' (1961), repr. ibid.

—— 'Two Kinds of Error in Action' (1963), repr. ibid.

AUSTIN, J. L., *How to Do Things with Words* (Cambridge, Mass.: Harvard University Press, 1962).

AYER, A. J., 'Negation', in his *Philosophical Essays* (London: Macmillan, 1954).

BENNETT, JONATHAN, 'Whatever the Consequences' (1966), repr. in Steinbock and Norcross, *Killing and Letting Die*, 167–91.

—— Untitled review of papers on imperative inference, *Journal of Symbolic Logic*, 35 (1970), 314–18.

—— 'Shooting, Killing, Dying', *Canadian Journal of Philosophy*, 2 (1973), 315–23.

—— *Kant's Dialectic* (Cambridge: Cambridge University Press, 1974).

—— 'Accountability', in Zak van Straaten (ed.), *Philosophical Subjects* (Oxford University Press: Oxford, 1980).

—— 'Morality and Consequences', in Sterling McMurrin (ed.), *The Tanner Lectures on Human Values*, ii (Salt Lake City: University of Utah Press, 1981).

—— 'Positive and Negative Relevance', *American Philosophical Quarterly*, 20 (1983), 185–94.

—— Critical Notice of Davidson's *Inquiries into Truth and Interpretation*, *Mind*, 94 (1985), 601–26.

—— *Events and their Names* (Oxford: Oxford University Press, 1988).

—— 'Two Departures from Consequentialism', *Ethics*, 100 (1989), 54–66.

—— *Linguistic Behaviour*, 2nd edn. (Indianapolis: Hackett, 1990).

—— 'The Necessity of Moral Judgments', *Ethics*, 103 (1993), 458–72.

BENTHAM, JEREMY, *An Introduction to the Principles of Morals and Legislation* (1780; repub. New York: Hafner Press, 1948).

BERGSTRÖM, LARS, *The Alternatives and Consequences of Actions* (Stockholm: Almqvist & Wiksell, 1966).

BERKELEY, GEORGE, *Alciphron; or, The Minute Philosopher* (1732), repr. in *The Works of George Berkeley*, ed. A. A. Luce and T. E. Jessop (London: Nelson, 1950).

BIGELOW, JOHN, 'Possible Worlds Foundations for Probability', *Journal of Philosophical Logic*, 5 (1976), 299–320.

BRANDT, RICHARD B., *A Theory of the Good and the Right* (New York: Oxford University Press, 1979).

BRINK, DAVID O., 'Utilitarianism and the Personal Point of View', *Journal of Philosophy*, 83 (1986), 417–38.

BROOK, RICHARD, 'Agency and Morality', *Journal of Philosophy*, 88 (1991), 190–212.

BROOME, JOHN, *Weighing Goods* (Oxford: Blackwell, 1991).

CAMPBELL, RICHMOND, and LANNING SOWDEN (eds.), *Paradoxes of Rationality and Cooperation: Prisoner's Dilemma and Newcomb's Problem* (Vancouver: University of British Columbia Press, 1985).

CARGILE, JAMES T., 'On Consequentialism', *Analysis*, 29 (1968–9), 78–88.

CASEY, JOHN, 'Actions and Consequences', in John Casey (ed.), *Morality and Moral Reasoning* (London: Methuen, 1971).

CASTAÑEDA, HECTOR-NERI, 'Intensionality and Identity in Human Action and Philosophical Method', *Nous*, 13 (1979), 235–60.

CHISHOLM, RODERICK M., *The First Person* (Minneapolis: University of Minnesota Press, 1981).

COLE, PETER (ed.), *Radical Pragmatics* (New York: Academic Press, 1981).

CONNELL, F. J., 'Double Effect, Principle of', in *The New Catholic Encyclopedia* (New York: McGraw Hill, 1967), iv.

CURRAN, CHARLES E., *Ongoing Revision in Moral Theology* (Notre Dame, Ind.: Notre Dame University Press, 1975).

D'ARCY, ERIC, *Human Acts: An Essay in their Moral Evaluation* (Oxford: Oxford University Press, 1963).

DAVIDSON, DONALD, 'Reply to Bruce Vermazen', in Bruce Vermazen and Merrill B. Hintikka (eds.), *Essays on Davidson: Actions and Events* (Oxford: Oxford University Press, 1985).

DAVIS, NANCY, 'Utilitarianism and Responsibility', *Ratio*, 22 (1980), 15–35.

DAVIS, STEVEN (ed.), *Pragmatics* (New York: Oxford University Press, 1991).

DI IANNI, ALBERT, 'The Direct/Indirect Distinction in Morals', in Charles E. Curran and Richard A. McCormick (eds.), *Readings in Moral Theology*, no. 1 (New York: Paulist Press, 1979).

DINELLO, DANIEL, 'On Killing and Letting Die' (1971), repr. in Steinbock and Norcross, *Killing and Letting Die*, 192–6.

DONAGAN, ALAN, *The Theory of Morality* (Chicago: University of Chicago Press, 1977).

FEINBERG, JOEL, 'Action and Responsibility' (1965), repr. in his *Doing and Deserving* (Princeton, NJ: Princeton University Press, 1970).

FINGARETTE, HERBERT, 'Some Moral Aspects of Good Samaritanship', in Ratcliffe, *The Good Samaritan and the Law*.

FISCHER, JOHN MARTIN, MARK RAVIZZA, and DAVID COPP, 'Quinn on Double Effect: The Problem of Closeness', *Ethics*, 103 (1993), 707–25.

FLETCHER, GEORGE P., 'Prolonging Life: Some Legal Considerations' (1967), repr. in Steinbock and Norcross, *Killing and Letting Die*, 88–102.

FOOT, PHILIPPA, 'The Problem of Abortion and the Doctrine of Double Effect' (1967), repr. in her *Virtues and Vices and Other Essays in Moral Philosophy* (Berkeley, Calif.: University of California Press, 1978), and in Steinbock and Norcross, *Killing and Letting Die*, 266–79.

—— 'Killing, Letting Die, and Euthanasia: A Reply to Holly Goldman', *Analysis*, 41 (1981), 159–60.

—— 'Utilitarianism and the Virtues', *Mind*, 94 (1985), 196–209.

FRANCKEN, PATRICK, and LAWRENCE BRIAN LOMBARD, 'How not to Flip the Switch with the Floodlight', *Pacific Philosophical Quarterly*, 73 (1992), 31–43.

FREGE, GOTTLOB, 'Negation' (1919), in *Translations from the Philosophical Writings of Gottlob Frege*, tr. and ed. Peter Geach and Max Black (Oxford: Blackwell, 1952).

FREY, R. G., 'Some Aspects of the Doctrine of Double Effect', *Canadian Journal of Philosophy*, 5 (1975), 259–83.

—— 'What a Good Man can Bring himself to Do', *Journal of Value Inquiry*, 12 (1978), 134–41.

FRIED, CHARLES, *Right and Wrong* (Cambridge, Mass.: Harvard University Press, 1978).

FUMERTON, RICHARD A., *Reason and Morality* (Ithaca, NY: Cornell University Press, 1990).

GALE, RICHARD M., *Negation and Non-Being*, American Philosophical Quarterly Monograph no. 10 (1976).

GIBBARD, ALLAN, 'Hare's Analysis of "Ought" and its Implications', in Seanor and Fotion, *Hare and Critics*.

—— *Wise Choices, Apt Feelings* (Cambridge, Mass.: Harvard University Press, 1990).

GINET, CARL, *Action* (Cambridge: Cambridge University Press, 1990).

GOLDMAN, ALVIN A., *A Theory of Human Action* (Princeton, NJ: Princeton University Press, 1970).

GREGORY, CHARLES O., 'The Good Samaritan and the Bad: The Anglo-American Law', in Ratcliffe, *The Good Samaritan and the Law*.

GRICE, H. P., 'The Causal Theory of Perception' (1961), repr. in his *Studies in the Way of Words*.

—— *Studies in the Way of Words* (Cambridge, Mass.: Harvard University Press, 1989).

Grisez, Germain, and Russell Shaw, *Beyond the New Morality* (Notre Dame, Ind.: Notre Dame University Press, 1974).

Gury, Jean Pierre, *Compendium Theologiae Moralis* (1850), 34th edn. (New York: Frederick Pustet, 1939).

Hampshire, Stuart, 'Morality and Pessimism' (1973), repr. in his *Morality and Conflict* (Cambridge, Mass.: Harvard University Press, 1983).

Hare, R. M., *The Language of Morals* (Oxford: Oxford University Press, 1952).

—— 'Universalisability' (1955), repr. in his *Essays on the Moral Concepts* (Berkeley, Calif.: University of California Press, 1972).

—— *Freedom and Reason* (Oxford: Oxford University Press, 1963).

—— 'Principles' (1972), repr. in his *Essays in Ethical Theory* (Oxford: Oxford University Press, 1989).

—— *Moral Thinking: Its Levels, Method and Point* (Oxford: Oxford University Press, 1981).

—— '*In Vitro* Fertilization and the Warnock Report' (1987), repr. in his *Essays on Bioethics* (Oxford: Oxford University Press, 1993).

—— 'Comments on Gibbard', in Seanor and Fotion, *Hare and Critics*.

Harris, John, 'The Marxist Conception of Violence', *Philosophy and Public Affairs*, 3 (1974), 192–220.

—— 'Williams on Negative Responsibility and Integrity', *Philosophical Quarterly*, 24 (1974), 265–73.

—— 'The Survival Lottery' (1975), repr. in Steinbock and Norcross, *Killing and Letting Die*, 257–65.

Honoré, Antony M., 'Law, Morals and Rescue', in Ratcliffe, *The Good Samaritan and the Law*.

Hornsby, Jennifer, *Actions* (London: Routledge & Kegan Paul, 1980).

Hudson, James L., 'Subjectivization in Ethics', *American Philosophical Quarterly*, 26 (1989), 221–9.

Jordan, Jeff, 'Why Negative Rights Only?', *Southern Journal of Philosophy*, 29 (1991), 245–55.

Kagan, Shelly, *The Limits of Morality* (Oxford: Oxford University Press, 1989).

Kamm, Frances Myrna, 'Killing and Letting Die: Methodological and Substantive Issues', *Pacific Philosophical Quarterly*, 64 (1983), 297–312.

—— 'Harming Some to Save Others', *Philosophical Studies*, 57 (1989), 227–60.

—— 'Non-consequentialism, the Person as an End-in-Itself, and the Significance of Status', *Philosophy and Public Affairs*, 21 (1992), 354–89.

Kant, Immanuel, *Critique of Pure Reason* (1781), tr. Norman Kemp Smith (London: Macmillan, 1929).

Kenny, Anthony, 'Intention and Purpose', *Journal of Philosophy*, 63 (1966), 642–51.

Kidder, Joel, 'Maxims, Freedom, and Laws', unpub. MS (1989).

Kleinig, John, 'Good Samaritanism', *Philosophy and Public Affairs*, 5 (1976), 382–407.

KUPPERMAN, JOEL, *Character* (New York: Oxford University Press, 1991).

LANGENFUS, WILLIAM L., 'Consequentialism in Search of a Conscience', *American Philosophical Quarterly*, 27 (1990), 131–41.

LEIBNIZ, G. W., *New Essays on Human Understanding* (1705), tr. and ed. Peter Remnant and Jonathan Bennett (Cambridge: Cambridge University Press, 1981).

LEWIS, DAVID, 'Insensitive Causation', in his *Philosophical Papers*, ii (New York: Oxford University Press, 1986).

LOCKE, DON, 'The Choice between Lives', *Philosophy*, 57 (1982), 453–75.

LOCKE, JOHN, *An Essay Concerning Human Understanding* (1695), ed. Peter H. Nidditch (Oxford: Oxford University Press, 1975).

MCFALL, LYNNE, 'Happiness, Rationality, and Individual Ideals', *Review of Metaphysics*, 38 (1984), 595–613.

—— 'Integrity', *Ethics*, 98 (1987), 5–20.

MACK, ERIC, 'Bad Samaritanism and the Causation of Harm', *Philosophy and Public Affairs*, 9 (1980), 230–59.

MACKIE, J. L., 'Causes and Conditions', *American Philosophical Quarterly*, 2 (1965), 245–64.

MCMAHAN, JEFF, 'Killing, Letting Die, and Withdrawing Aid' (1993), repr. in Steinbock and Norcross, *Killing and Letting Die*, 383–419.

MALM, HEIDI, 'Directions of Justification in the Negative–Positive Duty Debate', *American Philosophical Quarterly*, 27 (1990), 315–24.

MELE, ALFRED R., 'Recent Work on Intentional Action', *American Philosophical Quarterly*, 29 (1992), 199–217.

MELLOR, D. H., 'The Singularly Affecting Facts of Causation', in his *Matters of Metaphysics* (Cambridge: Cambridge University Press, 1991).

MILL, JOHN STUART, *Utilitarianism* (1861), ed. George Sher (Indianapolis: Hackett, 1979).

MILLER, DICKINSON S., 'Free Will as Involving Determination and Inconceivable without It' (1934), repr. in his *Philosophical Analysis and Human Welfare*, ed. Lloyd D. Easton (Dordrecht: Reidel, 1975).

MONTALDI, DANIEL F., 'A Defense of St Thomas and the Principle of Double Effect', *Journal of Religious Ethics*, 14 (1986), 296–332.

MOORE, G. E., *Principia Ethica* (Cambridge: Cambridge University Press, 1903).

NAGEL, THOMAS, 'War and Massacre' (1972), repr. in his *Mortal Questions*.

—— 'Moral Luck' (1976), repr. ibid.

—— *Mortal Questions* (Cambridge: Cambridge University Press, 1979).

—— 'The Limits of Objectivity', in Sterling McMurrin (ed.), *The Tanner Lectures on Human Values*, i (Salt Lake City: University of Utah Press, 1980).

—— *Equality and Partiality* (New York: Oxford University Press, 1991).

NIETZSCHE, FRIEDRICH, *The Gay Science* (1882), tr. Walter Kaufmann (New York: Random House, 1974).

OTTEN, JAMES, 'Even if One were Letting Another Innocent Person Die', *Southern Journal of Philosophy*, 14 (1976), 313–22.

PARFIT, DEREK, *Reasons and Persons* (Oxford: Oxford University Press, 1984).

POLLOCK, JOHN L., *Subjunctive Reasoning* (Dordrecht: Reidel, 1976).

PRICHARD, H. A., 'Duty and Ignorance of Fact' (1932), repr. in his *Moral Obligation* (Oxford: Oxford University Press, 1949).

—— 'Acting, Willing, Desiring' (1945), ibid.

QUINE, W. V., 'Two Dogmas of Empiricism' (1951), repr. in his *From a Logical Point of View* (Cambridge, Mass.: Harvard University Press, 1953).

—— 'The Problem of Meaning in Linguistics' (1951), ibid.

—— 'On the Nature of Moral Values', in Alvin I. Goldman and Jaegwon Kim (eds.), *Values and Morals* (Dordrecht: Reidel, 1978).

QUINN, WARREN S., 'Actions, Intentions, and Consequences: The Doctrine of Double Effect', *Philosophy and Public Affairs*, 18 (1989), 334–51.

—— 'Actions, Intentions, and Consequences: The Doctrine of Doing and Allowing' (1989), repr. in Steinbock and Norcross, *Killing and Letting Die*, 355–82.

RACHELS, JAMES, 'Active and Passive Euthanasia' (1975), repr. in Steinbock and Norcross, *Killing and Letting Die*, 122–19.

RAILTON, PETER, 'Alienation, Consequentialism, and the Demands of Morality', *Philosophy and Public Affairs*, 13 (1984), 134–71.

RAKOWSKI, ERIC, 'Taking and Saving Lives', *Columbia Law Review*, 93 (1993), 1063–1156.

RATCLIFFE, JAMES M. (ed.), *The Good Samaritan and the Law* (Garden City, NY: Doubleday, 1966; repr. Gloucester, Mass.: Peter Smith, 1981).

RORTY, RICHARD, 'Representation, Social Practises, and Truth' (1988), repr. in his *Objectivity, Relativism and Truth* (Cambridge: Cambridge University Press, 1991).

ROSS, W. D., *The Right and the Good* (Oxford: Oxford University Press, 1930).

RUDZINSKI, ALEKSANDER W., 'The Duty to Rescue: A Comparative Analysis', in Ratcliffe, *The Good Samaritan and the Law*.

RUSSELL, BRUCE, 'On the Relative Strictness of Negative and Positive Duties', *American Philosophical Quarterly*, 14 (1977), 87–97.

RYLE, GILBERT, *The Concept of Mind* (London: Hutchinson, 1949).

SACKS, OLIVER, 'The Disembodied Lady' (1983), repr. in his *The Man who Mistook his Wife for a Hat* (New York: Harper and Row, 1987).

SANFORD, DAVID H., 'Negative Terms', *Analysis*, 27 (1966–7), 201–5.

—— 'Symposium Contribution on *Events and their Names* by Jonathan Bennett', *Philosophy and Phenomenological Research*, 51 (1991), 633–6.

SANTAYANA, GEORGE, 'The Philosophy of Bertrand Russell', in his *The Winds of Doctrine* (London: Dent, 1913).

SARTORIUS, ROLF E., *Individual Conduct and Social Norms* (Encino, Calif.: Dickenson, 1975).

SARTORIUS, ROLF E., 'Utilitarianism, Rights, and Duties to Self', *American Philosophical Quarterly*, 22 (1985), 241–9.

SCANLON, T. M., 'Rights, Goals and Fairness', in Stuart Hampshire (ed.), *Public and Private Morality* (Cambridge: Cambridge University Press, 1978).

SCHEFFLER, SAMUEL, *The Rejection of Consequentialism* (Oxford: Oxford University Press, 1982).

SEANOR, DOUGLAS, and N. FOTION (eds.), *Hare and Critics* (Oxford: Oxford University Press, 1988).

SEARLE, JOHN R., *Intentionality* (Cambridge: Cambridge University Press, 1983).

SEN, AMARTYA, 'Rights and Agency', *Philosophy and Public Affairs*, 11 (1982), 3–39.

—— 'Evaluator Relativity and Consequential Evaluation', *Philosophy and Public Affairs*, 12 (1983), 113–32.

SHUN, KWONG-LOI, 'Intending as a Means', *Pacific Philosophical Quarterly*, 66 (1985), 216–23.

SIDGWICK, HENRY, *The Methods of Ethics*, 7th edn. (London: Macmillan, 1907; repub. Indianapolis: Hackett, 1981).

SINGER, PETER, 'Utility and the Survival Lottery', *Philosophy*, 52 (1977), 218–22.

SMART, J. J. C., 'An Outline of a System of Utilitarian Ethics', in J. J. C. Smart and Bernard Williams, *Utilitarianism For and Against* (Cambridge: Cambridge University Press, 1973).

SPINOZA, BENEDICT, *Ethics Demonstrated in Geometric Order* (1677), repr. in *The Collected Works of Spinoza*, tr. and ed. Edwin Curley (Princeton, NJ: Princeton University Press, 1985).

STALNAKER, ROBERT C., *Inquiry* (Cambridge, Mass.: MIT Press, 1984).

STEINBOCK, BONNIE, and ALASTAIR NORCROSS (eds.), *Killing and Letting Die*, 2nd edn. (New York: Fordham University Press, 1994).

STOCKER, MICHAEL, 'Intentions and Act Evaluations', *Journal of Philosophy*, 67 (1970), 589–602.

STRAWSON, P. F., 'Freedom and Resentment' (1962), repr. in his *Freedom and Resentment and Other Essays* (London: Methuen, 1974).

STROUD, A., *Mens Rea; or, Imputability under the Law* (London, 1914).

SUÁREZ, FRANCISCO, *Laws and God the Lawgiver* (1612), partly repr. in *Selections from Three Works of Francisco Suárez, SJ*, ed. James Brown Scott (Oxford: Oxford University Press, 1944).

TAUREK, JOHN, 'Should the Numbers Count?', *Philosophy and Public Affairs*, 6 (1977), 293–316.

THOMAS AQUINAS, *Summa Theologiae* (1266–73), tr. Fathers of the English Dominican Province (London: R. & T. Washbourne, 1918).

—— *Commentary on the Nicomachean Ethics* (c.1268), tr. C. I. Litzinger (Chicago: University of Chicago Press, 1964).

THOMAS, LAURENCE, *Living Morally: A Psychology of Moral Character* (Philadelphia: Temple University Press, 1989).

THOMSON, JUDITH JARVIS, 'A Defense of Abortion' (1971), repr. in her *Rights, Restitution, and Risk: Essays in Moral Theory*, ed. William Parent (Cambridge, Mass.: Harvard University Press, 1986).

—— 'Killing, Letting Die, and the Trolley Problem' (1976), repr. ibid.

—— *Acts and Other Events* (Ithaca, NY: Cornell University Press, 1977).

—— 'The Trolley Problem' (1985), repr. in her *Rights, Restitution, and Risk: Essays in Moral Theory*, ed. William Parent (Cambridge, Mass.: Harvard University Press, 1986).

—— *The Realm of Rights* (Cambridge, Mass.: Harvard University Press, 1990).

THOREAU, HENRY, *Walden*, ed. J. L. Shanley (Princeton, NJ: Princeton University Press, 1971).

TILES, J. E., *Things that Happen* (Aberdeen: Aberdeen University Press, 1981).

TOOLEY, MICHAEL, 'Abortion and Infanticide', *Philosophy and Public Affairs*, 2 (1972), 37–65.

TUNC, ANDRÉ, 'The Volunteer and the Good Samaritan', in Ratcliffe, *The Good Samariton and the Law*.

VENDLER, ZENO, 'Facts and Events', in his *Linguistics in Philosophy* (Ithaca, NY: Cornell University Press, 1967).

VERMAZEN, BRUCE, 'Negative Acts', in Bruce Vermazen and Merrill B. Hintikka (eds.), *Essays on Davidson: Actions and Events* (Oxford: Oxford University Press, 1985).

WALZER, MICHAEL, *Just and Unjust Wars* (New York: Basic Books, 1977).

WARNOCK, G. J., 'John Langshaw Austin: A Biographical Sketch', in K. T. Fann (ed.), *Symposium on J. L. Austin* (London: Routledge & Kegan Paul, 1969).

WILCOX, WILLIAM H., 'Egoists, Consequentialists, and their Friends', *Philosophy and Public Affairs*, 16 (1987), 73–84.

WILLIAMS, BERNARD, 'Morality and the Emotions' (1965), repr. in his *Problems of the Self* (Cambridge: Cambridge University Press, 1973).

—— *Morality: An Introduction to Ethics* (New York: Harper & Row, 1972).

—— 'A Critique of Utilitarianism', in J. J. C. Smart and Bernard Williams, *Utilitarianism For and Against* (Cambridge: Cambridge University Press, 1973).

—— 'Persons, Character and Morality' (1976), repr. in his *Moral Luck* (Cambridge: Cambridge University Press, 1981).

—— 'The Structure of Hare's Theory', in Seanor and Fotion, *Hare and Critics*.

WINKLER, EARL, 'Is the Killing/Letting-Die Distinction Normatively Neutral?', *Dialogue*, 30 (1991), 309–25.

WITTGENSTEIN, LUDWIG, *Philosophical Investigations* (Oxford: Blackwell, 1953).

WOLF, SUSAN, 'Moral Luck', forthcoming.

Working party, *Euthanasia and Clinical Practice*: *Trends, Principles and Alternatives*, Report of a Working Party (London: Linacre Centre, 1982).

ZUCCHI, ALESSANDRO, *The Language of Propositions and Events* (Dordrecht: Kluwer, 1993).

INDEX OF PERSONS

INDEX OF SUBJECTS

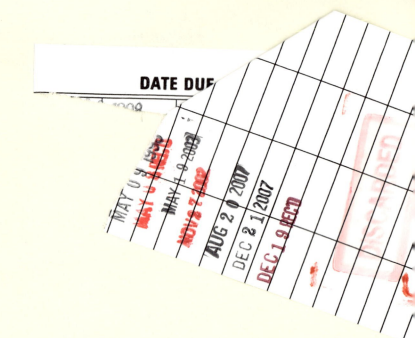